Human Remains: Another Dimension

Human Remains: Another Dimension

The Application of Imaging to the Study of Human Remains

Edited by

David Errickson
Teesside University, Middlesbrough, United Kingdom

Tim Thompson
Teesside University, Middlesbrough, United Kingdom

ACADEMIC PRESS

An imprint of Elsevier
elsevier.com

Academic Press is an imprint of Elsevier
125 London Wall, London EC2Y 5AS, United Kingdom
525 B Street, Suite 1800, San Diego, CA 92101-4495, United States
50 Hampshire Street, 5th Floor, Cambridge, MA 02139, United States
The Boulevard, Langford Lane, Kidlington, Oxford OX5 1GB, United Kingdom

British Library Cataloguing-in-Publication Data
A catalogue record for this book is available from the British Library

Library of Congress Cataloging-in-Publication Data
A catalog record for this book is available from the Library of Congress

ISBN: 978-0-12-804602-9

For Information on all Academic Press publications
visit our website at https://www.elsevier.com/books-and-journals

Working together
to grow libraries in
developing countries

www.elsevier.com • www.bookaid.org

Publisher: Sara Tenney
Acquisition Editor: Elizabeth Brown
Editorial Project Manager: Joslyn Chaiprasert-Paguio
Senior Production Project Manager: Priya Kumaraguruparan
Designer: Mark Rogers

Typeset by MPS Limited, Chennai, India

DEDICATION

For my parents and my grandparents.

—DE

For Becky (who is incredibly supportive) and Theo and Milo (who, if I am honest, are less fussed but like the cover).

—TJUT

CONTENTS

LIST OF CONTRIBUTORS

Owen J. Arthurs
Great Ormond Street Hospital for Children NHS Foundation Trust, London, United Kingdom; UCL Great Ormond Street Institute of Child Health, London, United Kingdom

Thomas Booth
Natural History Museum, London, United Kingdom

Summer Decker
University of South Florida Morsani College of Medicine, Tampa, FL, United States

Jenna M. Dittmar
University of Cambridge, Cambridge, United Kingdom

David Errickson
Teesside University, Middlesbrough, United Kingdom; Cranfield University, Cranfield, United Kingdom

Jonathan Ford
University of South Florida Morsani College of Medicine, Tampa, FL, United States

Ricardo M. Godinho
University of York, York, United Kingdom; University of Coimbra, Coimbra, Portugal

Samuel J. Griffith
University of Southampton, Southampton, United Kingdom

Andrew D. Holland
University of Bradford, Bradford, United Kingdom

Patrick Mahoney
University of Kent, Canterbury, United Kingdom

Nicholas Márquez-Grant
Cranfield University, Cranfield, United Kingdom

Justyna J. Miszkiewicz
Australian National University, Canberra, ACT, Australia

Kieron Niven
University of York, York, United Kingdom

Paul O'Higgins
University of York, York, United Kingdom

Julian D. Richards
University of York, York, United Kingdom

Tom Sparrow
University of Bradford, Bradford, United Kingdom

Charlotte E.L. Thompson
University of Southampton, Southampton, United Kingdom

Tim Thompson
Teesside University, Middlesbrough, United Kingdom

Priscilla F. Ulguim
Teesside University, Middlesbrough, United Kingdom

Jacquie Vallis
Teesside University, Middlesbrough, United Kingdom

Rick R. van Rijn
Netherlands Forensic Institute, The Hague, the Netherlands;
Academic Medical Centre Amsterdam, Amsterdam, the Netherlands;
Amsterdam Centre for Forensic Science and Medicine, Amsterdam,
the Netherlands

Mayonne van Wijk
Netherlands Forensic Institute, The Hague, the Netherlands

Marloes E.M. Vester
Netherlands Forensic Institute, The Hague, the Netherlands;
Academic Medical Centre Amsterdam, Amsterdam, the Netherlands;
Amsterdam Centre for Forensic Science and Medicine, Amsterdam,
the Netherlands

Andrew S. Wilson
University of Bradford, Bradford, United Kingdom

ACKNOWLEDGMENT

This book is the result of our shared work and interest in new and innovative ways of studying human skeletal remains. It is the outcome of countless discussions and conversations that we both had over the past few years—and we thank everyone who has engaged with us throughout this process. We would like to thank all of the contributors to this volume for their time and their expertise in writing the individual chapters.

Likewise, thank you to all of those who helped get this book through the manuscript editing phases. In particular we would like to thank our team of peer—reviewers, including Gordon Taylor Wilson, Kirsty Squires, Alexandra Wink, Matt Adamson, Claire Hodson, Nicholas Higgs, Roslyn DeBattista, Naomichi Ogihara and Nicolene Lottering.

We would also very much like to thank both Joslyn Chaiprasert—Paguio and Liz Brown at Elsevier for their continued advice and support from the beginning to the end of this project.

Finally, we would just like to note the valuable contribution that the various cafes, coffee shops and tea rooms around Middlesbrough have made during this process.

CHAPTER 1

Context

Tim Thompson
Teesside University, Middlesbrough, United Kingdom

1.1 INTRODUCTION

It is often said that "a picture says a thousand words"; in fact this is a phrase that is repeated so often that it has now slipped into cliché and as such, is rarely considered in any great depth. Although it has been attributed as an ancient Chinese proverb, its first use in the English language occurred just over one hundred years ago in the *Syracuse Post Standard* newspaper as part of a discussion on journalism and publicity. It has been repeated countless times in countless forms since, but always with the same intent—that displaying something visually is a more effective means of explaining something than describing it verbally or with the written word.

Indeed, it is possible to consider many different examples of where this is true. It is the absolute basis for all effective marketing and advertising—a concept which is vividly demonstrated in the M&C Saatchi (2011) training manual, later to be developed into their publication *Brutal Simplicity of Thought*. Many aspects of our day-to-day lives are also impacted by this philosophy, right down to how we dress as we leave the house—for example, with work showing that the use of imagery and color is vital in the communication of weather information (Sherman-Morris et al., 2015). However, while this type of association between imagery and products or concepts is often linked to making money or influencing behavior, in other contexts the use of imagery focusses on helping people to understand. An obvious example of this would be within the medical context where imaging

Human Remains: Another Dimension. DOI: http://dx.doi.org/10.1016/B978-0-12-804602-9.00001-1

modalities have been used and developed for many years with the aim of allowing clinicians to detect, diagnose, and treat a variety of medical conditions and problems which had previously been impossible. Often we think of the use of X-rays or CT scans, but equally, creative use of the more straightforward standard photography also continues to offer much in surgical contexts (Murphy et al., 2016). At a larger scale, the *Satellite Sentinel Project* (http://www.satsentinel.org/) has allowed those working within international criminal and humanitarian law contexts to image and visualize sites of mass violence and extrajudicial killings through the use of satellite remote imaging. This has facilitated a greater understanding of conflict at a regional and national level in a way which has not been possible before. Novel approaches to imaging and visualization also have the benefit of allowing nonexperts or those physically distanced from the object a greater chance of understanding it. Museums have been keen to exploit this and a vast array of cultural objects are now available to view and study through online portals (see, e.g., the interactive *Smithsonian X 3D* facility at https://3d.si.edu/).

It must be noted however, that a picture on its own does not always assist one to understand a given topic. Research has demonstrated that without any associated commentary, visualizations of complex data are as difficult to understand as the raw data itself (Stofer, 2016). As a further example, within the learning and teaching context students of human anatomy and physiology who use physical plastic models can achieve higher exam scores than those who use virtual images of the body (Lombardi et al., 2014), while those teaching osteology have consistently argued that digital images are not as effective for learning as actual skeletal specimens (Betts et al., 2011; Niven et al., 2009). As with many new developments, a degree of caution is worthwhile as new methods and techniques are adopted into practice.

Across the sciences the development of innovative methods of imaging and visualization has led to a greater understanding of our bodies. The anatomical sciences are a wonderful example of this, with the internal workings of the body being recorded first through hand drawings, then photography, then microscopic photography, and now full three-dimensional imaging of everything from bone cells up to entire systems (e.g., see the likes of Alers-Hankey and Chisholm, 2006; Rifkin et al., 2006). However, for some disciplines, the very images themselves are open to question. Within the forensic sciences, there has historically been much discussion regarding the acceptance and admission of color and then digital photography from crime scenes into the courtroom (Thompson, 2008), while current debate focusses on the admissibility of 3D digitizations largely from the perspective of validation of methods and the CSI Effect on jurors (Errickson et al., 2014).

1.2 HUMAN REMAINS—ANOTHER DIMENSION

Human remains are studied and analyzed in a wide range of disciplines as researchers attempt to understand more about our bodies, our past, and our societies. In recent years, there has been an increased interest in new methods and approaches to visualizing aspects of the human body and ways in which this can be applied to new and developing disciplines. The aim of this volume is to explore this new frontier of human study by examining the application of a number of imaging and visualization approaches and methodologies to human remains in varying conditions from diverse contexts. We have three key themes that our contributors have brought together within each chapter—a method of imaging, an interesting context of application, and a practical consideration associated with the visualization of human remains.

With this in mind, each chapter explores different methods, contexts, and issues—thus each chapter touches upon different aspects of the three key themes of the book.

The human body is a complex structure, and human osteologists have been extremely comfortable in exploiting many new methods of imaging and visualization in order to more effectively study people from modern and ancient contexts. Booth provides a wonderful example of this through the use of widely available low-powered microscopy to assess bioerosion of buried archeological remains; this is followed by Miszkiewicz and Mahoney who also use this approach to examine bone histology to demonstrate how viewing bone from a different perspective can allow greater understanding of how a person lived their life; Dittmar then applies high-powered microscopy in the examination of trauma, in this case cut-marks on bone; Vallis then emphasizes the important role of imaging human remains in disaster victim identification contexts and the considerations of undertaking this; next, the power of digital visualization in field archeology and in the interpretation of taphonomic factors is discussed by Ulguim; Errickson subsequently provides an example demonstrating the applicability (without ignoring the accompanying challenges) of developing new methods for the visualization of bone surfaces. Despite the successes, many attempts to create osteo-profiles are hampered by bone diagenesis and other taphonomic factors, and this is specifically addressed in this volume by Griffiths and Thompson through the application of noncontact laser surface scanning to bone recovered from the water. Wilson and colleagues tackle similar challenges associated with viewing and assessing the modification of bone when developing a digital bioarcheology approach of study—this time by laser scanning bony modifications caused by illness and disease; Godinho and O'Higgins demonstrate how a greater understanding of human evolution is possible through the strategic use of modern imaging modalities, and the advantages that such an approach has when material is missing or fragmented; and finally, revolutions in the practice of pediatric medicine (with a particular emphasis on cases of suspected child abuse) as a consequence of new approaches to imaging are highlighted by van Wijk and colleagues.

Moving away from the body itself, it is obvious that a broad array of contexts of study may benefit from the availability of such a range of potential methods of imaging and visualizations. However, there is more to debate than just the method and context of application, and so our volume ends with a consideration of an often overlooked aspect of imaging and visualization—the data produced. The relative ease of digitally visualizing the complex body results in a mass of new data being produced, with few academics addressing the key resultant questions: What this data may mean; who owns the data of the dead; is it right to display visualizations of the dead in a public arena; how should we store and preserve this data; and so on. Thus, we conclude our book with discussions on the nature of this digital bodily archive. Niven and Richards of the Archaeology Data Service (University of York, UK) tease out the thorny issues of digital preservation and significance of data formats; Decker and Ford develop these ideas further in their chapter on digital data; and finally, Marquez-Grant and Errickson highlight and explore the challenging ethical debates involved in the display and dissemination of data collected from the imaging of human remains.

It is the aim of this volume to highlight the current state-of-play while crucially providing a springboard for greater discussion of the methods and issues surrounding attempts to visualize the human body—either living or dead, fully fleshed or skeletalized, and across disciplinary boundaries.

REFERENCES

Alers-Hankey, V., Chisholm, J., 2006. Inside the Body: Fantastic Images From Beneath the Skin. Cassell Illustrated, UK.

Betts, M., Maschner, H., Schou, C., Schlader, R., Holmes, J., Clement, N., et al., 2011. Virtual zooarchaeology: building a web-based reference collection of northern vertebrates for archaeofaunal research and education. J. Archaeol. Sci. 38, 755–762.

Errickson, D., Thompson, T.J.U., Rankin, B.W.J., 2014. The application of 3D visualization of osteological trauma for the courtroom: a critical review. J. Forensic Radiol. Imaging 2, 132–137.

Lombardi, S.A., Hicks, R.E., Thompson, K.V., Marbach-Ad, G., 2014. Are all hands-on activities equally effective? Effect of using plastic models, organ dissections, and virtual dissections on student learning and perceptions. Adv. Physiol. Educ. 38, 80–86.

Murphy, B.L., Boughey, J.C., Degnim, A.C., Hieken, T.J., Harmsen, W.S., Keeney, G.L., et al., 2016. A picture is worth a thousand words: intraoperative photography as a quality metric for axillary dissection. Ann. Surg. Oncol. Available from: http://dx.doi.org/10.1245/s10434-016-5271-7.

M&C Saatchi, 2011. Brutal Simplicity of Thought. Ebury Press, UK.

Niven, L., Steele, T., Finke, H., Gernat, T., Hublin, J., 2009. Virtual skeletons: using a structured light scanner to create a 3D faunal comparative collection. J. Archaeol. Sci. 36, 2018–2023.

Rifkin, B.A., Ackerman, M.J., Folkenberg, J., 2006. Human Anatomy: Depicting the Body From the Renaissance to Today. Thames & Hudson, Ltd, London.

Sherman-Morris, K., Antonelli, K.B., Williams, C.C., 2015. Measuring the effectiveness of the graphical communication of hurricane storm surge threat. Weather Clim. Soc. 7, 69–82.

Stofer, K.A., 2016. When a picture isn't worth 1000 words: learners struggle to find meaning in data visualizations. J. Geosci. Educ. 64 (3), 231–241.

Thompson, T.J.U., 2008. The role of the photograph in the application of forensic anthropology and the interpretation of clandestine scenes of crime. Photogr. Cult. 1 (2), 163–182.

CHAPTER 2

The Rot Sets In: Low-Powered Microscopic Investigation of Taphonomic Changes to Bone Microstructure and its Application to Funerary Contexts

Thomas Booth

Natural History Museum, London, United Kingdom

Bone has a distinctive microscopic structure that can be examined using low-powered transmitted light microscopy applied to transversely orientated histological bone thin sections. Woven bone, which consists of irregular organizations of collagen fibrils, is the primary bone microstructure and is gradually replaced by organized parallel lamellae $3-7\,\mu m$ thick (Junqeira et al., 1986). Circumferential lamellae form the outer (periosteal) and inner (endosteal) surfaces (Fig. 2.1). Osteonal bone forms when lamellae are laid down around longitudinally orientated blood vessels, producing a central cavity known as a Haversian canal (Fig. 2.2). Osteons that form as a result of remodeling (secondary osteons) are defined by a mineralized barrier called a cement or reversal line. Haversian canals are connected by transverse Volkmann's canals (Fig. 2.3). Interstitial bone consists of parallel lamellae lying between osteons. Star-shaped osteocyte lacunae, which contain osteocyte cells,

Human Remains: Another Dimension. DOI: http://dx.doi.org/10.1016/B978-0-12-804602-9.00003-5

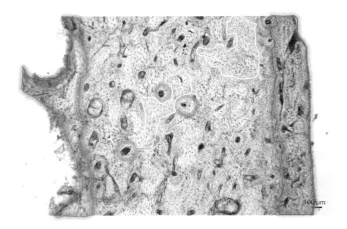

Figure 2.1 Micrograph of a transverse human femoral thin section from a modern cadaver (University of Sheffield School of Medicine and Biological Sciences) with main organizational features highlighted. Red (gray in print version), endosteal circumferental lamellar bone; blue (dark gray in print verison), periosteal circumferential lamellar bone; green (light gray in print version), osteonal lamellar bone; yellow (white in print version), interstitial lamellar bone.

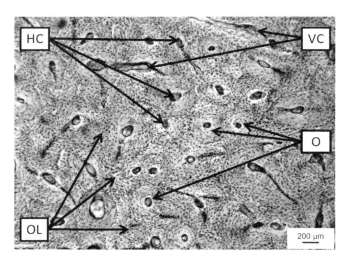

Figure 2.2 Micrograph of a transverse human femoral thin section from a modern cadaver (University of Sheffield School of Medicine and Biological Sciences) with labeled microstructures. HC, Haversian canal, cavities which in life contained circulatory, lymphatic, and nervous structures; OL, osteocyte lacunae, which in life contain the osteocyte cell; VC, Volkmann's canal, which connect Haversian canals longitudinally; O, osteons, the Haversian canal plus the encircling lamellar bone.

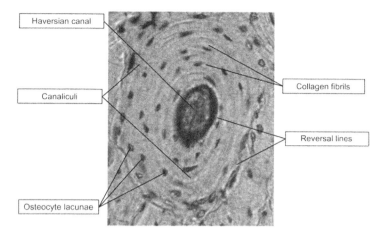

Figure 2.3 Anatomy of an osteon.

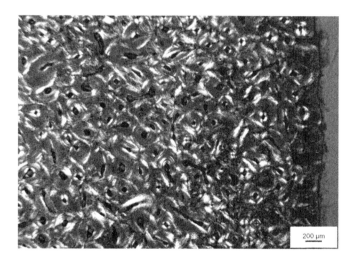

Figure 2.4 Micrograph of a transverse human femoral thin section from a modern cadaver (University of Sheffield School of Medicine and Biological Sciences) under polarized light. The bone microstructure appears birefringent when viewed under polarized light. Intensity of birefringence is often diminished by diagenesis.

pervade all bone microstructures and are connected to each other and Haversian canals by fine canaliculi. Bone is birefringent, meaning that the arrangement of internal microstructure becomes more distinct when viewed under polarized light (Fig. 2.4).

Thin section light microscopy can also be used to examine taphonomically significant diagenetic alterations to the internal microstructure of archaeological bone (Hollund et al., 2012; Booth, 2016). Bone diagenesis refers to any taphonomic process that degrades or alters bone, leading to its destruction or fossilization (Hedges et al., 1995; Lee-Thorp and Sealy, 2008). Bone diagenesis also encompasses changes that do not necessarily involve degradation, such as infiltration by extraneous substances (Garland, 1987; Grupe and Dreses-Werringloer, 1993; Shahack-Gross et al., 1997). Most archaeological bones have been subjected to one or a combination of three diagenetic processes: chemical degradation of the organic phase (accelerated collagen hydrolysis), chemical degradation of both the organic and mineral phases (catastrophic dissolution), and biological degradation of the organic and mineral phases (microbial bioerosion) (Nielsen-Marsh et al., 2007; Smith et al., 2007).

Microbial bioerosion is the most common form of diagenesis found in archaeological bones from temperate environments (Hedges, 2002; Turner-Walker et al., 2002; Jans et al., 2004). Invasive microorganisms degrade bone proteins, forming characteristic tunnels in the internal microstructure (Hackett, 1981). Hackett (1981, p. 250) identified four categories of tunneling or micro-foci of destruction (MFD): linear longitudinal, budded, lamellate (non-Wedl), and Wedl. Wedl tunneling is characteristic of bone deposited in aquatic environments where it has been linked to cyanobacteria (blue-green algae), but appears irregularly in bone from terrestrial contexts, where it has been linked with saprophytic fungi (Marchiafava et al., 1974; Bell and Elkerton, 2008; Fernández-Jalvo et al., 2010; Pesquero et al., 2010; Fig. 2.5). In archaeological contexts, Wedl tunneling occurs more frequently in butchered faunal bones than in articulated human and faunal skeletons (Jans et al., 2004; Nielsen-Marsh et al., 2007). The distribution of Wedl tunneling among archaeological human remains is loosely associated with caves and other open contexts, suggesting that Wedl-type attack is encouraged by deposition of defleshed or partially fleshed bones in open, aerated environments, perhaps because these environments provide greater access to fungal spores (Booth, 2014).

The three forms of non-Wedl MFD are found almost ubiquitously in archaeological human bone from terrestrial contexts and have been associated with bacteria (Balzer et al., 1997; Jackes et al., 2001; Turner-Walker and Syversen, 2002; Fig. 2.6). They tend to be concentrated around osteocyte lacunae in osteons while avoiding peripheral circumferential periosteal and endosteal lamellar bone, even in samples

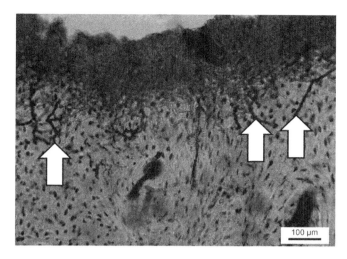

Figure 2.5 Micrograph of a transverse thin section of a 11th century AD frontal bone recovered from the River Wye near Bakewell, UK. Meandering, branched Wedl tunneling can be observed penetrating the periosteal surface (arrows).

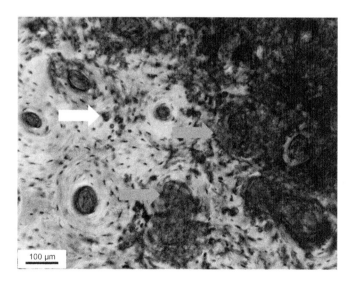

Figure 2.6 Micrograph of a transverse femoral thin section from an 19th century cemetery at Coronation street, South Shields, UK. Discrete linear longitudinal and budded MFD can be observed developing around osteocyte lacunae (yellow (white in print version) arrow). Amalgamations of all three forms of non-Wedl MFD have severely altered bone microstructures (blue (gray in print version) arrows).

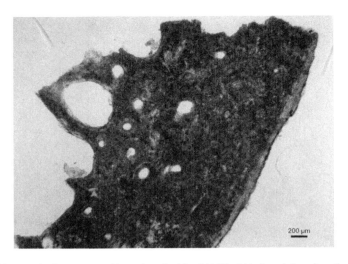

Figure 2.7 Micrograph of a transverse thin section of a Mesolithic/Neolithic foot phalanx from the Havnø shell midden, Denmark. The bone microstructure has been extensively bioeroded by bacteria, leaving slithers of preserved bone at the periosteal and endosteal surfaces. This pattern of attack is typical of most archaeological human bones, particularly those from articulated skeletons.

that have been extensively bioeroded by bacteria (Bell et al., 1996; Hedges, 2002; Jans et al., 2004; Fig. 2.7). This patterning suggests that osteolytic bacteria access the bone microstructure through Haversian systems, rather than invading directly through external surfaces. Early studies assumed soil bacteria were responsible for non-Wedl MFD, however more recent investigations suggest that an organism's endogenous gut bacteria may be involved (Child, 1995; Bell et al., 1996; Jans et al., 2004; White and Booth, 2014). In the first few days after death, visceral bacteria transmigrate around the body via the circulatory system and are principally involved in the initial putrefactive stage of bodily decomposition (Polson et al., 1985; Janaway, 1996; Child, 1995; Gill-King, 1997). These bacteria can access the internal bone microstructures using vascular structures in Haversian canals.

Several histological studies of archaeological and forensic human and faunal remains from around temperate Europe have found that the extent of bacterial bioerosion broadly correlates with early postmortem treatment, but not chronological age or soil type (Bell et al., 1996; Jans et al., 2004; Nielsen-Marsh et al., 2007; White and Booth, 2014; Booth, 2016). The specific processes observed to influence bacterial bone bioerosion all affect the extent to which the bone is exposed to bacterial soft tissue decomposition. For instance, butchered archaeological faunal remains are often free from bacterial attack whereas bones from articulated human or faunal skeletons have usually been extensively bioeroded by bacteria (Jans et al., 2004; Nielsen-Marsh et al., 2007). Butchery rapidly separates organs and soft tissue from bones, ensuring that the bones are exposed to minimal soft tissue decomposition. Unburied corpses decompose and disarticulate rapidly, therefore most articulated archaeological skeletons must have been buried as intact bodies soon after death and exposed to maximal levels of bacterial soft tissue decomposition (Jans et al., 2004; Duday, 2006; Booth, 2016; Fig. 2.8). Bones from subaerially-exposed (excarnated) human and animal carcasses, where soft tissue would have been rapidly removed by scavengers and carnivorous invertebrates, usually show lower levels of bacterial bioerosion than bones from buried remains (Rodriguez and Bass, 1983; Bell et al., 1996; Simmons et al., 2010; White and Booth, 2014). Consistencies in levels of bacterial attack in historical articulated human skeletons suggest that processes which affect the rate rather than the extent of bacterial soft tissue decomposition (e.g., seasonality, coffin burial) have no detectable impact on bacterial bone bioerosion (Booth, 2016).

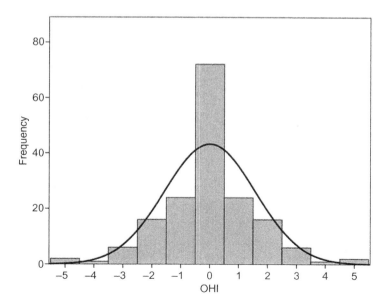

Figure 2.8 Mirrored distribution of OHI scores allocated to samples of articulated human skeletons from historical (43 AD–present) British archaeological contexts indicative of the expected distribution from a population who were mostly buried intact soon after death and exposed to high levels of bacterial soft tissue decomposition (Booth et al., 2015).

The link between bodily decomposition and putrefactive gut bacteria ostensibly suggests that an endogenous model of bacterial bioerosion provides the best explanation for the relationship between bacterial attack and early postmortem treatment (Jans et al., 2004). However, this relationship could also be explained by an exogenous model of bone bioerosion if soil bacteria are primarily attracted to bone that retains soft tissue. In either scenario, the extent of bacterial bone bioerosion seems to be predictable based on the level of soft tissue decomposition a bone would have been exposed to in different taphonomic scenarios (Nielsen-Marsh et al., 2007; Booth, 2016). Therefore, combining histological analysis of bacterial bone bioerosion with forensic models of bodily decomposition may provide unprecedented insight into past funerary behavior (Parker Pearson et al., 2005; Booth et al., 2015; Booth and Madgwick, 2016). There is no relationship between the external appearance of a bone and the microbial degradation of its internal microstructure, therefore microscopic analysis represents a novel source of taphonomic information (Hanson and Buikstra, 1987; Jans et al., 2004; Booth, 2016).

At the most basic level, histological analysis of diagenetic change in archaeological bone could be used to distinguish the number of taphonomic trajectories or funerary processes represented at a site (Booth and Madgwick, 2016). The extent of bacterial bioerosion as it relates to soft tissue decomposition could then be used to support or refute particular taphonomic or funerary scenarios. However, patterns of bacterial bioerosion associated with certain taphonomic processes represent tendencies rather than absolute relationships (Booth, 2016). Therefore, it would be problematic to make inferences about funerary behavior based solely on histological investigations of a single bone. Ideally, studies intending to use microscopic analysis of archaeological bone to investigate past funerary practices would assess a substantial assemblage of samples to establish consistent patterns of bacterial attack. Useful inferences regarding funerary processes are only possible when results are combined with complementary taphonomic information, such as state of skeletal articulation, completeness, cortical erosion, etc. (Carr and Knüsel, 1997; Duday, 2006; Carr, 2007; Booth, 2016; Booth and Madgwick, 2016).

Anoxic and waterlogged environments inhibit soft tissue decomposition and have a similar effect on bacterial bone bioerosion (Janaway, 1996; Turner and Wiltshire, 1999; Turner-Walker and Jans,

2008; Hollund et al., 2012; Booth, 2016). Patterns of bacterial bioerosion in bone from anoxic or waterlogged sediments cannot be used to infer aspects of funerary treatment. There must be reasonable grounds for rejecting environmental explanations of bacterial bone bioerosion before anthropogenic interpretations can be invoked. Large proportions of archaeological human young infant (aged using diaphyseal length at 1 month or younger) skeletons are free from bacterial bioerosion, which is best explained by the remains of stillborn or short-lived infants who died before their osteolytic gut microbiota had developed (White and Booth, 2014; Booth, 2016; Booth et al., 2016). An absence of bacterial bioerosion from young infant skeletons cannot be related to funerary treatment. However, the ability to identify archaeological stillborn and short-lived infants has positive applications to funerary archaeology, particularly in investigating differential treatment of these remains (for instance Irish Catholic cillíní; Murphy, 2008; Booth et al., 2016).

Interactions with exogenous substances produce localized discoloration of bone microstructures (staining) and the accumulation of foreign elements in microporosities (inclusions) (Garland, 1987; Grupe and Dreses-Werringloer, 1993; Hanson and Cain, 2007). Dark microstructural staining can sometimes be mistaken for bioerosion (Grupe and Dreses-Werringloer, 1993). Bioerosion has a distinct morphology (MFD) and tends to be absent from the periosteal and endosteal fringes, whereas staining is amorphous and more often concentrated at the peripheries.

Most inclusions are composed of minerals from the surrounding soil deposited by percolating groundwater, particularly iron oxides and manganese, or products of bone decomposition, such as calcite (Marchiafava et al., 1974; Grupe and Dreses-Werringloer, 1993). Framboidal pyrite inclusions form as a result of organic decomposition by anaerobic sulfate-reducing bacteria (Bottrell et al., 1998; Turner-Walker, 1999; Turner-Walker and Jans, 2008). Their presence suggests that a bone decomposed under anoxic or waterlogged conditions at some point during its depositional history. Subsequent oxidation of framboidal pyrite produces iron oxides and organic acids that create localized orange staining and acidic degradation. The link between pyrite framboids and anoxic decomposition means that inclusions and staining have to be considered carefully when interpreting patterns of bacterial bioerosion (Turner-Walker and Jans, 2008; Hollund et al.,

2012; van der Sluis et al., 2014). For instance, the presence of pyrite framboids in bone that shows limited bacterial tunneling may suggest that soft tissue decomposition was inhibited by an anoxic or water-logged environment.

2.1 METHODS AND ASSESSMENT

There are two necessarily destructive methods of producing archaeo-logical bone thin sections: grinding and cutting. Both require a suitably sized bone fragment (~ 1 cm $\times$ cm covering the bone cross section down to the medullary cavity). This can be a preexisting fragment, but in most cases a sample has to be cut from a bone using an electric hand saw. To produce a ground thin section, the bone sample is embedded in epoxy resin and reduced on a Grinder—Polisher until it is of an appropriate thickness (usually below 100 µm—see Miszkiewicz and Mahoney, 2016). The cutting method requires a saw microtome to cut a suitably sized thin section directly from a bone sample. Most archaeological bone samples do not have to be embedded in epoxy resin to be cut on a saw microtome, however embedding is sometimes necessary to prevent the disintegration of friable samples (see Booth, 2016). Thin sections can be mounted onto microscope slides under a glass cover slip with a mounting medium.

The standard method for assessing bone bioerosion is the Oxford Histological Index (OHI), which is an ordinal measure of bioerosion relating to the percentage of unaltered bone microstructure (Hedges et al., 1995; Millard, 2001; Table 2.1). The OHI correlates with abso-lute measures of diagenesis such as protein/collagen yield, suggesting that it is a useful measure of biodeterioration (Hedges et al., 1995; Haynes et al., 2002; Nielsen-Marsh et al., 2007; Smith et al., 2007; Ottoni et al., 2009; Sosa et al., 2013). Both chemical and biological diagenesis produce a reduction in bone birefringence, which is mea-sured using the Birefringence Index (BI) when observing archaeological bone thin sections under polarized light (Jans et al., 2004). The BI is a simple measure involving three grades assessing whether a bone has normal (1), reduced (0.5), or obliterated (0) birefringence. The BI par-ticularly useful for recording chemical diagenesis, which is not as apparent in bone thin sections viewed under normal transmitted light. Staining and inclusions are usually recorded qualitatively.

Table 2.1 Oxford Histological Index (Hedges et al., 1995; Millard, 2001)		
OHI Score	Percentage of Microstructure Remaining	Description
0	<5%	No original features identifiable, except Haversian canals
1	<15%	Small areas of well-preserved bone present, or the lamellate structure is preserved by the pattern of destructive foci
2	<50%	Some well-preserved bone present between destroyed areas
3	>50%	Larger areas of well-preserved bone present
4	>85%	Bone is fairly well preserved with minor amounts of destroyed areas
5	>95%	Very well preserved, similar to modern bone

Bioerosion has been noted to vary between skeletal elements and sometimes through the same bone (Hanson and Buikstra, 1987; Nicholson, 1996; Hollund et al., 2015). Tooth dentine and cementum particularly show lower levels of bioerosion than bone from the same individual, possibly because teeth are more mineralized and less vascularized than bone (Hollund et al., 2015). Intraskeletal studies of bioerosion have sometimes produced contradictory findings, but generally bones consisting predominantly of trabecular bone tend to show higher levels of bacterial bioerosion than those which are mostly composed of cortical bone (Hanson and Buikstra, 1987; Jans et al., 2004; Booth, 2016). This may be expected given that ratios of cortical/trabecular bone will dictate the surface area exposed to diagenetic processes. Articular ends of long bones, which are mostly composed of trabecular bone, as well as trabecular diploë in the cranium are more susceptible to bacterial attack than cortical structures in the same bones (Booth, 2014). Under an endogenous model of bacterial bioerosion, anatomical proximity to the gut as the potential source of osteolytic bacteria has also been suggested as an influential factor affecting intraskeletal diagenesis (Jans et al., 2004). Bones located away from the gut, such as those of the extremities (particularly metcarpals/tarsals and phalanges) may be less susceptible to bacterial attack. Intraskeletal variation in osteonal porosity, which is ultimately dictated by remodeling, may also affect how easily osteolytic bacteria are able to access the microstructure (Turner-Walker, 2008).

Long bone (most often femoral) mid-shafts are usually targeted by histological studies of bone diagenesis, often for the sake of consistency, but also as they are consistently composed of cortical bone and may be close enough to the gut to act as a reliable gage of any associated osteolytic bacterial activity (Jans et al., 2004). Recent micro-CT analysis of archaeological human remains has suggested that bacterial bioerosion does not vary significantly along long bone diaphyses and that results from single long bone thin sections should be representative and comparable (Dal Sasso et al., 2014; Booth et al., 2016). The following case studies illustrate how histological analysis of diagenetic changes to ancient bone microstructure may be used in combination with contextual, taphonomic, archaeological, and historical information to produce refined interpretations of past funerary practices.

2.2 DANEBURY IRON AGE HILLFORT AND SUDDERN FARM SETTLEMENT, HAMPSHIRE, UK

Danebury, Hampshire, UK, is an Iron Age hillfort that was occupied from approximately 550–100 BC (Cunliffe et al., 2015). Over 300 deposits of human remains have been recovered from Danebury in various states of articulation, as part of single and multiple burials from various dispersed features (Walker, 1984; Cunliffe and Poole, 2000). Some of the bones were covered by a layer of natural silt, suggesting bodies had been left to decompose in open pits. Suddern Farm is an enclosed Iron Age settlement located around 5 km to the west of Danebury (Cunliffe and Poole, 2000). A quarry located to the southwest of the enclosure had been used as a cemetery from the Early to Middle Iron Age (ca. 700–100 BC). Human remains representing a minimum of 60 individuals were recovered from quarry pits dug directly into the chalk rubble. Configurations of skeletal remains were very similar to what was observed among the Danebury burials. All of the burial sediments were composed of free-draining chalk silt and there was no evidence that any of the burial contexts were intrinsically anoxic or had been waterlogged.

Femoral thin sections of 20 human individuals from Danebury and Suddern Farm were analyzed using transmitted light microscopy to investigate the diversity and nature of funerary practices at the sites (Booth and Madgwick, 2016). All but one of the samples examined had been extensively bioeroded by bacteria (OHI < 3), suggesting that individuals had been treated in ways which exposed the bones to extensive soft tissue decomposition. Isolated disarticulated bones all showed maximal levels of bacterial attack (OHI = 0), suggesting that they had been buried as part of intact bodies before the bones were exhumed and redeposited (Fig. 2.9).

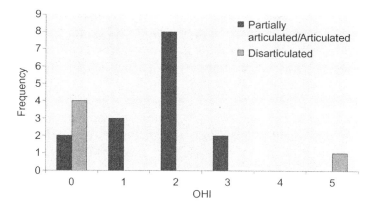

Figure 2.9 Histogram showing the distribution of OHI scores among the Danebury human bone thin sections assemblage, separated by state of articulation.

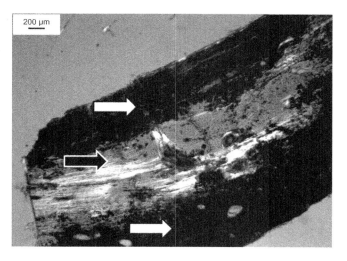

Figure 2.10 Micrograph of a transverse femoral thin section from partially articulated Danebury Deposit 37 under polarized light showing intermediate levels of bacterial bioerosion (white arrows), leaving a large well-preserved birefringent midsection (black arrow).

Bacterial bioerosion was significantly less severe (OHI = 0−3) in bones from skeletons recovered in partial or full anatomical articulation (Fig. 2.10). No experimental studies of bone diagenesis have replicated these intermediate signatures of bioerosion. However, indoor or enclosed environments delay rapid soft tissue loss by invertebrates, allowing bacterial bodily decomposition to progress further than it would in an outdoor environment (Goff, 1991; Terrell-Nield and MacDonald, 1997; Anderson, 2011). However, the anatomical articulation of some of these skeletal remains suggested that the pits represented their primary depositional context (Cunliffe, 1984). These pits were steep-sided and would have silted up rapidly. Therefore, one plausible scenario is that whole bodies were deposited in open pits, with rapid silting subsequently sheltering bodies and reducing insect-mediated soft tissue loss. It is difficult to say whether rapid silting would prolong bacterial soft tissue decomposition in a way that would promote intermediate levels of bacterial bioerosion. Therefore, an alternative possible scenario is that pits were sealed or covered while bodies decomposed (Booth and Madgwick, 2016). Selective retrieval and redeposition of parts of decomposing bodies would account for disturbed and partial deposits. Rates of Wedl tunneling among the articulated/partially articulated bones were also elevated, which is consistent with these bodies having decomposed in open pits (Booth, 2014).

A thin section from a single discrete disarticulated bone fragment showed limited levels of bacterial bioerosion. This sample represented a third taphonomic process that had resulted in the bone being exposed to only limited bacterial decomposition, characteristic of excarnation (Bell et al., 1996; White and Booth, 2014). This bone was also the only sample that showed severe cortical weathering, consistent with excarnation (Carr and Knüsel, 1997; Craig et al., 2005; Carr, 2007; Redfern, 2008). Birefringence was reduced in areas of this sample that were unaffected by bacterial attack, suggesting that the bone had been affected by accelerated hydrolytic reactions. Exposure to the elements, particularly rapid wetting/drying, is thought to promote accelerated collagen hydrolysis of bone (Smith et al., 2002, 2007). Therefore, there is reasonable evidence to suggest that this sample originated from an individual that had been excarnated.

2.3 CHURCH OF ST. MARY AND ST. LAURENCE, BOLSOVER, DERBYSHIRE, UK

The 13th century church of Saint Mary and Saint Laurence is located in Bolsover, near Chesterfield, Derbyshire, UK. A total of 70 articulated skeletons as well as additional disarticulated material were excavated from the church and associated churchyard (Foster, 1992). The disarticulated human bone had accumulated through disturbance of decomposed bodies during grave digging or construction. None of the burial sediments were anoxic or showed signs of previous waterlogging. Children and infant skeletons were predominant among remains recovered from the churchyard north of the church. Documentary evidence suggests that this area was reserved for burials of unbaptized infants and social deviants, such as cases of suicide (Kerr, 1994). Femoral thin sections of 28 human skeletons were analyzed histologically as part of a study into bacterial bioerosion among European archaeological remains (Economous, 2003; Booth, 2014, 2016).

The majority of bone thin sections had been extensively bioeroded by bacteria (OHI < 2; Fig. 2.11). This result was consistent with the knowledge that these samples had come from a historic Christian cemetery where the majority of individuals were buried intact soon after death and exposed to maximal bacterial soft tissue decomposition. However, five thin sections were entirely free from bacterial bioerosion. Four out of five of these unbioeroded samples were from skeletons of perinates or infants less than 1 month old. All four of these skeletons came from the north side of the church, which is consistent with the suggestion that this area was reserved for the burial of unbaptized infants (Kerr, 1994). A single adult sample was

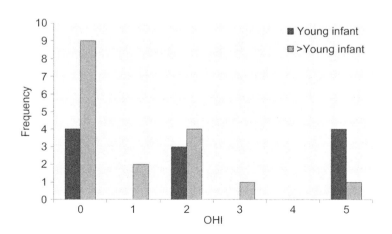

Figure 2.11 Histogram showing the distribution of OHI scores among human bone thin sections from the Church of St. Mary and St. Laurence, separated by whether the sample came from a young infant/perinate or an older individual.

anomalously free from bioerosion. This bone was recovered as part of the disarticulated charnel assemblage and there was little supplementary information that could be used to assess whether the taphonomic history of this individual was divergent. This sample could represent an outlier in the natural distribution of OHI scores associated with intact burial (Booth, 2016).

2.4 EAST SMITHFIELD, LONDON, UK

Articulated skeletons representing 1012 individuals were recovered from the East Smithfield cemetery in the city of London, UK (Grainger et al., 2008). The first burial phase is associated with a cemetery founded to accommodate the volume of dead produced by the 1348−50 AD Black Death epidemic. Soil slumping in the bases of some graves suggested that they had been left open for a time. Some skeletons were recovered in various stages of articulation in graves that showed no signs of revisiting, suggesting that there had been a delay between death and burial. The second phase of burial at East Smithfield was associated with a churchyard dating to ca. 1360−1650 AD (Grainger and Phillpotts, 2011). Several skeletons were excavated from beneath the associated abbey church and two of these were surrounded by quicklime. Quicklime inhibits early bodily decomposition and this practice was thought to represent an attempt to temporarily preserve bodies for display (Grainger and Phillpotts, 2011, p. 104; Schotsmans et al., 2012). The burial sediments consisted of free-draining sandy gravel and there was no evidence that any of the graves had ever been waterlogged (Grainger et al., 2008; Grainger and Phillpotts, 2011).   .

Femoral thin sections from 38 individuals were assessed for a study of archaeological human bone diagenesis across temperate Europe (Tryzelaar, 2003; Booth, 2016). The majority of samples from the later churchyard had been extensively bioeroded by bacteria (OHI < 2), consistent with them having originated from bodies that had been buried intact soon after death and exposed to high levels of bacterial bodily decomposition. Most of the samples from the Black Death cemetery had also been bioeroded extensively by bacteria, but a significant proportion showed lower levels of bioerosion, inconsistent with immediate burial (OHI = 3−5; Fig. 2.12; Booth, 2014).

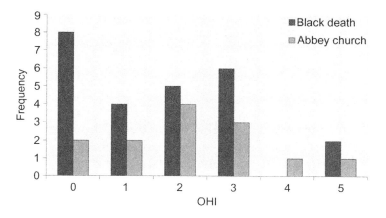

Figure 2.12 Histogram showing the distribution of OHI scores among human bone thin sections from the East Smithfield cemetery, separated by context.

These results suggested that the early taphonomic histories of some of the skeletons from the Black Death cemetery differed from those of individuals buried in the later churchyard. This is consistent with archaeological and osteological evidence suggesting that there was a delay between the death and the burial of certain individuals from the Black Death cemetery. These delays may have occurred as a result of the transportation of bodies to the site from outlying parishes, gaps between the death and the discovery of the deceased, and bodies being left in open graves for a time in anticipation of further burials (Grainger et al., 2008, p. 19). The intermediate levels of bacterial bioerosion observed in a proportion of the Black Death samples are consistent with a delay between death and burial, as unburied bodies would have been rapidly defleshed (Rodriguez and Bass, 1983; Campobasso et al., 2001; Simmons et al., 2010; Vass, 2011). Once the bodies were buried, the bones would have been subject to limited bacterial decomposition, determined by the initial exogenous loss of soft tissue.

The bone thin section of the skeleton from the Abbey Church that had been surrounded by quicklime was entirely free from bioerosion. An absence of bacterial bioerosion is characteristic of bone from mummified bodies (Booth et al., 2015). The presence of this signature in this sample was consistent with suggestions that the body had been deliberately preserved for display through the application of quicklime (Grainger and Phillpotts, 2011, p. 104).

2.5 SUMMARY

Variation in bacterial bioerosion in bones from archaeological and forensic studies suggests that it is associated with early bodily decomposition. Depositional environments that affect bodily decomposition (anoxic or waterlogged) will primarily control levels of bacterial bioerosion in a bone. However, outside of these conditions, variation in bacterial bioerosion can be linked to early postmortem events and combined with complementary taphonomic, archaeological, and historical information to make inferences about taphonomic histories and funerary treatment of individuals and populations. The striking absence of bacterial bioerosion from a large proportion of young infant remains suggests that microscopic analysis of bone diagenesis may also be useful for identifying stillborn infants in both forensic and archaeological contexts. Therefore, low-powered microscopic analysis of taphonomically significant changes to bone microstructure using thin section light microscopy has useful applications to investigations of taphonomic histories and past funerary treatment.

REFERENCES

Anderson, G.S., 2011. Comparison of decomposition rates and faunal colonisation of carrion in indoor and outdoor environments. J. Forensic Sci. 56 (1), 136–142.

Balzer, A., Gleixner, G., Grupe, G., Schmidt, H.L., Schramm, S., Turban-Just, S., 1997. In vitro decomposition of bone collagen by soil bacteria: the implications for stable isotope analysis in archaeometry. Archaeometry 39 (2), 415–429.

Bell, L.S., Elkerton, A., 2008. Unique marine taphonomy in human skeletal material recovered from the Medieval warship Mary Rose. Int. J. Osteoarchaeol. 18, 523–535.

Bell, L.S., Skinner, M.F., Jones, S.J., 1996. The speed of *post mortem* change to the human skeleton and its taphonomic significance. Forensic Sci. Int. 82, 129–140.

Booth, T.J., 2014. An Investigation into the Relationship Between Bone Diagenesis and Funerary Treatment. University of Sheffield, PhD Thesis.

Booth, T.J., 2016. An investigation into the relationship between bacterial bioerosion and funerary treatment in European archaeological human bone. Archaeometry 58 (3), 484–499.

Booth, T.J., Madgwick, R., 2016. New evidence for diverse secondary burial practices in Iron Age Britain: a histological case study. J. Archaeol. Sci. 67, 14–24.

Booth, T.J., Chamberlain, A.T., Parker Pearson, M., 2015. Mummification in Bronze Age Britain. Antiquity 89 (347), 1155–1173.

Booth, T.J., Redfern, R.C., Gowland, R.L., 2016. Immaculate conceptions: micro-CT analysis of diagenesis in Romano-British infant skeletons. J. Archaeol. Sci. 74, 124–134.

Bottrell, S.H., Hannam, J.A., Andrews, J.A., Maher, B.A., 1998. Diagenesis and remobilization of carbon and sulfur in mid-Pleistocene organic-rich freshwater sediment. J. Sediment. Res. 68 (1), 37–42.

Campobasso, C.P., Giancarlo, D.V., Introna, F., 2001. Factors affecting decomposition and Diptera colonization. Forensic Sci. Int. 120, 18−27.

Carr, G., 2007. Excarnation to cremation: continuity or change? In: Haselgrove, C., Moore, T. (Eds.), The Later Iron Age in Britain and Beyond. Oxbow, Oxford, pp. 446−455.

Carr, G.C., Knüsel, C., 1997. The ritual framework of excarnation by exposure as the mortuary practice of the early and middle Iron Ages of central southern Britain. In: Gwilt, A., Haselgrove, C. (Eds.), Reconstructing Iron Age Societies, 71. Oxbow Monograph, Oxford, pp. 167−173.

Child, A.M., 1995. Towards an understanding of the microbial decomposition of archaeological bone in the burial environment. J. Archaeol. Sci. 22, 165−174.

Craig, R.C., Knüsel, C.J., Carr, G.C., 2005. Fragmentation, mutilation and dismemberment: an interpretation of human remains on Iron Age sites. In: Parker Pearson, M., Thorpe, I.J.N. (Eds.), Warfare, Violence and Slavery in Prehistory. BAR International Series 1374, Oxford, pp. 165−180.

Cunliffe, B., 1984. Danebury: An Iron Age Hillfort in Hampshire Vol. 2: The Finds. Council for British Archaeology, London.

Cunliffe, B., Poole, C., 2000. Suddern Farm, Middle Wallop, Hants., 1991 and 1996. English Heritage and Oxford University Committee for Archaeology Monograph, Oxford, No. 49.

Cunliffe, B., Farrell, P., Dee, M., 2015. A happening at Danebury hillfort—but when? Oxford J. Archaeol. 34, 407−414.

Dal Sasso, G., Maritan, L., Usai, D., Angelini, I., Artioli, G., 2014. Bone diagenesis at the micro-scale: bone alteration patterns during multiple burial phases at Al Khiday (Khartoum, Sudan) between the Early Holocene and the II century AD. Palaeogeogr. Palaeoclimatol. Palaeoecol. 416, 30−42.

Duday, H., 2006. L'archéothanatologie ou l'archéologie de la mort (Archaeothanatology or the archaeology of death). In: Gowland, R., Knüsel, C. (Eds.), Social Archaeology of Funerary Remains. Oxbow, Oxford, pp. 30−56.

Economous, C., 2003. Behind the North Wall of Sleep. Microbial Degradation of Foetal and Neonatal Bone, With a Case Study from Bolsover. University of Sheffield, Unpublished MSc Dissertation.

Fernández-Jalvo, Y., Andrews, P., Pesquero, D., Smith, C., Marín-Monfort, D., Sánchez, B., et al., 2010. Early bone diagenesis in temperate environments Part I: Surface features and histology. Palaeogeogr. Palaeoclimatol. Palaeoecol. 288, 62−81.

Foster P. 1992. Excavations at the Parish Church of St. Mary & St. Lawrence, Bolsover. *Creswell Heritage Trust Report*.

Garland, A.N., 1987. A histological study of archaeological bone decomposition. In: Boddington, A., Garland, A.N., Janaway, R.C. (Eds.), Death, Decay and Reconstruction: Approaches to Archaeology and Forensic Science. Manchester University Press, Manchester, pp. 109−126.

Gill-King, H., 1997. Chemical and ultrastructural aspects of decomposition. In: Haglund, W.D., Sorg, M.H. (Eds.), Forensic Taphonomy: The Postmortem Fate of Human Remains. CRC Press, Boca Raton, FL, pp. 93−108.

Goff, M.L., 1991. Comparison of insect species associated with decomposing remains recovered from inside dwellings and out-doors on the Island of Oahu, Hawaii. J. Forensic Sci. 36, 748−753.

Grainger I & Phillpotts C. 2011. The Cistercian Abbey of St. Mary Graces, East Smithfield, London. Museum of London Archaeology Monograph 44, London.

Grainger I, Hawkins D, Cowal L. & Mikulski R. 2008. The Black Death Cemetery, East Smithfield, London. Museum of London Archaeology Monograph 43, London.

Grupe, G., Dreses-Werringloer, U., 1993. Decomposition phenomena in thin-sections of excavated human bones. In: Grupe, G., Garland, A.N. (Eds.), Histology of Ancient Human Bone: Methods and Diagnosis. Springer-Verlag, Berlin, pp. 27−36.

Hackett, C.J., 1981. Microscopical focal destruction (tunnels) in exhumed human bones. Med. Sci. Law 21 (4), 243–266.

Hanson, D.B., Buikstra, J.E., 1987. Histomorphological alteration in buried human bone from the Lower Illinois Valley: implications for palaeodietary research. J. Archaeol. Sci. 14, 549–563.

Hanson, M., Cain, C.R., 2007. Examining histology to identify burned bone. J. Archaeol. Sci. 34, 1902–1913.

Haynes, S., Searle, J.B., Bretman, A., Dobney, K.M., 2002. Bone preservation and ancient DNA: the application of screening methods for predicting DNA survival. J. Archaeol. Sci. 29 (6), 585–592.

Hedges, R.E.M., 2002. Bone diagenesis: an overview of processes. Archaeometry 44 (3), 319–328.

Hedges, R.E.M., Millard, A.R., Pike, A.W.G., 1995. Measurements and relationships of diagenetic alteration of bone from three archaeological sites. J. Archaeol. Sci. 22, 201–209.

Hollund, H.I., Jans, M.M.E., Collins, M.J., Kars, H., Joosten, I., Kars, S.M., 2012. What happened here? Bone histology as a tool in decoding the postmortem histories of archaeological bone from Castricum, the Netherlands. Int. J. Osteoarchaeol. 22 (5), 537–548.

Hollund, H.I., Arts, N., Jans, M.M.E., Kars, H., 2015. Are teeth better? Histological characterisation of diagenesis in archaeological bone—tooth pairs and a discussion of the consequences for archaeometric sample selection and analyses. Int. J. Osteoarchaeol. 25 (6), 901–911.

Janaway, R.C., 1996. The decay of buried human remains and their associated material. In: Hunter, J., Roberts, C., Martin, A. (Eds.), Studies in Crime: An Introduction to Forensic Archaeology. Butler & Tanner, Frome, pp. 58–85.

Jans, M.M.E., Nielsen-Marsh, C.M., Smith, C.I., Collins, M.J., Kars, H., 2004. Characterisation of microbial attack on archaeological bone. J. Archaeol. Sci. 31, 87–95.

Jackes, M., Sherburne, R., Lubell, D., Barker, C., Wayman, M., 2001. Destruction of microstructure in archaeological bone: a case study from Portugal. Int. J. Osteoarchaeol. 11, 415–432.

Junqeira, L.C., Carneiro, J., Long, J.A., 1986. Basic Histology, Fifth ed. Prentice-Hall, London.

Kerr N. 1994. Report of Human Remains from Bolsover, Derbyshire. University of Sheffield, Unpublished Certificate of Archaeology Dissertation.

Lee-Thorp, J.A., Sealy, J.C., 2008. Beyond documenting diagenesis: the fifth international bone diagenesis workshop. Palaeogeogr. Palaeoclimatol. Palaeoecol. 266, 129–133.

Marchiafava, V., Bonucci, E., Ascenzi, A., 1974. Fungal osteoclasia: a model of dead bone resorption. Calcif. Tissue Res. 14, 195–210.

Millard, A., 2001. The deterioration of bone. In: Brothwell, D., Pollard, A.M. (Eds.), Handbook of Archaeological Sciences. John Wiley & Sons, Chichester, pp. 637–647.

Miszkiewicz, J.J., Mahoney, P., 2016. Ancient human bone microstructure in medieval England: comparisons between two socio-economic groups. Anat. Rec. 299 (1), 42–59.

Murphy, E.M., 2008. Deviant Burial in the Archaeological Record. Oxbow, Oxford.

Nicholson, R.A., 1996. Bone degradation, burial medium and species representation: debunking the myths, an experimental-based approach. J. Archaeol. Sci. 23, 513–533.

Nielsen-Marsh, C.M., Smith, C.I., Jans, M.M.E., Nord, A., Kars, H., Collins, M.J., 2007. Bone diagenesis in the European Holocene II: taphonomic and environmental considerations. J. Archaeol. Sci. 34 (9), 1523–1531.

Ottoni, C., Koon, H.E., Collins, M.J., Penkman, K.E., Rickards, O., Craig, O.E., 2009. Preservation of ancient DNA in thermally damaged archaeological bone. Naturwissenschaften 96 (2), 267–278.

Parker Pearson, M., Chamberlain, A., Craig, O., Marshall, P., Mulville, J., Smith, J., et al., 2005. Evidence for mummification in Bronze Age Britain. Antiquity 79, 529–546.

Pesquero, M.D., Ascaso, C., Alcalá, L., Fernández-Jalvo, Y., 2010. A new taphonomic bioerosion in a Miocene lakeshore environment. Palaeogeogr. Palaeoclimatol. Palaeoecol. 295, 192–198.

Polson, C.J., Gee, D.J., Knight, B., 1985. The Essentials of Forensic Medicine. Pergamon Press, Oxford.

Redfern, R., 2008. New evidence for Iron Age secondary burial practice and bone modification from Gussage All Saints and Maiden Castle (Dorset, England). Oxford J. Archaeol. 27 (3), 281–301.

Rodriguez, W.C., Bass, W.M., 1983. Insect activity and its relationship to decay rates of human cadavers in East Tennessee. J. Forensic Sci. 28 (2), 423–432.

Schotsmans, E.M.J., Denton, J., Dekeirsschieter, J., Ivaneanu, T., Leentjes, S., Janaway, R.C., et al., 2012. Effects of hydrated lime and quicklime on the decay of buried remains using pig cadavers as human body analogues. Forensic Sci. Int. 217, 50–59.

Shahack-Gross, R., Bar-Yosef, O., Weiner, S., 1997. Black-coloured bones in Hyonim Cave, Israel: differentiating between burning and oxide staining, J. Archaeol. Sci., 24. pp. 439–446.

Simmons, T., Cross, P.A., Adlam, R.E., Moffatt, C., 2010. The influence of insects on decomposition rate in buried and surface remains. J. Forensic Sci. 55 (4), 889–892.

Smith, C.I., Nielsen-Marsh, C.M., Jans, M.M.E., Arthur, P., Nord, A.G., Collins, M.J., 2002. The strange case of Apigliano: early 'fossilisation' of medieval bone in southern Italy. Archaeometry 44 (3), 405–415.

Smith, C.I., Nielsen-Marsh, C.M., Jans, M.M.E., Collins, M.J., 2007. Bone diagenesis in the European Holocene I: patterns and mechanisms. J. Archaeol. Sci. 34 (9), 1485–1493.

Sosa, C., Vispe, E., Núñez, C., Baeta, M., Casalod, Y., Bolea, M., et al., 2013. Association between ancient bone preservation and DNA yield: a multidisciplinary approach. Am. J. Phys. Anthropol. 151, 102–109.

Terrell-Nield, C., MacDonald, J., 1997. The effects of decomposing animal remains on cave invertebrate communities. Cave Karst Sci. 24 (2), 53–65.

Tryzelaar L. 2003. Histological Study of the Destruction of Bone at the Royal Mint. University of Sheffield, Unpublished MSc Dissertation.

Turner, B., Wiltshire, P., 1999. Experimental validation of forensic evidence: a study of the decomposition of buried pigs in a heavy clay soil. Forensic Sci. Int. 101, 113–122.

Turner-Walker, G., 1999. Pyrite and bone diagenesis in terrestrial sediments evidence from the West Runton freshwater bed. Bull. Geol. Soc. Norfolk 48, 3–26.

Turner-Walker, G., 2008. The chemical and microbial degradation of bones and teeth. In: Pinhasi, R., Mays, S. (Eds.), Advances in Human Palaeopathology. John Wiley & Sons, Chichester, pp. 3–30.

Turner-Walker, G., Syversen, U., 2002. Quantifying histological changes in archaeological bones using BSE-SEM image analysis. Archaeometry 44 (3), 461–468.

Turner-Walker, G., Jans, M.M.E., 2008. Reconstructing taphonomic histories using histological analysis. Palaeogeogr. Palaeoclimatol. Palaeoecol. 266, 227–235.

Turner-Walker, G., Nielsen-Marsh, C.M., Syversen, U., Kars, H., Collins, M.J., 2002. Submicron spongiform porosity is the major ultra-structural alteration occurring in archaeological bone. Int. J. Osteoarchaeol. 12, 407−414.

van der Sluis, L.G., Hollund, H.I., Buckley, M., De Louw, P.G.B., Rijsdijk, K.F., Kars, H., 2014. Combining histology, stable isotope analysis and ZooMS collagen fingerprinting to investigate the taphonomic history and dietary behaviour of extinct tortoises from the Mare aux Songes deposit on Mauritius. Palaeogeogr. Palaeoclimatol. Palaeoecol. 416, 80−91.

Vass, A.A., 2011. The elusive universal post-mortem interval formula. Forensic Sci. Int. 204, 34−40.

Walker, L., 1984. The deposition of the human remains. In: Cunliffe, B.W. (Ed.), Danebury: An Iron Age Hillfort in Hampshire, vol 2, Excavation 1968-78: The Finds. Council for British Archaeology, London, pp. 442−462.

White, L., Booth, T.J., 2014. The origin of bacteria responsible for bioerosion to the internal bone microstructure: results from experimentally-deposited pig carcasses. Forensic Sci. Int. 239, 92−102.

CHAPTER 3

Human Bone and Dental Histology in an Archaeological Context

Justyna J. Miszkiewicz[1] and Patrick Mahoney[2]

[1]Australian National University, Canberra, ACT, Australia [2]University of Kent, Canterbury, United Kingdom

3.1 INTRODUCTION

Histological studies of ancient human skeletons can reveal biological processes and structures that underlie skeletal growth and adaptation in individuals and populations from the archeological past. This information can be accessed from bones and teeth, which provide two different types of microstructural data. Human bone reflects indicators of its metabolic activity which remodels the skeleton throughout our lifespan, adapting, and responding to external and internal factors and stimuli (such as physical activity, dietary change, disease, aging). Tooth enamel structures, on the other hand, serve as a permanent record of skeletal growth during childhood, because once formed enamel does not remodel. The aim of this chapter is to provide an overview of

Human Remains: Another Dimension. DOI: http://dx.doi.org/10.1016/B978-0-12-804602-9.00004-7

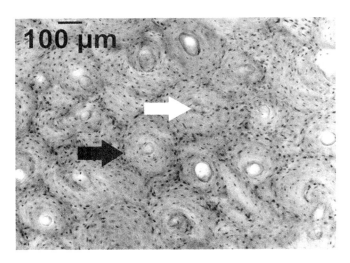

Figure 3.1 Human femoral cortical bone viewed at 10× magnification. White arrow indicates a Haversian canal, black arrow points to an intact osteon. This image shows excellent preservation of bone micro-anatomy in a British Medieval male from Canterbury, UK.

histological approaches to archeological human adult bone and juvenile teeth. We then apply this methodology to a British Medieval population from Canterbury (11th−16th centuries AD) revealing aspects of their skeletal biology.

3.2 BONE

Bone histology, the study of the microscopic anatomy of cells and tissues, has been traditionally examined in bioscience research and clinical diagnosis (Müller et al., 1998), often relied upon in paleobiology (Sander et al., 2006), and now its value unfolds in anthropological studies of ancient humans (Crowder and Stout, 2011). Thin sections from well-preserved ancient samples may be examined to visualize biological changes, processes, and structural features at the microscopic level (Stout and Teitelbaum, 1976). Both qualitative (e.g., morphological appearance, brightness) and quantitative (e.g., densities, dimensions) data can be collected (Crowder and Stout, 2011) (Figs. 3.1−3.2). Contextual evidence, such as cultural and/or lifestyle background of a population, gathered from archeological and historical records can be used in combination with bone histological insights to reconstruct ancient human adaptation (e.g., Miszkiewicz and Mahoney, 2016).

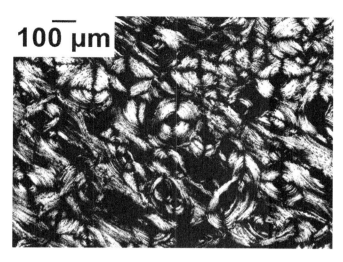

Figure 3.2 Medieval human femoral cortical bone viewed at 10× magnification using polarized light to reveal different types of collagen fiber orientation ("bright" and "dark" osteons).

Bone is a mineralized connective, yet flexible living tissue which changes throughout human lifespan via two key processes known as modeling and remodeling (Boyce and Xing, 2008). The living skeleton undergoes transformation from juvenile to adult form by shaping its morphology and depositing mature bone tissue (modeling) and continues to renew itself once adulthood is reached (remodeling). This metabolic activity allows bone to respond and adapt to external and internal factors and stimuli (such as physical activity, diet, disease, aging), which may be reconstructed from histological indicators in ancient samples (Crowder and Stout, 2011). Histology of adult compact (cortical) bone in particular offers a substantial research potential when examined in archeological samples. Tightly packed secondary osteons that are on average 200−300 μm in diameter feature central Haversian canals that facilitate blood supply in live cortical tissue (Figs. 3.1−3.2). Each osteon, composed of lamellae (bone layers) and bordered by a cement line, displays numerous 5−20 μm small cavities (lacunae) for osteocytes (bone maintenance cells) which interact with each other via canal processes (canaliculi) (Fig. 3.3). Once imaged under a high-powered microscope, healthy or abnormal appearance and changes in bone are visualized, and evaluated in relation to other biological variables that affect or underlie bone modeling and remodeling. For example, this may include function and mobility as bone microstructure adapts itself to accommodate mechanical load (Robling

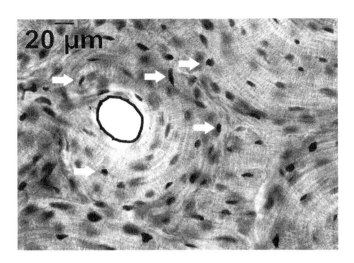

Figure 3.3 Medieval human femoral cortical bone viewed at 40× magnification showing multiple osteocyte lacunae (white arrows), and indicating that Haversian canal area (white circle with black outline) can be recorded in thin sections.

et al., 2006), and aspects of growth or age-at-death estimation as osteons increase in numbers with age (Currey, 1964).

In cases where considerable taphonomic and diagenetic change originating from archeological matrix alters histology, micro-anatomical interpretations are limited, though past taphonomic histories may be reconstructed (e.g., Hollund et al., 2012; Booth and Madgwick, 2016). Thin sections, usually from the rib or femur, with no or minimal taphonomic alteration have been successfully used to evaluate aging (e.g., Thompson and Gunness-Hey, 1981), behavior (e.g., Robling and Stout, 2003; Miszkiewicz and Mahoney, 2016), disease (e.g., Schultz, 2001, 2003), diet (e.g., Richman et al., 1979), and sex-specific (Mulhern and Van Gerven, 1997; Mulhern, 2000) variation and environmental adaptation in the human past.

Early histological studies of ancient bone primarily explored bone preservation, composition, and diagnosed paleopathology through descriptive accounts of micro-anatomical appearance (e.g., Dubois, 1937; Graf, 1949). Later studies focused on ancient "paleophysiology" which aimed to reconstruct the fundamentals of physiological bone processes in the context of human age, sex, and lifestyle (Stout, 1978, p. 603). Most recently, utilizing larger samples and inferential statistics, ancient bone metabolic activity in a biomechanical context has been investigated (e.g., Pfeiffer et al., 2006; Miszkiewicz and Mahoney, 2016). Using principles of bone functional adaptation in relation to different mechanical loading regimes, changes in density and geometric properties of bone histology features have been measured and interpreted in the light of information about past behavior (e.g., Robling and Stout, 2003; Miszkiewicz and Mahoney, 2016). For example, human femora from a physically active group had higher density of osteons when compared to sedentary humans from ancient Peru (Robling and Stout, 2003).

Analytical approaches range from counting or measuring osteons (histomorphometry) in images captured under normal transmitted light (e.g., Miszkiewicz, 2015) (Figs. 3.1−3.2), qualitative evaluation of collagen fiber orientation (CFO) under polarized light (histomorphology) (e.g., Schultz, 2001) (Fig. 3.2) where osteon birefringent "rings" can be scored (Skedros et al., 2013), to the use of geographical information systems in mapping cortical bone variation (e.g., Rose et al., 2012; Gocha and Agnew, 2016). One may be more suitable over the other depending on research questions posed. For example, reconstructing populational trends, such as gender division in labor or the effect of socioeconomic status on bone health, from microstructural variation has been achieved using femoral cortical histomorphometry (e.g., Mulhern, 2000; Miszkiewicz and Mahoney, 2016) because it allows for localized bone functional adaptation to be measured. Mechanical load adaptation at the osteon level may be better understood from CFO at sites of lower limb tension or compression, because mechanical properties of individual osteons are largely determined by the arrangement of lamellar collagen fibers (Goldman et al., 2003).

3.3 TEETH

The secretory stage of tooth enamel growth commences in deciduous incisors, early in the second trimester (Kraus and Jordan, 1965; Mahoney, 2015). The first molar is the only permanent tooth to commence enamel growth in utero, usually a few weeks before birth (Mahoney, 2008), but this varies greatly between individuals. Growth continues after birth in all deciduous and permanent tooth types, finishing in permanent third molar crowns in the late childhood to early teenage years (Reid and Dean, 2006; Mahoney, 2015).

Although tooth enamel continues to mature after the crown has formed, it does not remodel, unlike bone. Thus, tooth crowns preserve within their structure a permanent record of their own growth, in the form of incremental markings. These markings develop as ameloblasts differentiate along the dentin—enamel junction (DEJ), and move away from the DEJ, as tooth crowns increase in height and thickness (Boyde, 1989). Ameloblasts are cells that secrete enamel matrix proteins. Ameloblast differentiation and secretion is not consistent, which produces incremental markings in the form of cross striations (Fig. 3.4) and Retzius lines (Fig. 3.5). Cross striations occur at a rate that corresponds to a circadian rhythm (Lacruz et al., 2012; Zheng et al., 2013).

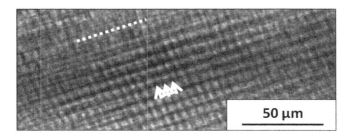

Figure 3.4 Cross striations (white arrows) in tooth enamel viewed at 40× magnification. Dashed white line indicates prism direction.

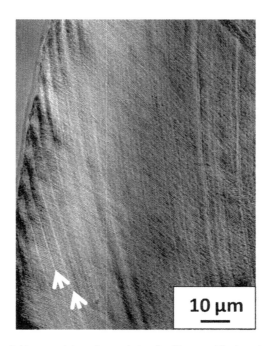

Figure 3.5 Retzius lines (white arrows) in tooth enamel viewed at 10× magnification using polarized light.

Retzius lines occur with a periodicity that ranges between 4 and 12 days when compared between humans (Mahoney et al., 2016). A third type of incremental marking is a neonatal line, a prominent marking that occurs at birth (e.g., Sabel et al., 2008). The neonatal line subdivides enamel growth into pre- and postnatal periods.

Several macroscopic methods are available to reconstruct tooth enamel growth (e.g., Liversidge et al., 1993; Liversidge and Molleson, 2004). Histological methods rely upon imaging microstructure, in thin sections, to reconstruct growth by counting and measuring cross striations and Retzius lines. Histological analyses of incremental markings in archeological samples of modern human deciduous teeth have been used to document the timing and rate of prenatal enamel growth (Mahoney, 2015), estimate age-at-death (Boyde, 1964), explore the evolution of modern human life history (Mahoney, 2015), and reveal biorhythms underlying enamel and bone growth (Mahoney et al., 2016).

3.4 TECHNICAL CONSIDERATIONS

Samples removed for histological analyses of bone can be sufficiently small ($0.5-1$ cm in height), making the technique minimally invasive (e.g., Pfeiffer et al., 2006; Miszkiewicz and Mahoney, 2016). Dental histology studies can also rely on sampling one tooth per individual (e.g., Mahoney, 2008). Accepted standards and ethics for destructive sampling should be followed (Mays et al., 2013). Increasingly efficient and cost-effective ancient skeletal sample preparation techniques and ways of equipping laboratories are available (De Boer et al., 2012, 2013; Paine, 2007), encouraging the inclusion of histology in bioarchaeological schools and research centers. Extracted skeletal samples require embedding in resin or plastic and are then usually cut on a precision low speed saw, ground, and polished (Bancroft and Gamble, 2002) to yield final thin sections that can be stored for future analyses. These normally range from 50 to 100 µm in thickness (Crowder and Stout, 2011). A high-powered microscope (e.g., Olympus BX, or less expensive CX series) is necessary to achieve a relatively high magnification ($60 \times$ to $100 \times$) if cell-related features (e.g., osteocyte lacunae) are to be studied, though a range of $10 \times$ to $40 \times$ magnification suffices for the examination of osteons, and their features. Images of thin sections are captured with a mounted microscope camera (e.g., Olympus DP, or less expensive CS series). Data are recorded and quantified using an imaging software with a range of drawing and point counting tools (e.g., CELL Live Biology Imaging, Olympus Stream, or free and open access ImageJ).

Given that bone undergoes remodeling, the selection of regions of interest (ROIs) within a thin section should be consistent to ensure replicability of studies, meaningful data comparisons, and appropriate evaluation of research questions. Different techniques have been reported, including the use of an eyepiece grid micrometer (e.g., Mulhern and Van Gerven, 1997), evaluation of bone strips (Robling and Stout, 2003), subparts of the cortex (Miszkiewicz, 2015; Miszkiewicz and Mahoney, 2016), examining countable osteons (e.g., Pfeiffer et al., 2006) or entire thin section (Thompson and Gunness-Hey, 1981). However, localized taphonomic and diagenetic change may complicate study design. Though it has been shown that different ROI selection procedures yield matching results (Villa and Lynnerup, 2010), it is recommended that a minimum of 25−50 osteons should be studied per thin section (Crowder and Stout, 2011).

Standard histological sectioning of teeth relies upon capturing one 2D plane that travels through the tip of the enamel cusp, the tip of the dentin horn, and into the most cervical enamel. Mineralization of teeth (and in particular enamel) is much higher compared to bone, which means that dental samples are less susceptible to diagenetic and taphonomic change (Hollund et al., 2015). The thickness of sections will vary depending upon the degree of mineralization within a crown. Usually, sections of deciduous teeth are between 70 and 120 μm in thickness. Cross striations and Retzius lines are recorded at a magnification of $20 \times$ to $60 \times$. The region examined within a tooth crown will depend upon the variable that is recorded. Cross striations can be used to calculate the rate of enamel secretion in cuspal (occlusal) enamel, which is usually subdivided into inner, mid, and outer regions. Retzius lines can be used to calculate periodicity of lateral enamel regions. Image capturing and recording is undertaken with appropriate software such as Olympus DP and CELL Live Biology Imaging.

3.5 HUMAN SKELETAL HISTOLOGY IN MEDIEVAL CANTERBURY, UK: SHORT STUDY

The Skeletal Biology Research Centre at the University of Kent (Canterbury, UK) curates several hundred human skeletons that include subadults and adults, males and females, and individuals with a range of pathologies. The collection represents a late Medieval (11th–16th centuries AD) British population from high-status St. Gregory's Priory and adjacent low-status cemetery in Canterbury (see Hicks and Hicks, 2001; Miszkiewicz, 2012). As revealed through archeological excavations, the high-status group had few and rich burials located inside the Priory (Hicks and Hicks, 2001). Historical evidence identifies the adjacent cemetery to be designated for poor and sick peasants and those who could not afford burial in the higher status site (Brent, 1879). Over the past few years we have been exploring the bioarchaeology of these individuals using skeletal histology.

Recently, we reported significant variation in femoral bone microstructure between the two distinct burial groups (Miszkiewicz and Mahoney, 2016). We demonstrated that differences in histomorphometric parameters (such as secondary osteon density, area and dimeter of transverse cross-sectional osteon and vascular surfaces) corresponded with adult lifestyle information for each status groups. When compared to those of low status, high-status adults had increased osteon densities with larger osteon and Haversian canal surfaces, indicating good health, nutrition, but sedentary lifestyle. Our interpretations were based on basic engineering principles of bone microstructure functional adaptation which indicate the deposition of smaller osteons with increasing load (e.g., van Oers et al., 2008), and dietary influences on bone remodeling which suggest an increase in bone density with surplus of calories (e.g., Richman et al., 1979; Paine and Brenton, 2006).

Dental histology research on juveniles from this archeological site revealed that deciduous enamel growth commenced in deciduous incisors early in the second trimester and finished around the end of the first postnatal year in second molars (Mahoney, 2015). Enamel growth appears to be coordinated, to some extent, with primary bone growth (Mahoney et al., 2016). An underlying biorhythm corresponds with greater production of enamel and primary bone matrix.

In this brief study, we extend the above findings to demonstrate the application of histology images from archeological bones and teeth:

1. We compare femoral histology data within the low-status cemetery between two adult age groups to explore ancient aging and behavior. Though all low-status individuals usually undertook physically

active occupations (Dyer, 1989), we predict bone microstructure to reflect adaptation to larger and more frequent mechanical load resulting from more regular and strenuous activities in the younger males (Dyer, 2000, 2002) when compared to the middle-aged males.

2. Using cross striations, Retzius and neonatal lines in teeth, we compare the proportion of pre- and postnatal enamel growth in deciduous maxillary molars.

3.5.1 Materials and Methods

A total of 199 femora from adult British Medieval males from Canterbury were selected for a histomorphometric analysis. Age-at-death and sex were estimated following standard anthropological methods based on gross skeletal anatomy examination (Buikstra and Ubelaker, 1994). Two age groups of "young" 20–34 ($n = 44$) and "middle-aged" 35–50 years old ($n = 155$) individuals were created. Osteon population density (OPD as #/mm^2) and Haversian canal area (H.Ar in μm^2) were recorded in images of thin sections removed from the posterior femur (see Miszkiewicz, 2015 and Miszkiewicz and Mahoney, 2016) and compared between the young and middle-aged adults using a Mann–Whitney U test accounting for unequal sample size.

Forty-eight deciduous maxillary molars (dm^1, dm^2) from juveniles recovered in Medieval Canterbury were sectioned using standard histological methods (see Mahoney, 2015; and new data here). Total crown formation times, subdivided by the proportion of pre- and postnatal enamel in these tooth types, were calculated from daily enamel secretion rates, Retzius periodicity, and measures of enamel thickness combined with the location of the neonatal line.

3.5.2 Results

Both OPD ($n = 186$, $U = 3813.000$, $p = 0.006$) and H.Ar ($n = 199$, $U = 4200.000$, $p = 0.019$) were significantly higher in middle-aged males when compared to the younger group (Fig. 3.6). The total crown formation time was 415 days for dm^1 and 539 days for dm^2. Thirty-three percent of dm^1 enamel and 15% of dm^2 enamel formed before birth (Fig. 3.7).

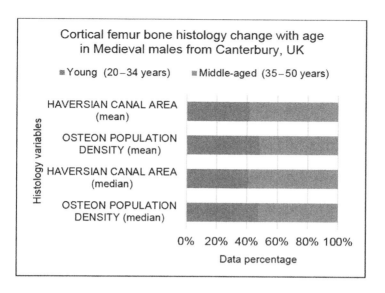

Figure 3.6 Graph illustrating OPD and Haversian canal area differences between the two age groups of males.

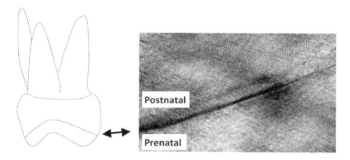

Figure 3.7 Pre- and postnatal enamel growth in a maxillary deciduous first molar. Black arrow points to the neonatal line.

3.5.3 Discussion and Summary

Our aim in this brief study was to demonstrate that skeletal micro-structure data can be recorded in images captured from thin sections and used to reconstruct aspects of ancient human life in the past. We found an increase in OPD (#/mm^2) from young to middle-aged adults in agreement with previous ancient bone histology research (e.g., Thompson and Gunness-Hey, 1981) and attribute it to age-related increase in osteons (Currey, 1964). As predicted, we also observed the young males to have smaller Haversian canals (μm^2) indicating adaptation to larger strains (Miszkiewicz and Mahoney, 2016), and thus corresponding with the age-specific differences in Medieval lifestyles and occupations (Bennett and Hollister, 2006; Dyer, 1989, 2000, 2002). For example, younger Medieval peasant males tended to engage in agricultural occupations that involved heavy load carrying subjecting their lower limbs to rigorous walking and additional stress originating from the carried weight (Gransden, 1972). While the older peasant males also engaged in substantial walking, their load carrying responsibilities would have been reduced (if not abandoned completely) due to health deterioration, aging, and age group specific division of labor (Bennett and Hollister, 2006). However, we emphasize that the intricate processes of bone growth require cautious interpretations of ancient human past and, ideally, comparisons with experimental or contemporary data.

The average proportion of enamel growth in this sample of deciduous *maxillary* molars is slightly greater when compared to samples of *mandibular* molars from Medieval Canterbury (Mahoney, 2011; $dm^1 = 29\%$, $dm^2 = 16\%$). This is most likely due to slight differences in enamel initiation times in utero, in order to facilitate slightly thicker maxillary molar enamel within the total crown formation period. Knowledge of the proportions of pre- and postnatal enamel growth can be used to assess changes in growth trajectories in ancient compared to modern day populations. They can also contribute to age-at-death estimations in a bioarchaeological and forensic context. Taken together, our results reveal insights into skeletal growth and adaptation in this Medieval population.

3.6 CONCLUSIONS

Histological analyses of ancient human skeletons can reveal the underlying mechanisms that facilitate morphological change during growth, aging, and disease. Imaging and analyzing these microscopic structures holds great potential for revealing the skeletal biology of past human populations.

ACKNOWLEDGMENTS

We thank Tim Thompson for inviting us to contribute to this volume and two reviewers for invaluable feedback. The Royal Society funded equipment (PM), bone histology data were collected during a PhD studentship (JJM) funded by the School of Anthropology and Conservation, University of Kent. Elle Grono (Geoarchaeology, Australian National University) facilitated microscope imaging in Figs. 3.1 and 3.3.

REFERENCES

Bancroft, J.D., Gamble, M., 2002. Theory and Practice of Histological Techniques. Churchill Livingstone, London.

Bennett, J., Hollister, C.W., 2006. Medieval Europe: A Short History. McGraw-Hill, New York.

Booth, T.J., Madgwick, R., 2016. New evidence for diverse secondary burial practices in Iron Age Britain: a histological case study. J. Archaeol. Sci. 67, 14–24.

Boyce, B.F., Xing, L., 2008. Functions of RANKL/RANK/OPG in bone modeling and remodeling. Arch. Biochem. Biophys. 473, 139–146.

Boyde, A., 1964. Estimation of age at death of young human skeletal remains from incremental lines in dental enamel. Third International Meeting in Forensic Immunology, Medicine, Pathology and Toxicology, Plenary Session 11A. 16–24 April 1963, London. Excerpta Med Int Congr Ser, vol. 80.

Boyde, A., 1989. Enamel. In: Berkovitz, B.K.B., Boyde, A., FrankRM, Hohling, H.J., Moxham, B.J., Nalbandian, J., Tonge, C.H. (Eds.), Teeth. Handbook of Microscopic Anatomy. Springer-Verlag, Berlin, pp. 309–473.

Brent, J., 1879. Canterbury in the Olden Time. Simpkin, Marshall and Co, London.

Buikstra, J.E., Ubelaker, D.H. 1994. Standards for Data Collection from Human Skeletal Remains. Arkansas Archaeology Survey, Fayetteville.

Crowder, C., Stout, S., 2011. Bone Histology: An Anthropological Perspective. CRC Press, Boca Raton, FL.

Currey, J.D., 1964. Some effects of ageing in human Haversian systems. J. Anat. 98 (1), 69–75.

De Boer, H.H., Aarents, M.J., Maat, G.J.R., 2012. Staining ground sections of natural dry bone tissue for microscopy. Int. J. Osteoarchaeol. 22, 379–386.

De Boer, H.H., Aarents, M.J., Maat, G.J.R., 2013. Manual for the preparation and staining of embedded natural dry bone tissue sections for microscopy. Int. J. Osteoarchaeol. 23, 83–93.

Dubois, E., 1937. The osteone arrangement of the thigh-bone compacta of man identical with that first found of *Pithecanthropus*. Proc. R. Acad. Amsterdam 38, 850–852.

Dyer, C., 1989. Standards of Living in the Later Middle Ages: Social Change in England, 1200–1520. Cambridge University Press.

Dyer, C., 2000. Everyday Life in Medieval England. Cambridge University Press.

Dyer, C., 2002. Making a Living in the Middle Ages. Yale University Press.

Gocha, T.P., Agnew, A.M., 2016. Spatial variation in osteon population density at the human femoral midshaft: histomorphometric adaptations to habitual load environment. J. Anat. 228 (5), 733–745.

Goldman, H.M., Bromage, T.G., Thomas, C.D.L., Clement, J.G., 2003. Preferred collagen fiber orientation in the human mid-shaft femur. Anat. Rec. 272A, 434–445.

Graf, W., 1949. Preserved histological structures in Egyptian mummy tissues and ancient Swedish skeletons. Cells Tissues Organs 8, 236–250.

Gransden, A., 1972. Childhood and youth in Mediaeval England. Nottingham Medieval Studies 16 (1), 3–19.

Hicks, M., Hicks, A., 2001. St. Gregory's Priory, Northgate, Canterbury Excavations 1988-1991 (p. Volume II). Canterbury Archaeological Trust Ltd.

Hollund, H.I., Jans, M.M.E., Collins, M.J., Kars, H., Joosten, I., Kars, S.M., 2012. What happened here? Bone histology as a tool in decoding the postmortem histories of archaeological bone from Castricum, the Netherlands. Int. J. Osteoarchaeol. 22 (5), 537–548.

Hollund, H.I., Arts, N., Jans, M.M.E., Kars, H., 2015. Are teeth better? Histological characterization of diagenesis in archaeological bone–tooth pairs and a discussion of the consequences for archaeometric sample selection and analyses. Int. J. Osteoarchaeol. 25 (6), 901–911.

Kraus, B., Jordan, R., 1965. The Human Dentition Before Birth. Lea & Febiger, Philadelphia.

Lacruz, R.S., Hacia, J.G., Bromage, T.G., Boyde, A., Lei, Y., Xu, Y., et al., 2012. The circadian clock modulates enamel development. J. Biol. Rhythms 27 (3), 237–245.

Liversidge, H.M., Molleson, T.I., 2004. Variation in crown and root formation and eruption of human deciduous teeth. Am. J. Phys. Anthropol. 123 (2), 172–180.

Liversidge, H.M., Dean, M.C., Molleson, T.I., 1993. Increasing human tooth length between birth and 5.4 years. Am. J. Phys. Anthropol. 90, 307–313.

Mahoney, P., 2008. Intraspecific variation in M 1 enamel development in modern humans: implications for human evolution. J. Hum. Evol. 55, 131–147.

Mahoney, P., 2011. Human deciduous mandibular molar incremental enamel development. Am. J. Phys. Anthropol. 144, 204–214.

Mahoney, P., 2015. Dental fast track: prenatal enamel growth, incisor eruption, and weaning in human infants. Am. J. Phys. Anthropol. 156, 407–421.

Mahoney, P., Miszkiewicz, J.J., Pitfield, R., Schlecht, S.H., Deter, C., Guatelli-Steinberg, D., 2016. Biorhythms, deciduous enamel thickness, and primary bone growth in modern human children: a test of the Havers–Halberg Oscillation hypothesis. J. Anat. 228, 919–928.

Mays, S., Elders, J., Humphrey, L., White, W., Marshall, P., 2013. Science and the Dead: A Guidelines for the Destructive Sampling of Archaeological Human Remains for Scientific Analysis. Advisory Panel on the Archaeology of Burials in England. English Heritage.

Miszkiewicz, J.J., 2012. Linear enamel hypoplasia and age-at-death at Medieval (11th–16th centuries) St. Gregory's Priory and Cemetery, Canterbury, UK. Int. J. Osteoarchaeol. 25, 79–87.

Miszkiewicz, J.J., 2015. Investigating histomorphometric relationships at the human femoral midshaft in a biomechanical context. J. Bone Miner. Metab. 34, 179–192.

Miszkiewicz, J.J., Mahoney, P., 2016. Ancient human bone microstructure and behaviour in medieval England: comparisons between two socio-economic groups. Anat. Rec. 299, 42–59.

Mulhern, D.M., 2000. Rib remodeling dynamics in a skeletal population from Kulubnarti, Nubia. Am. J. Phys. Anthropol. 111, 519–530.

Mulhern, D.M., Van Gerven, D.P., 1997. Patterns of femoral bone remodeling dynamics in a Medieval Nubian population. Am. J. Phys. Anthropol. 104, 133–146.

Müller, R., Van Campenhout, H., Van Damme, B., Van der Perre, G., Dequeker, J., Hildebrand, T., et al., 1998. Morphometric analysis of human bone biopsies: a quantitative structural comparison of histological sections and micro-computed tomography. Bone 23, 59–66.

Paine, R.R., 2007. How to equip a basic histological lab for the anthropological assessment of human bone and teeth. J. Anthropol. Sci. 85, 213–219.

Paine, R.R., Brenton, B.P., 2006. Dietary health does affect histological age assessment: an evaluation of the Stout and Paine (1992) age estimation equation using secondary osteons from the rib. J. Forensic Sci. 51, 489–492.

Pfeiffer, S., Crowder, C., Harrington, L., Brown, M., 2006. Secondary osteon and Haversian canal dimensions as behavioral indicators. Am. J. Phys. Anthropol. 468, 460–468.

Reid, D.J., Dean, M.C., 2006. Variation in modern human enamel formation times. J. Hum. Evol. 50, 329–346.

Richman, E.A., Ortner, D.J., Schulter-Ellis, F.P., 1979. Differences in intracortical bone remodeling in three aboriginal American populations: possible dietary factors. Calcif. Tissue Int. 28, 209–214.

Robling, A.G., Stout, S.D., 2003. Histomorphology, geometry, and mechanical loading in past populations. In: Agarwal, S.C., Stout, S.D. (Eds.), Bone Loss and Osteoporosis: An Anthropological Perspective. Kluwer Academic/Plenum Publishers, New York, pp. 189–206.

Robling, A.G., Castillo, A.B., Turner, C.H., 2006. Biomechanical and molecular regulation of bone remodeling. Annu. Rev. Biomed. Eng. 8, 455–498.

Rose, D.C., Agnew, A.M., Gocha, T.P., Stout, S.D., Field, J.S., 2012. Technical note: the use of geographical information systems software for the spatial analysis of bone microstructure. Am. J. Phys. Anthropol. 148, 648–654.

Sabel, N., Johansson, C., Kuhnisch, J., Robertson, A., Steiniger, F., Norén, J.G., et al., 2008. Neonatal lines in the enamel of primary teeth—a morphological and scanning electron microscopic investigation. Arch. Oral. Biol. 53, 954–963.

Sander, P.M., Mateus, O., Laven, T., Knötschke, N., 2006. Bone histology indicates insular dwarfism in a new Late Jurassic sauropod dinosaur. Nature 441, 739–741.

Schultz, M., 2001. Paleohistopathology of bone: a new approach to the study of ancient diseases. Am. J. Phys. Anthropol. 116, 106–147.

Schultz, M., 2003. Light microscopic analysis in skeletal paleopathology. In: Ortner, D.J. (Ed.), Identification of Pathological Conditions in Human Skeletal Remains. Elsevier Science, London, pp. 73–109.

Skedros, J.G., Keenan, K.E., Williams, T.J., Kiser, C.J., 2013. Secondary osteon size and collagen/lamellar organization ("osteon morphotypes") are not coupled, but potentially adapt independently for local strain mode or magnitude. J. Struct. Biol. 181 (2), 95–107.

Stout, S.D., 1978. Histological structure and its preservation in ancient bone. Curr. Anthropol. 19, 601–604.

Stout, S.D., Teitelbaum, S.L., 1976. Histological analysis of undecalcified thin sections of archeological bone. Am. J. Phys. Anthropol. 44, 263–269.

Thompson, D.D., Gunness-Hey, M., 1981. Bone mineral-osteon analysis of Yupik-Inupiaq skeletons. Am. J. Phys. Anthropol. 55, 1–7.

van Oers, R.F., Ruimerman, R., van Rietbergen, B., Hilbers, P.A., Huiskes, R., 2008. Relating osteon diameter to strain. Bone 43, 476–482.

Villa, C., Lynnerup, N., 2010. Technical note: a stereological analysis of the cross-sectional variability of the femoral osteon population. Am. J. Phys. Anthropol. 142, 491–496.

Zheng, L., Seon, Y.J., Mourão, M.A., Schnell, S., Kim, D., Harada, H., et al., 2013. Circadian rhythms regulate amelogenesis. Bone 55, 158–165.

CHAPTER 4

"Cut to the Bone": The Enhancement and Analysis of Skeletal Trauma Using Scanning Electron Microscopy

Jenna M. Dittmar
University of Cambridge, Cambridge, United Kingdom

4.1 CASE STUDY: TOOL MARKS AND HUMAN DISSECTION

4.2 IDENTIFICATION OF SAWS AND KNIVES USED IN HUMAN DISSECTION

4.3 SAWS

4.4 KNIVES

4.5 SEM ANALYSIS: FOR MORE THAN JUST THE ENHANCEMENT OF TOOL MARKS

4.6 CONCLUSIONS

ACKNOWLEDGMENTS

REFERENCES

The examination and identification of traumatic lesions within forensic and archaeological contexts is a crucial element in understanding the events surrounding the death and postmortem treatment of an individual. In recent decades, many technological advances have allowed for the enhancement and visualization of traumatic lesions, but none have been more influential to the study of tool marks on bone than scanning electron microscopy. Scanning electron microscopes (SEMs) became commercially available in 1965 (McMullan, 1995). By 1970, their application to criminal investigations had been recognized (Korda et al., 1970). Since that time, SEMs have been increasingly used to enhance the detail of traumatic lesions, fibers, and biological materials—as this form of microscopy has several advantages over conventional light microscopes (Rose, 1983; Tucker et al., 2001; Domínguez-Rodrigo et al., 2009; Symes et al., 2010; Reichs, 1998; Bromage and Boyde, 1984). A SEM, for example, has superior

Human Remains: Another Dimension. DOI: http://dx.doi.org/10.1016/B978-0-12-804602-9.00005-9

resolution of three-dimensional structures, increased depth of field, and the capacity for higher magnification. These features allow for variations to be identified which are not always visible to the naked eye or when using light microscopy (Hayat, 1978; Watt, 1985; Tucker et al., 2001).

The enhanced imaging capabilities of a SEM allows for human interactions, primarily in the form of interpersonal violence, to be interpreted based on tool or weapon marks found on human skeletal remains. Within forensic contexts, scanning electron microscopy has been used to examine gunshot defects (Rickman and Smith, 2014) and weapon marks in bone (Quatrehomme et al., 2005; Symes et al., 2010), but interest in the enhancement of traumatic lesions is not restricted to forensic scientists. The interpretation of trauma is also of particular interest to the study of people from past societies. Although tool marks on bones from archaeological contexts are relatively rare, when they are identified, the analysis of the trauma using a SEM can provide key information about the activities of past people. Such activities include, funerary practices (White, 1986), butchery practices (Shipman and Rose, 1983; Perez et al., 2005; Johnson and Bement, 2009; Thompson and Henshilwood, 2014) warfare (Fiorato et al., 2000), and more extraordinary activities such as cannibalism (Mays and Beattie, 2015) and postmortem medical intervention (Dittmar and Mitchell, 2016; Dittmar-Blado and Wilson, 2012; Valentin and d'Errico, 1995).

This chapter will discuss how scanning electron microscopy enables the interpretation of traumatic lesions on bone in order to gain increased information about peri-mortem treatment of bodies in both modern and past societies. This is illustrated by examining the tool marks from postmortem medical procedures during early anatomical education. The utilization of a SEM to analyze the tool marks associated with human dissection provides an excellent example of how the application of forensic methods to archaeological skeletal remains can provide not only information on the tools used, but also about the treatment and perception of bodies within specific contexts.

4.1 CASE STUDY: TOOL MARKS AND HUMAN DISSECTION

Since the medieval period, anatomical dissection has been performed to acquire "perfect knowledge" of the body. To achieve this,

anatomists spent hours extensively examining the anatomical structures. As a result of this process, tool marks created by various instruments are left on the skeleton, as is evidenced by the number of
archaeological excavations that have uncovered human skeletal
remains presenting evidence of sharp-force trauma consistent with
human dissection in recent decades (Chamberlain, 2012; Dittmar and
Mitchell, 2015; Fowler and Powers, 2012; Mitchell, 2012).

Within the archaeological record, the most common sign that a
body has been examined for medical purposes after death is the presence of a craniotomy along the axial plane (Fig. 4.1). In this procedure, the top of the cranium is sawn open so that the brain and
internal structures can be examined. In addition to this procedure,
another commonly identified component of dissection was to open the
chest through a procedure called a thoracotomy. This procedure was
accomplished by sawing through the sternum, via a sternotomy (Ellis,
1840), or by sawing through the costoclavicular cartilage connecting
the ribs on each side (Harris, 1887; Holden and Langton, 1868;
Virchow, 1880). In addition to the procedures described above, surgical tool marks have been identified in a variety of locations on dissected skeletons, some of which indicate that bodies were dismembered
to facilitate learning among student dissectors. This practice, known as

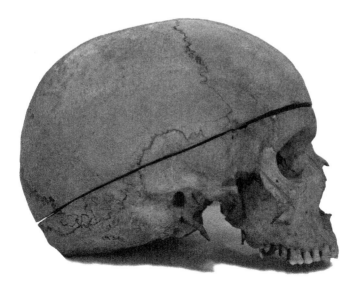

Figure 4.1 Skull of a dissected adult with a craniotomy at the University of Cambridge, 19th century.

cadaver sharing, is noted within several dissected populations (Dittmar, 2016; Fowler and Powers, 2012).

This body of evidence provides a unique opportunity to enhance our understanding of human dissection in early modern anatomical education in England by investigating the surgical practices and tools used by anatomists. The analysis of the tool marks found on these dissected individuals enables a temporal examination of dissection practices as well as an examination into the evolution of surgical instruments; an area which has received very little research. In order to do this, a SEM was used to analyze the sharp-force trauma identified on multiple ($n = 31$) individuals who were dissected at the University of Cambridge between ca. 1769 and ca. 1913. Alec Tiranti RTV putty silicone was used to create molds of the tool marks as outlined in the work of Dittmar et al. (2015). Each silicone mold was then analyzed using a Hitachi 3000 Tabletop SEM on topographical mode.

As the types of surgical instruments used during the 18th and 19th centuries (handsaws, knives) are similar to the types of tools commonly examined within modern forensic investigations, an analysis of the morphological characteristics was undertaken based on the analyses of sharp-force trauma described within forensic literature (Saville et al., 2007; Symes et al., 2010). Sharp-force trauma is identifiable in many violent crimes in the United Kingdom (Office of National Statistics, 2016) and as a result, the ability to identify and classify weapon marks is of paramount importance to the forensic investigation. Extensive research has been conducted on knife marks (Saville et al., 2007; Thompson and Inglis, 2009), as stab wounds are common. Saw marks, however, is not commonly found on homicide victims, as dismemberment is a relatively rare occurrence (Porta et al., 2016). The fascination and horror inflicted by the dismemberment of a corpse has led to a number of published case reports but very few synthetic studies of tool marks exist apart from the seminal work by Symes et al. (2010). Research by Houck (1998), Bartelink et al. (2001), Hutchinson and Humphrey (2001), Tucker et al. (2001), and Alunni-Perret et al. (2005) has contributed to the development of metal tool classification criteria and was referred to during this work to complement the classification of tools based on morphological characteristics by Symes et al. (2010).

4.2 IDENTIFICATION OF SAWS AND KNIVES USED IN HUMAN DISSECTION

Recognizing the differences between cut marks caused by knife blades and those caused by a saw is essential in tool mark identification, especially since both classes of tool mark are often together on dismembered and dissected remains (Symes et al., 2010; Dittmar and Mitchell, 2015). Of particular importance to this research are kerfs, incomplete saw cuts, and incisions made by knives. Scanning electron microscopy aids the differentiation of saw marks and knife marks as it enhances the morphology of the tool marks (Saville et al., 2007; Symes et al., 2010).

4.3 SAWS

The morphology of a saw mark is dependent on numerous factors including the shape of the blade that created the kerf (straight, circular, etc.), the size of the teeth, the blade width and tooth set, the material cut, and the actions of the individual creating the kerf marks (Andahl, 1978; Symes et al., 2002, p. 408). A saw blade is comprised of teeth which each cut into the bone, and the action of multiple cutting surfaces for each tooth removes a part of the material being cut, essentially shaving or chiseling through the material (Symes et al., 2010). The movement of the saw leaves a series of macroscopically visible fine lines, called striations, which indicate the direction of the sawing and the type of saw used.

Saws are categorized by the design (rip or crosscut) and set of their teeth (alternating, raker, wavy) (Symes et al., 2010). While all saws produce kerfs that are relatively square in shape, the cross-sectional shape of the kerf enables more information about the blade to be discerned. Crosscut saws, designed to cut across the grain of wood, create kerfs that have a convex kerf floor, while rip saws, designed to cut along the grain of the wood, leave a flat or concave floor (Symes, 1992; Symes et al., 2010). The morphology of the kerf allows the set of the saw's teeth to be identified. Alternate set saws have teeth that are angled outward, away from the midline in opposite directions and create kerfs that have a convex floor that can have a W-shaped cross section. Raker set saws have angled teeth pointing away from the midline in alternating directions in addition to teeth positioned straight along the midline. The complex design of raker saws creates kerfs with straight walls with numerous parallel striae on the floor of the kerf. Saws with wavy set teeth consist of a series of teeth with alternating directions on a wave-shaped edge, which create long, parallel striae on the floor of the kerf (Symes et al., 2010). Saws with the teeth positioned straight along the midline of the blade produce a kerf with a flat or slightly rounded bottom (Symes et al., 2010).

Microscopic analysis enables these features to be examined in detail and the analysis of the striations can permit the individualization of a cut mark to a specific tool (Houck, 1998). In order to enable a comparison, the features of a number of historic saws, housed at the Whipple Museum at the University of Cambridge and the Thackray Museum in Leeds, were recoded. This analysis was supplemented by examining the results of experimental sawing research undertaken by Fisher (2014).

The SEM analysis of the surgical tool marks was able to provide further information on the type of saw used to open the skull during dissection. This research was restricted to an examination of the incomplete saw kerfs. Unfortunately, specific saws were unable to be identified based on the morphological characteristics of the kerf floor and walls. However, this assessment was able to exclude a number of saws based on the analysis of the morphological features on the kerf floors and minimum kerf widths. Within this sample, kerf floors presenting a pointed mound in the center of two, V-shaped furrows on either side were most commonly identified. The morphology of these kerfs is consistent with a crosscut saw with alternating teeth. As a result, it is possible to exclude a number of surgical saws, primarily those with raker or wavy set teeth (Fig. 4.2).

This finding is consistent with the historical surgical catalogs that illustrate crosscut saws with alternate set teeth as commonly used in Britain by the late 18th century. A standard construction for saws used to cut through bone was published by J. H. Savigny in a catalog distributed from 1793 to 1795. These saws were described as having teeth "very regularly bent outwards in opposite directions," which is equivalent to a modern alternate set saw blade (Savigny, 1793–1795). The reason for this construction method was described by Savigny:

12 teeth an inch" serves its' "purpose (severing bone) most completely", if they are finer they will produce a smoother surface of the bone, and occasion fewer splinters, they become clogged during the operation and produce a violent agitation of the limb and splinter the edges of the bone to a degree that they afterwards become troublesome

Savigny, 1793–1795, p. 65.

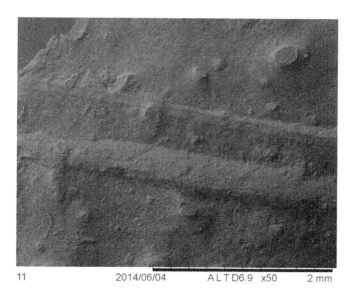

11   2014/06/04   A L T D6.9 x50   2 mm

Figure 4.2 SEM micrograph (×50) of an alternate set saw kerf taken from a silicon cast from a dissected individual.

The practicality of this construction likely influenced the general design for surgical saws, with most conforming to the standard described by Savigny, however Savigny admits that it was impossible to fix an exact standard. The variation in construction standards between surgical instrument makers or even batches of instruments made by the same maker is supported by the analysis of the minimum kerf widths on the skeletal remains of dissected individuals. Width measurements of the saw kerfs revealed that the width of the saw blades used in dissection at the University of Cambridge varied greatly (0.45–1.25 mm) (Dittmar, 2016). Some of this variation likely resulted from the individual who created the kerf, however it is believed that the substantial variation between surgical tools made by different makers is responsible for the variation in kerf widths.

4.4 KNIVES

A knife incision occurs when a sharp edged tool superficially cuts the surface of the bone, often while following the contour of a bone (Symes et al., 2010). Cut marks retain the characteristics of the inflicting blade, including striations, and engraved patterns, which can be used to reconstruct the shape of a knife blade and the blade angle

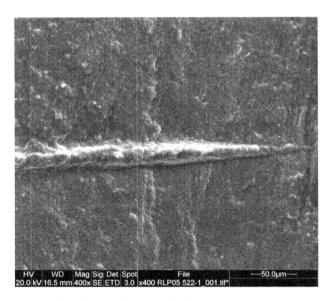

Figure 4.3 SEM micrograph (× 400) of knife incision taken from a silicon cast from RLP05 522.

(Shaw et al., 2011; Thompson and Inglis, 2009). These cut marks are characterized by narrow blade dimensions, a V-shaped cross section and striations perpendicular to the kerf (Shaw et al., 2011).

The SEM analysis of the incisions on the bones revealed that all knife marks were created by a straight knife without a serrated edge. There were no discernable differences between knife marks present on individuals in this sample. This suggests that there was very little variation in the type of knife blades used in human dissection at the University of Cambridge (Fig. 4.3).

4.5 SEM ANALYSIS: FOR MORE THAN JUST THE ENHANCEMENT OF TOOL MARKS

As is often the case with archaeological skeletal remains, the analysis of sharp-force trauma can reveal more than just the morphological characteristics of the tools used. Specifically, within the context of early modern anatomical education much about the perception and varying treatment of medical bodies by anatomists is also discernable. A recent study conducted on a historically documented collection from the former anatomical museum at the University of Cambridge revealed much about the treatment of fetal and infant bodies by early modern anatomists (Dittmar and Mitchell, 2016).

Very few fetal and infant skeletal remains presenting evidence of tool marks associated with human dissection have been found at archaeological sites. Therefore, this important subgroup has been overlooked within historical and archaeological scholarship. In their study, Dittmar and Mirchell observed that the surgical tool marks on the skeletal remains of fetal and infant bodies ($n = 54$) dissected at the University of Cambridge revealed that the bodies of individuals within this subgroup were treated very differently to adults. Most of these fetal and infant bodies were dissected in a way that did not result in substantial damage to the skeletal system, allowing them to be displayed in the anatomical museum (Dittmar and Mitchell, 2016). SEM analysis of silicone casts taken from the endocranial surface of these skulls has revealed numerous fine, linear striations. The morphological characteristics of these striae in addition to their proximity to each other suggest that a tool with multiple fine bristles, like a brush, was used on these skulls (Dittmar, 2016). The brush marks were likely created during the preparatory process prior to display within the museum and indicate that great care was taken to preserve these valuable sources of anatomical knowledge.

4.6 CONCLUSIONS

Within both forensic and archaeological contexts, scanning electron microscopy allows for increased information about peri-mortem treatment of bodies in both modern and past societies. This analysis of the tool marks on dissected human skeletal remains has allowed for an increase of information about the history of medicine and medical education. This includes the types of surgical instruments used. The morphological examination of the tool marks revealed that knives and crosscut saws with alternate set teeth were used during dissections conducted by students at the University of Cambridge throughout the late 18th and 19th centuries. Finally, the analysis of sharp-force trauma can reveal more than just the morphological characteristics of the tools responsible. This provides insight into the perception and treatment of medical bodies within the context of early modern anatomical education.

ACKNOWLEDGMENTS

I would like to thank Josh Nall at the Whipple Museum at the University of Cambridge and Lauren Ryall-Stockton of the Thackray Musuem, Leeds for allowing me to examine historical surgical instruments within their collections. I would also like to thank Hallie Smith-Lloyd for her comments.

REFERENCES

Alunni-Perret, V., Muller-Bolla, M., Laugier, J.P., Lupi-Pegurier, L., Bertrand, M.F., Staccini, P., et al., 2005. Scanning electron microscopy analysis of experimental bone hacking trauma. J. Forensic Sci. 50 (4), 796–801.

Andahl, R.O., 1978. The examination of saw marks. J. Forensic Sci. Soc. 18, 31–46.

Bartelink, E., Wiersema, J., Demaree, R., 2001. Quantitative analysis of sharp-force trauma: an application of scanning electron microscopy in forensic anthropology. J. Forensic Sci. 46 (6), 1288–1293.

Bromage, T.G., Boyde, A., 1984. Microscopic criteria for the determination of directionality of cutmarks on bone. Am. J. Phys. Anthropol. 65, 359–366.

Chamberlain, A., 2012. Morbid osteology: evidence for autopsies, dissection and surgical training from the Newcastle Infirmary burial ground (1753–1845). In: Mitchell, P.D. (Ed.), Anatomical Dissection in Enlightenment England and Beyond: Autopsy, Pathology and Display. Ashgate, Farnham, pp. 11–22.

Dittmar, J.M., 2016. An Archaeological Examination of Human Dissection and its Role in Anatomical Education in England from 1600–1900. University of Cambridge, PhD Thesis.

Dittmar, J.M., Mitchell, P.D., 2015. New criteria for identifying and differentiating human dissection and autopsy in archaeological assemblages. J. Archaeol. Sci. Rep. 3, 73–79.

Dittmar, J.M., Mitchell, P.D., 2016. From cradle to grave via the dissection room: the role of foetal and infant bodies in anatomical education from the late 1700s to early 1900s. J. Anat. Available from: http://dx.doi.org/10.1111/joa.12515.

Dittmar, J.M., Errickson, D., Cafell, A., 2015. A comparison of silicone casting materials for archaeological applications. J. Archaeol. Sci. Rep. 4, 559–564.

Dittmar-Blado, J.M., Wilson, A.S., 2012. Microscopic examination of the tool marks. In: Powers, N., Fowler, L. (Eds.), Doctors, Dissection and Resurrection Men: Excavations in the 19th-Century Burial Ground of the London Hospital, 2006. MOLA Monograph Series 62. Lavenham Press, London, pp. 180–184.

Domínguez-Rodrigo, M., De Juana, S., Galán, A.B., Rodríguez, M., 2009. A new protocol to differentiate trampling marks from butchery cut marks. J. Archaeol. Sci. 36 (12), 2643–2654.

Ellis, G.V., 1840. Demonstrations of Anatomy; Being a Guide to the Dissection of the Human Body. Taylor and Walton, London. Available from Internet Archive [4 April 2016].

Fiorato, V., Boylston, A., Knüsel, C., 2000. Blood Red Roses: The Archaeology of a Mass Grave from the Battle of Towton AD 1461. Oxbow Books, Oxford.

Fisher, J., 2014. Cut Mark Analysis of Post-Medieval Medical Instrument on Bone. University of Bradford, MSc Dissertation.

Fowler, L., Powers, N., 2012. Doctors, Dissection and Resurrection Men: Excavations in the 19th-Century Burial Ground of the London Hospital, 2006. MOLA Monograph Series 62. Laverham Press, London.

Harris, T., 1887. Post-Mortem Handbook or How to Conduct Post-Mortem Examinations for Clinical and for Medico-Legal Purposes. Smith, Elder & Co., London.

Hayat, M.A., 1978. Introduction to Biological Scanning Electron Microscopy. University Park Press, Baltimore, MD.

Holden, L., Langton, J. (Eds.), 1868. Holden's Manual of the Dissection of the Human Body. 3rd ed. J. Churchill, London.

Houck, M., 1998. Skeletal trauma and the individualization of knife marks in bone. In: Reichs, K.J. (Ed.), Forensic Osteology: Advances in the Identification of Human Remains, 2nd ed. Charles C Thomas, Springfield, IL, pp. 410–424.

Hutchinson, D.L., Humphrey, J.H., 2001. Macroscopic characteristics of hacking trauma. J. Forensic Sci. 46 (2), 228–233.

Johnson, E., Bement, L.C., 2009. Bison butchery at Cooper, a Folsom site on the southern plains. J. Archaeol. Sci. 36 (7), 1430–1446.

Korda, E.J., MacDonell, H.L., Williams, J.P., 1970. Forensic applications of the scanning electron microscope. J. Crim. Law Criminol. Police Sci. 61, 453–458.

Mays, S., Beattie, O., 2015. Evidence for end-stage cannibalism on Sir John Franklin's last expedition to the Arctic, 1845. Int. J. Osteoarchaeol.Online 4 August. http://dx.doi.org/10.1002/oa.2479.

McMullan, D., 1995. Scanning electron microscopy 1928–1965. Scanning 17 (3), 175–185.

Mitchell, P.D. (Ed.), 2012. Anatomical Dissection in Enlightenment England and Beyond: Autopsy, Pathology and Display. Ashgate, Farnham.

Office of National Statistics 2016. Crime in England and Wales: Year ending December 2015. Published online 21 April 2016. Available from: http://www.ons.gov.uk/peoplepopulationandcommunity/crimeandjustice/bulletins/crimeinenglandandwales/yearendingdecember2015.

Perez, V.R., Godfrey, L.R., Nowak-Kemp, M., Burney, D.A., Ratsimbazafy, J., Vasey, N., 2005. Evidence of early butchery of giant lemurs in Madagascar. J. Hum. Evol. 49, 722–742.

Porta, D., Amadasi, A., Cappella, A., Mazzarelli, D., Magli, F., Gibelli, D., et al., 2016. Dismemberment and disarticulation: a forensic anthropological approach. J. Forensic Leg. Med. 38, 50–57.

Quatrehomme, G., Laugier, J.P., Lupi-Pégurier, L., Bolla, M., Bertrand, M.F., Muller-Bolla, M., et al., 2005. Scanning electron microscopy analysis of experimental bone hacking trauma. J. Forensic Sci. 50 (4), 796–801.

Reichs, K.J., 1998. Postmortem dismemberment: recovery, analysis and interpretation. In: Reichs, K.J. (Ed.), Forensic Osteology Advances in the Identification of Human Remains, 2nd ed. Charles C. Thomas, Springfield, IL, pp. 353–388.

Rickman, J.M., Smith, M.J., 2014. Scanning electron microscope analysis of gunshot defects to bone: an underutilized source of information on ballistic trauma. J. Forensic Sci. 59 (6), 1473–1486.

Rose, J.J., 1983. A replication technique for scanning electron microscopy: applications for anthropologists. Am. J. Phys. Anthropol. 62, 255–263.

Savigny, J.H., 1793–1795. A Collection of Engravings Presenting the Most Modern and Approved Instruments Used in the Practice of Surgery with Appropriate Explanations. Surgeon's instrument-maker, The Letter-Press by T Bensley, London.

Saville, P.A., Hainsworth, S.V., Rutty, G.N., 2007. Cutting crime: the analysis of the "uniqueness" of saw marks on bone. Int. J. Leg. Med. 121 (5), 349–357.

Shaw, K.P., Chung, J.H., Chung, F.C., Tseng, B.Y., Pan, C.H., Yang, K.T., et al., 2011. A method for studying knife tool marks on bone. J. Forensic Sci. 56 (4), 967—971.

Shipman, P., Rose, J.J., 1983. Evidence of butchery and hominid activity at Torralba and Ambrona: an evaluation using microscopic techniques. J. Archaeol. Sci. 10 (3), 465—474.

Symes, S.A., 1992. Morphology of Saw Marks in Human Bone: Identification of Class Characteristics. University of Tennessee, PhD Thesis. <http://trace.tennessee.edu/utk_graddiss/1253>.

Symes, S.A., Williams, J.A., Murray, E.A., Hoffman, J.M., Holland, T.D., Saul, J.M., et al., 2002. Taphonomic context of sharp-force trauma in suspected cases of human mutilation and dismemberment. Advances in Forensic Taphonomy: Method, Theory, and Archaeological Perspectives. pp. 403—434.

Symes, S.A., Chapman, E.N., Rainwater, C.W., Cabo, L.L., Myster, S.M.T., 2010. Knife and Saw Tool Mark Analysis in Bone: A Manual Designed for the Examination of Criminal Mutilation and Dismemberment. National Institute of Justice, Report number: NCJ 232227.

Thompson, J.C., Henshilwood, C.S., 2014. Tortoise taphonomy and tortoise butchery patterns at Blombos Cave, South Africa. J. Archaeol. Sci. 41, 214—229.

Thompson, T.J.U., Inglis, J., 2009. Differentiation of serrated and non-serrated blades from stab marks in bone. Int. J. Leg. Med. 123 (2), 129—135.

Tucker, B.K., Hutchinson, D.L., Gilliland, M.F., Charles, T.M., Daniel, H.J., Wolfe, L.D., 2001. Microscopic characteristics of hacking trauma. J. Forensic Sci. 46 (2), 234—240.

Valentin, F., d'Errico, F., 1995. Skeletal evidence of operations on cadavers from Sens (Yonne, France) at the end of the XVth century. Am. J. Phys. Anthropol. 98, 375—390.

Virchow, R., 1880. A Description and Explanation of the Method of Performing Post-Mortem Examinations in the Dead House of the Berlin Charité Hospital. J & A Church Hill, London.

Watt, I.M., 1985. The Principles and Practice of Electron Microscopy. Cambridge University Press, New York.

White, T.D., 1986. Cut marks on the Bodo cranium: a case of prehistoric defleshing. Am. J. Phys. Anthropol. 69, 503—509.

CHAPTER 5

The Role of Radiography in Disaster Victim Identification

Jacquie Vallis

Teesside University, Middlesbrough, United Kingdom

REFERENCES

The use of radiography in Disaster Victim Identification (DVI) is well established (Rutty et al., 2013); Kahana and Hiss (1999) claimed that 55% of victims from major catastrophes are identified using a variety of radiological comparisons. Meyer (2003) concurs, stating that DNA, forensic odontology, and radiology currently provide the highest yield in terms of positive identification. The role of radiography in DVI is to assist with identification, cause of death, and the location of evidence (forensic and personal artefacts). Furthermore, radiography is essential for screening the body bags when they are received at the mortuary, to determine if there are any health and safety risks for staff in the mortuary. The range of imaging modalities that can be utilized in DVI will be critiqued for their role in various types of mass fatalities incidents, a summary is given in Table 5.1. DVI incorporates the processes and procedures for recovering and identifying deceased people and human remains in mass fatalities (College of Policing, 2013). The Home Office (2004, p. 3) define a mass fatalities incident as one "where the number of fatalities is greater than normal local arrangements can manage." Interpol (2014) categorize identification methods in relation to their accuracy and reliability. Primary methods (the most accurate) include fingerprints, dental, DNA, unique serial number from medical implants, while secondary methods include medical findings, personal description, tattoos, property and clothing, and X-rays. While X-rays are generally defined as a secondary method, dental X-rays contribute significantly as a primary identification method.

A radiographer utilizes a variety of imaging modalities to produce high-quality images of the body with some radiographers qualified to

Human Remains: Another Dimension. DOI: http://dx.doi.org/10.1016/B978-0-12-804602-9.00006-0

Table 5.1 Summary of the Role of Different Imaging Modalities in DVI		
Imaging Modality	Uses Ionizing Radiation	Uses in DVI
Digital/ conventional	Yes	• Good for AM and PM comparisons • Good for imaging body parts/small evidence bags, when there is lots of fragmentation • Demonstrates trauma • Imaging of unique skeletal material
Dental intraoral	Yes	• Contributes as a primary identification method • Required in all DVI incidents • Quick, cheap, highly efficient, and reliable • Provides images of all the dentition and surrounding anatomy • Assists the odontologist in examination of the dentition and surrounding anatomy • Nomad—will require lead rubber aprons for protection
Fluoroscopy	Yes	• Real-time imaging of the body bag • Health and Safety survey of the bag to alert staff to hazards • Excellent for locating artefacts, including bomb fragments, personal artefacts (phones, jewelry, etc.). • Demonstrates contents of the bag, commingling, fragmentation • Completed within 10 minutes including documentation
Multislice computed tomography	Yes—highest radiation exposure	• Quick imaging of the body bag contents • Shows internal structures clearly (removing superimposing structures) • Produces 3D reconstructions and multiplanar reformats • Clearly identifies metal and skeletal material • Most expensive modality • Still requires dental imaging or extra software and staff to undertake the post-processing required • Requires storage capacity for large amounts of data • Review of images is more time-consuming

provide a report on the images (SCoR, 2016). A radiologist is a doctor who has specialized in radiology, reports on the images, and undertakes interventional procedures (RCR, 2016).

Radiography is very useful when identifying the deceased, as the bones and teeth are the last tissues to change after death (Jenson, 2000), and these can provide essential information about the deceased. It is particularly useful for imaging decomposed bodies as was the case following the Boxing Day Tsunami 2004 (BBC News, 2005). Radiography provides a permanent record of the evidence captured. Radiography can provide evidence for reconstructive and comparative identification. In terms of reconstructive identification, radiography of the skeleton can provide a general classification of each victim, building up a profile of each individual in relation to the sex of the individual, age, height, and race. In terms of comparative identification, radiography undertaken postmortem (PM) can be compared with antemortem (AM) radiographic imaging. As the frontal sinuses are unique to each individual, comparing AM and PM images of the frontal sinuses may give this form of identification the same potential value as fingerprints (Quatrehomme et al., 1996). With living patients only having a Multislice Computed Tomography (MSCT) scan of their sinuses now, rather than conventional plain film, research has been undertaken to confirm the reliability of MSCT for comparison of AM and PM images, including the ability in the software to undertake measurements directly of the internal structures (Tatlisumak et al., 2007). In addition, radiography may demonstrate the presence of medical intervention, such as prostheses, pins, plates, and evidence of embolization, where evidence such as prostheses has their own unique number engraved on it to confirm identity of the individual. Comparing the position of pins between AM and PM images has been utilized for identification purposes. Furthermore, Mann (1998) found that the bone trabeculae could be utilized to establish a positive identification, with no two bones being identical in the pattern and appearance of the trabeculae. Sanders et al. (1972) also identified a deceased individual from a single clavicle using the trabecular pattern. Others have also reported identifying the deceased using osteological features of the thorax, shoulder, vertebrae (Atkins and Potsaid, 1978), vascular grooves of the skull (Messmer and Fierro, 1986), and mastoid process and sphenoid sinus (Rhine and Sperry, 1991). Radiography demonstrating the effects of disease processes on the skeleton may also be utilized for identification purposes, building up the profile of the deceased or comparing with AM data.

As with imaging of the living, radiography can provide evidence of the trauma and/or pathology sustained, which can be utilized to determine cause of death, and therefore, can also contribute to enhancing safety of vehicles, etc. MSCT is increasingly being utilized to determine cause of death.

Radiography is excellent for locating personal artefacts or fragments from bombs or aircraft. For instance, a body that has been exposed to fire may have a necklace that is hidden in the charred soft tissues or may demonstrate a bullet or other artefact. As a mass fatalities incident may also be a crime scene, such as in the 2005 London Bombings, radiography is excellent for locating bomb fragments and any other such critical evidence.

The type of imaging modality utilized in DVI really depends on the nature and scale of the incident itself, the degree of fragmentation, availability of equipment, the chosen method of identification, and AM data available. For instance, dental radiography was the only imaging required following the Great Heck (Selby) rail crash in 2001 (BBC News, 2001), to identify all 10 of the victims. In addition, during the aftermath of the 2005 London Bombings (Xograph, 2007), considerable fragmentation of some of the victims meant that radiographers spent whole days X-raying small evidence bags, making digital imaging the best modality in this scenario; however, dental imaging was also required as a primary method of identification for larger parts/ whole bodies.

In terms of flow through the DVI mortuary, Fluoroscopy or MSCT is the first modality utilized. Fluoroscopy provides real-time imaging of a body bag prior to any other processes undertaken. It can give a quick evaluation of what exactly is contained in the body bag, and if there are any health and safety risks that those handling the body need to be aware of (sharps, explosives, ballistic material, etc.). For example, in the excavation of the mass graves in Kosovo, some bodies were found to be booby-trapped, and fluoroscopy quickly detected such hazards within the body bag (Viner, 2014). In addition, fluoroscopy can be used to identify commingling in the body bag, resulting from a bomb blasting fragments/body parts into another body, a mother holding a child to protect them when trapped in a fire, etc. Furthermore, fluoroscopy will demonstrate the location of skeletal material, personal artefacts that may aid identification, and clothing (belts, shoes, etc.). This evaluation of the body bag may take no more than 10 minutes by an experienced forensic radiographer, and digital or hard copy evidence can be provided as a permanent record along with accompanying documentation to identify what was located where in the bag. More recently MSCT has been utilized instead of fluoroscopy to evaluate the body bag contents.

The use of MSCT in forensic practice has been increasing throughout the world, with research demonstrating its effectiveness in determining cause of death. With the public demanding a minimally invasive MSCT scan rather than an invasive autopsy (R v H M Coroner for Inner London District Greater London, 2014), MSCT is becoming more routinely utilized. Research has demonstrated that MSCT could be utilized to determine cause of death, reporting that the frequency of major discrepancies between MSCT and the autopsy report was 33%, an error rate that Roberts et al. (2012) argue is similar to that for clinical death certificates. Focus has since looked at the contribution MSCT could make in DVI, and indeed MSCT has since been utilized for Victorian Bushfires (2009), MH17 (2014), and Shoreham Aircraft Disaster (2015) producing positive results. MSCT produces slices through the body demonstrating internal structures clearly (removing superimposing structures), and, with 3D reconstructions and multiplanar reformats possible, enables this modality to be excellent at demonstrating the various components of a body bag, with metal easily identified (using Maximum Intensity Projection—enabling color coding of the metal), and skeletal material. MSCT is the most expensive of the modalities discussed here and has the highest radiation exposure. It can be taken to the scene or emergency mortuary, as with the other modalities. MSCT of the body bag is quick; however, with the vast amount of information gained, longer time is required to view and postprocess the images (O'Donnell et al., 2011). MSCT has also been utilized for the mortuary exercise, Operation Torch (2008), that responded to the need to prepare for Chemical, Biological, Radiological, and Nuclear incidents (Brough et al., 2015).

Sidler et al. (2007) demonstrated that the information gained from MSCT could be used to complete 60% of Section D of the Interpol DVI form, completing aspects such as height, weight, age, etc. They argued that MSCT would reduce the time needed with the body and would not disrupt the body any further. This Interpol DVI form has been considerably reduced in size and updated since, with Brough et al. (2015) still concurring that the majority of the form can be completed using only MSCT. The Interpol DVI forms consist of yellow AM forms (normally completed by the Police) and identical pink PM forms (completed in the mortuary) that document morphological characteristics, clothing, personal possessions, fingerprints, pathology, odontology, and DNA samples taken (Interpol, 2013). The AM and PM data are then compared and a comparison report completed to present to the Identification Commission. This process can be undertaken manually; however, various software including Plass Data enables the AM and PM data to be entered, which then automatically searches all the data and provides possible matches to be verified by a forensic specialist (Plass Data, 2016). Plass Data was successfully used in the Boxing Day Tsunami 2004 (Tsokos et al., 2006).

MSCT made an essential contribution to DVI in the 2009 Victorian bushfires where it aided the identification of 161 deceased of the 164 people reported missing (O'Donnell et al., 2011). In this incident, MSCT was used to screen/triage the 255 body bags received at the mortuary. O'Donnell et al. (2011) developed a proforma to document the findings for each body bag, using the MSCT data to determine gender, presence of disease, medical devices, skeletal remains, metallic items (personal artefacts such as jewelry, phones, etc.), teeth, location of identifying features in heavily disfigured bodies, and estimation of age. Gender was possible to determine in 61% of cases utilizing presence of internal and external genitalia on the scan images (with only two cases being incorrect), and age was determined in 94% of cases with an accuracy of 76% (O'Donnell et al., 2011). Radiography of fire victims is essential as when the body is subjected to extreme heat, charred remains may be unrecognizable anatomically and may obscure any personal artefacts present. Furthermore, the body can become fragmented and fragile, and using MSCT reduces handling of the body/body part therefore, minimizing further disruption. In addition, bodies from a fire are often found in a pugilistic position, which may make it difficult for the body to fit through the gantry of the MSCT scanner. This was the case for two bodies of the Victorian bushfires; however, anatomical dissection of the upper limbs facilitated the full MSCT scans (O'Donnell et al., 2011). Morgan et al. (2014) stipulate that such manipulation, including the breaking of rigor mortis, must be undertaken by the pathologist and fully documented accordingly.

The ability to apply various algorithms (soft tissue, bone, etc.) to the MSCT data facilitates viewing of the body's soft tissues, bone, organs, and metal without any disruption to the body. Digital cleansing is useful for anthropologists to undertake anthropological assessment of the skeleton without any need for the preparation of bones (removing the soft tissues) that would otherwise be necessary and time-consuming (O'Donnell et al., 2011). Due to the vast amount of data produced with MSCT, capacity for secure storage of data is required, with consideration given to how other professionals (pathologist, anthropologist, odontologist, etc.) can view the images (Rutty et al., 2013; Viner et al., 2015). The benefit of copious data available consequently means that the review and post-processing of the images is more time-consuming (O'Donnell et al., 2011). Therefore, it is recommended that extra staff are trained to undertake this important role in DVI. Storage and availability of data additionally enables a digital exhumation (O'Donnell et al., 2011) if required, to review the body again, and to allow other experts to evaluate the images.

It has been suggested by some that MSCT reduces handling of the body and minimizes the psychological aspects of imaging the deceased, as the body can be scanned within the body bag so the radiographer does not need to see the deceased. However, with the excellent contrast resolution that MSCT provides, soft tissue algorithms result in very clear images of the deceased (that some have argued could be utilized for a visual identification), and bone algorithms clearly present the significant trauma and fragmentation sustained. Furthermore, when imaging deceased victims that are rapidly decomposing, the distinctive smell is a significant factor still for those involved. In addition, the radiographers involved in imaging the victims of MH17 (The Guardian, 2014), were involved in significant handling of the deceased (moving body bags from coffins on to the scan table), and due to the presence of formaldehyde were required to wear Personal Protective Equipment to protect them (making working conditions more difficult). The presence of formaldehyde was an issue also for those working in Fulham Mortuary identifying the repatriated victims of the Boxing Day Tsunami 2004. Moreover, MSCT Staff are still exposed to the harrowing consequences of mass fatalities, with the bereaved being ever present, and the intense media scrutiny.

Lessons learned from the use of MSCT in previous incidents and exercises in DVI are that MSCT staff should also be trained in DVI, protocols should be adapted according to the MSCT scanner available and for DVI/Forensic work (rather than clinical), and consideration needs to be given to tube loading (to not overheat the tube and therefore, make it unable to scan until it cools). Furthermore, the body bags may leak and so the MSCT table needs to be protected appropriately. Capacity for provision of MSCT needs to be enhanced by training more staff in MSCT and/or DVI to facilitate a shift system, and to enable more than one mobile MSCT scanner to be deployed if necessary.

Dental imaging (intraoral) may often be the only modality utilized in DVI and complements the odontologist's examination of the deceased, providing a primary method of identification. The teeth provide a wealth of information to contribute to identification and age estimation. Intraoral radiography demonstrates the morphology and pathology of the teeth and the surrounding bones and will demonstrate dental restorations, such as root canal work, and is particularly useful for showing tooth-colored restorations that may be difficult to identify with the naked eye (Kieser et al., 2006). While PM dental imaging may be challenging, experienced and trained forensic radiographers can produce images of all the teeth in a short amount of time. It is recommended to obtain as much information as possible in the mortuary, providing full anatomic coverage, as it may not be known at that time what AM data is available for comparison (Wood and Kogon, 2010). This will save time in not having to return to the body later to take further images. Digital sensors for dental imaging may be less tolerated by the living patients; however, they are ideal for imaging of the deceased as image acquisition is quick and can be checked without removing the sensor from the mouth, thereby allowing easy adjustments of the sensor for a high-quality image. The disadvantage is that the size of the sensors does not allow for occlusal images. A favorite of the odontologists is the Nomad, which is a hand-held dental X-ray machine that is easily transported to where it is needed, and was first utilized in a mass fatalities incident in the Boxing Day Tsunami 2004 (Pittayapat et al., 2012). Care must be taken with this particular equipment; however, as the radiation protection shield is designed for patients sitting upright. PM imaging is undertaken with the individual supine, which limits the level of protection given by the shield. Therefore, radiation protection advisors have advocated that lead rubber aprons must be worn as with any other form of imaging equipment in the mortuary environment.

PM identification is only possible with available, good quality AM data with which to make comparisons. In the Boxing Day Tsunami 2004, substantial AM dental records were available for the victims from Europe, North America, Oceania, and Africa. Conversely, the availability and quality of dental records for the Thai victims was reported to be useless, lacking content in 90% of cases. This resulted in only 2% of Thai victims being identified by dental records, whereas the figures were much higher for victims of other countries for whom

46.2% dental was the primary identifier (Petju et al., 2007). Fingerprints were the primary identifier for more than half of the Thai victims as this data was available from the production of their identity cards (Rai and Anand, 2006). This demonstrates the importance of using the right modality and method of identification in relation to the AM data available, and population involved. Furthermore, Kieser et al. (2006) stressed the important role of dental radiography and photographs in assessing the accuracy and quality in the completion of PM dental records. They found that only 68% of the radiographs and 49% of photographs confirmed the accompanying dental charting, attributing this to the inexperience of those charting, fatigue, poor working conditions, and tooth-colored fillings (Kieser et al., 2006). This demonstrates that, without radiography, some critical dental data may be inaccurate or missed and could delay identification of the deceased.

With the recent use of MSCT in DVI, research has been undertaken to assess the effectiveness of MSCT in dental identification. Bassed and Hill (2011) utilized MSCT in the Victorian Bushfires 2009, to estimate the age of the victims involved using the MSCT images of the dentition. In a closed disaster situation, they advocate that MSCT can be used to estimate age with a view to enabling discrimination between individuals (as in this disaster they were often identifying people from the same house). However, they also found that MSCT could not discriminate very well between different types of restorations and the metal artefacts resulted in insufficient detail to compare with AM dental records, which could prove difficult in an open disaster incident. Instead they advocated that dual-energy CT would provide more detail, and O'Donnell et al. (2011) has recommended the use of cone-beam CT to provide more detail and reduce the effects of metal artefacts. However, these modalities may not be easily available in a mass fatalities situation. Furthermore, the reconstruction and evaluation of MSCT images of the dentition for the MH17 victims was found to be too time-consuming and other methods were utilized to provide a more timely identification. Therefore, due to dental being a relatively cheap primary method of identification that has been critical in many DVI incidents, O'Donnell et al. (2011) propose that conventional dental imaging is still the mainstay of the dental examination.

Digital imaging is ideal for imaging smaller evidence bags when there are lots of body parts and for producing a permanent record of other unique skeletal material. The images can be obtained very quickly (3 s until can view image) facilitating significantly reduced examination times. Digital images are often used for anthropological assessment of the skeleton, and for the anthropologists to determine whether the body part is human or animal. Digital equipment is relatively cheap and is easily transported, such as the Canon DRagon that can be folded away and transported in the back of an estate car. An added benefit is that the detector panels can be left in place until the image is checked and easily adjusted if necessary (as with dental imaging). Digital imaging was essential for imaging the many body parts following the 2005 London Bombings, providing a quick evaluation of the contents of the evidence bags. Following the 2004 Boxing Day Tsunami, a team worked at Fulham to establish the true identity of the bodies repatriated back to the United Kingdom (Venables, 2016). Bodies were arriving with the Interpol documentation completed and identification established; however, this identification was not correct on a couple of occasions in the early weeks. With one such body, a quick digital X-ray of the pelvis identified the sterilization clips that were documented in her medical records. While this was not a feature on its own to identify the deceased, it helped to narrow the field of who it could be, quickened the identification process, and demonstrated the importance of all disciplines in the mortuary working together as a team.

As all of the modalities discussed utilizes ionizing radiation, a risk assessment must be undertaken to determine the location of the equipment and to minimize radiation dose to staff in the mortuary. While a mobile MSCT scanner has its own radiation protection measures, leakage of radiation around the lorry has been recorded. This does not pose a problem in its usual location (a hospital car park), as people are not next to the lorry for a significant period of time. However, the location of the lorry within the mortuary or at the scene should have sufficient space around it that is clear and cordoned off and does not have staff permanently working there.

To summarize, radiography has a well established role in DVI that provides information to assist with identification of the deceased, cause of death, and to locate forensic and personal artefacts/evidence, providing a permanent record of evidence. To determine which modality should be utilized, consideration should be given to the degree of fragmentation of the victims, availability of equipment, the chosen methods of identification to be used, and the AM data likely to be available. Fluoroscopy and digital imaging are quick, cheap, and easily available, with fluoroscopy utilized for screening of the body bags on entering the mortuary to provide an overview of the contents of the bag, and digital for greater image detail of unique skeletal material and for imaging smaller evidence bags. Dental imaging is quick, cheap, highly efficient, reliable, and has been validated for long AM/PM intervals (Schuller-Gotzburg and Suchanek, 2007; Wood and Kogon, 2010). MSCT is the more expensive modality for DVI; however, it also provides better contrast resolution, removes overlying structures, 3D reconstruction, multiplanar reformats, different algorithms can be applied to demonstrate, for example, bone and soft tissue, and color coding of the metal content of the body bag to allow easy visualization. MSCT has been successfully utilized in DVI incidents (Victorian Bushfires, MH17, and the Shoreham Air Disaster), with dental contributing to determining between individuals in the Victorian Bushfires; however, the processing of MSCT data for dental information was found to be too time-consuming for other DVI incidents and it was reported that this was abandoned. As dental imaging provides critical information as a primary method of identification, provision must be made for dental radiography of the victims in DVI to expedite identification. If only MSCT is utilized, consideration must be given to how data of the dentition can be obtained, by making any necessary software available on DVI MSCT scanners, by training additional staff to undertake post-processing of MSCT data for the odontologists, or by providing a separate dental imaging facility.

REFERENCES

Atkins, L., Potsaid, P.S., 1978. Roentgenographic identification of human remains. J. Am. Med. Assoc. 240, 2307–2308.

Bassed, R.B., Hill, A.J., 2011. The use of computed tomography (CT) to estimate age in the 2009 Victorian Bushfire Victims: a case report. Forensic Sci. Int. 205 (1–3), 48–51.

BBC News, 2001. Rail crash death toll reduced to 10. http://news.bbc.co.uk/1/hi/uk/1199346.stm (accessed 26.09.16).

BBC News, 2005. Timeline: Asian tsunami disaster. http://news.bbc.co.uk/1/hi/world/asia-pacific/4154791.stm (accessed 26.09.16).

Brough, A.L., Morgan, B., Rutty, G.N., 2015. The basics of disaster victim identification. J. Forensic Radiol. Imaging 3 (1), 29–37.

College of Policing, 2013. Disaster victim identification. https://www.app.college.police.uk/app-content/civil-emergencies/disaster-victim-identification/ (accessed 22.09.16).

Home Office, 2004. Guidance on Dealing with Fatalities in Emergencies. Home Office, London.

Interpol, 2013. DVI forms. http://www.interpol.int/INTERPOL-expertise/Forensics/DVI-Pages/Forms (accessed 26.09.16).

Interpol, 2014. DVI guide. http://www.interpol.int/INTERPOL-expertise/Forensics/DVI-Pages/DVI-guide (accessed 26.08.16).

Jenson, R.A., 2000. Mass Fatality and Casualty Incidents: A Field Guide. CRC Press, Boca Raton, FL.

Kahana, T., Hiss, J., 1999. Forensic radiology. Br. J. Radiol. 72 (854), 129–133.

Kieser, J.A., Laing, W., Herbison, P., 2006. Lessons learned from the large-scale comparative dental analysis following the South Asian Tsunami of 2004. J. Forensic Sci. 51 (1), 109–112.

Mann, R.W., 1998. Use of bone trabeculae to establish positive identification. Forensic Sci. Int. 98, 91–99.

Messmer, J.M., Fierro, M.F., 1986. Personal identification by radiographic comparison of vascular groove patterns of the calvarium. Am. J. Forensic Med. Pathol. 7 (2), 159–162.

Meyer, H.J., 2003. The Kaprun cable car fire disaster—aspects of forensic organisation following a mass fatality with 155 victims. Forensic Sci. Int. 138, 1–7.

Morgan, B., Alminyah, A., Cala, A., O'Donnell, C., Elliott, D., Gorincour, G., et al., 2014. Use of post-mortem computed tomography in Disaster Victim Identification. Positional Statement of the members of the Disaster Victim Identification working group of the International Society of Forensic Radiology and Imaging. J. Forensic Radiol. Imaging 2 (3), 114–116.

O'Donnell, C., Iino, M., Mansharan, K., Leditscke, J., Woodford, N., 2011. Contribution of post-mortem multidetector CT scanning to identification of the deceased in a mass disaster: experience gained from the 2009 Victorian bushfires. Forensic Sci. Int. 205 (1–3), 15–28.

Petju, M., Suteerayongprasert, A., Thongpud, R., Hassiri, K., 2007. Importance of dental records for victim identification following the Indian Ocean tsunami disaster in Thailand. Public Health 121, 251–257.

Pittayapat, P., Jacobs, R., De Valck, E., Vandermeulen, D., Willems, G., 2012. Forensic odontology in the disaster victim identification process. J. Forensic Odontostomatol. 30 (1), 1–12.

Quatrehomme, G., Fronty, P., Sapanet, M., Grévin, G., Bailet, P., Ollier, A., 1996. Identification by frontal sinus pattern in forensic anthropology. Forensic Sci. Int. 83, 147–153.

Rai, B., Anand, S., 2006. Role of forensic odontology in tsunami disasters. Int. J. Forensic Sci. 2 (1), 1–5.

Rhine, S., Sperry, K., 1991. Radiographic identification by mastoid sinus and arterial pattern. J. Forensic Sci. 36 (1), 272–279.

Roberts, I., Benamore, R.E., Benbow, E.W., Lee, S.J., Harris, J.H., Jackson, A., et al., 2012. Post-mortem imaging as an alternative to autopsy in the diagnosis of adult deaths: a validation study. Lancet 379 (9811), 136–142.

Royal College of Radiologists (RCR), 2016. Clinical Radiology. https://www.rcr.ac.uk/clinical-radiology/careers-and-recruitment (accessed 22.09.16).

Rutty, G.N., Alminyah, A., Cala, A., Elliott, D., Fowler, D., Hofman, P., et al., 2013. Use of radiology in disaster victim identification: positional statement of the members of the Disaster Victim Identification working group of the International Society of Forensic Radiology and Imaging. J. Forensic Radiol. Imaging 1 (4), 218.

R v H M Coroner for Inner London District Greater London, 2014. EWHC 3889 (Admin).

Sanders, I., Woesner, M.E., Ferguson, R.A., Noguchi, T.T., 1972. A new application of forensic radiology: identification of deceased from a single clavicle. Am. J. Roentgenol. 115 (3), 619–622.

Schuller-Gotzburg, P., Suchanek, J., 2007. Forensic odontologists successfully identify tsunami victims in Phuket, Thailand. Forensic Sci. Int. 171 (2–3), 204–207.

Sidler, M., Jackowski, C., Dirnhofer, R., Vock, P., Thali, M., 2007. Use of multislice computed tomography in disaster victim identification—advantages and limitations. Forensic Sci. Int. 169, 118–128.

Society and College of Radiographers (SCoR), 2016. A career in radiography. http://www.sor. org/about-radiography/career-radiography (accessed 22.09.16).

Tatlisumak, E., Ovali, G.Y., Aslan, A., Asirdizer, M., Zeyfeoglu, Y., Tarhan, S., 2007. Identification of unknown bodies by using CT images of frontal sinus. Forensic Sci. Int. 166, 42–48.

The Guardian, 2014. Malaysia Airlines flight MH17 crashes in east Ukraine. https://www.the-guardian.com/world/2014/jul/17/malaysia-airlines-plane-crash-east-ukraine (accessed 26.09.16).

Tsokos, M., Lessig, R., Grundmann, C., Benthaus, S., Peschel, O., 2006. Experiences in tsunami victim identification. Int. J. Leg. Med. 120 (3), 185–187.

Venables, R., 2016. A Life in Death. Thistle Publishing, London.

Viner, M.D., 2014. The use of radiology in mass fatality events. In: Adams, B.J., Byrd, J.E. (Eds.), Commingled Human Remains: Methods in Recovery, Analysis, and Identification. Elsevier, Oxford.

Viner, M.D., Alminyah, A., Apostol, M., Brough, A., Develter, W., O'Donnell, C., et al., 2015. Use of radiography and fluoroscopy in Disaster Victim Identification: positional statement of the members of the Disaster Victim Identification working group of the International Society of Forensic Radiology and Imaging. J. Forensic Radiol. Imaging 3 (2), 141–145.

Wood, R.E., Kogon, S.L., 2010. Dental radiology considerations in DVI incidents: a review. Forensic Sci. Int. 201 (1–3), 27–32.

Xograph, 2007. Dragon mobile DR system used by Association of Forensic Radiographers following London transport bombings. http://www.xograph.com/news-and-events/news/dragon-mobile-dr-system-used-by-association-of-forensic-radiographers-following-london-transport-bombings/ (accessed 26.09.16).

CHAPTER 6

Recording In Situ Human Remains in Three Dimensions: Applying Digital Image-Based Modeling

Priscilla F. Ulguim
Teesside University, Middlesbrough, United Kingdom

6.1 INTRODUCTION

Context is essential in archaeology and requires meaningful recording systems for reference and interpretation. When archaeologists record sites they enter an inherent process of data creation (Dallas, 2015) and if recording contextual information is data creation then these records "create" the archaeological site itself (Frankel, 1993). This perspective eschews the notion that excavation is "destruction" (Barker, 1982, p. 12), in the digital era "creating" the archaeological site increasingly implies digitization (Roosevelt et al., 2015).

Contextual recording relied on imaging from the earliest documentation of archaeological sites in sketches and photographs. In the latter half of the nineteenth century, Pitt Rivers used "piece plotting" and stratigraphic recording to determine dates (Thompson, 1977; Trigger, 2006). Planning and imaging formed an important component of early twentieth century "stratigraphic" excavation (Browman and Givens, 1996) and later supported the single context recording and Harris Matrix methods (Harris, 1979; MoLAS, 1994). As technology developed, other imaging methods were applied, from aerial photography

Human Remains: Another Dimension. DOI: http://dx.doi.org/10.1016/B978-0-12-804602-9.00007-2

and photogrammetry, to ground penetrating radar, electrical resistivity, LiDAR, laser scanning, and digital image-based modeling (IBM).

This chapter focuses on the application of digital IBM for three-dimensional (3D) digitization of human remains in situ and its significance for bioarchaeology. In particular, funerary taphonomy: the reconstruction of funerary practices using taphonomic evidence (Knüsel and Robb, 2016). First, this chapter summarizes 3D archaeological recording using optical methods and then discusses advances in computer vision which enabled the development of 3D models from two-dimensional (2D) images. Later it explores works which build 3D models of human remains in situ and integrate these with site data for refined interpretations. Finally, the chapter considers different perspectives on issues concerning these methods.

6.2 DIGITAL IBM AND THE "DIGITAL TURN"

Digital IBM refers to the creation of digital 3D models using data extracted from 2D images. This data may be obtained via passive optical methods for the acquisition of 3D geometries using algorithms from computer vision. These passive methods rely on ambient reflected light within the scene rather than actively obtaining range data, as in terrestrial laser scanning (TLS) or structured light scanning (SLS) (also known as active stereo) (Curless and Seitz, 2000; Remondino and El-Hakim, 2006) (Fig. 6.1). The emergence of robust combinations of algorithms to calculate image correspondences, solve structure from motion (SfM), i.e., extract 3D shape and texture from unordered images of unknown calibration and pose, and build dense point clouds, have provided the tools to regularly create accurate 3D meshes and

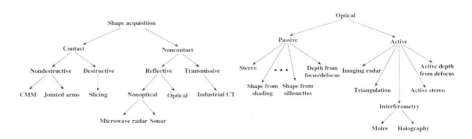

Figure 6.1 Taxonomy of 3D shape acquisition methods. (Source: Curless, 2000).

photorealistic textures from photographs. These have widespread real-world applications, including archaeological recording (Curless and Seitz, 2000; Pollefeys et al., 2004).

Passive optical methods were first developed in photogrammetry, which is the measurement of corresponding points within stereoscopic or overlapping images. This field was rapidly established following the invention of daguerreotypes and photographs (Ebert, 1984) as the fascination for stereoscopic imaging developed. This is reflected in Holmes's (1859) statement: "give us a few negatives of a thing worth seeing, taken from different points of view, and that is all we want of it." Examples from paleoanthropology include stereo-grams of the La Chapelle-aux-Saints Neanderthal cranium (Boule, 1911). Stereoscopic aerial photos were used to create orthogonal maps in the early 20th century archaeology (Reeves, 1936), and "close-range" or "terrestrial" photogrammetry was used to document standing sites from 1885 in Persepolis (Carbonnell, 1968 in Fussell, 1982). It was more regularly applied from the 1950s on excavations (Sjöqvist, 1960; Whittlesey, 1966; Ebert et al., 1979; Kimata, 1980), underwater archaeology (Rosencrantz, 1975), rock art (Clouten, 1974; Turpin et al., 1979; Rivett, 1980; Bezerra Mendonça, 1992), architecture (Dallas et al., 1995), artefacts (Campana, 1977), and human bone elements (Savara, 1965; Teaford, 1982). However, applications were limited by the expense of metric cameras and hours of manual labor on "stereo-plotters" by qualified photogrammetrists, "an extremely skilled job which few people would consider enjoyable" (Anderson, 1982). The development of digital technology culminated in new approaches in the 1980s including "soft-copy" or digital photo-grammetry (Garrison, 1992), for example, in 1996 Miyatsuka published a system for surveying archaeological sites using digital cameras and stereo-matching, a similar system used ground control points (GCPs) (Nagano et al., 1997). Nevertheless, methods generally required cali-brated cameras and costs remained relatively high (Ebert, 1984).

Other methods were more rapidly adopted as part of the "digital turn" in archaeology: Total Station 3D survey data, Geographical Information Systems (GIS) (Harris and Lock, 1996; Wheatley and Gillings, 2002; Barceló et al., 2003), digital recording workflows (May and Crosby, 2010; Issavi and Taylor, 2014), and active optical techni-ques like TLS and SLS (Curless and Seitz, 2000) in the burgeoning field of virtual archaeology (Reilly, 1990; Forte, 1997). Yet, at the same time, research in computer vision continued to refine the accuracy of passive 3D methods (Hartley and Zisserman, 2003). Combining improvements in feature correspondence using affine-invariant feature descriptors (see Lowe, 2004), with innovations in SfM solutions developed in the 1970s and 1980s (Ullman, 1979; Longuet-Higgins, 1981) such as bundle adjustment (Triggs et al., 1999) accurate sparse point clouds became available (Snavely et al., 2007). When united with methods such as multi-view stereo (MVS) dense point clouds (Furukawa et al., 2010) could be created to support accurate 3D meshes and textures. Cultural heritage and archaeology were active components in the development of these methods, for example at the site of Sagalassos, in Turkey where researchers applied SfM and noted potential for recording "3D stratigraphy" (Pollefeys et al., 1999, 2000a,b, 2003; Koch et al., 2000; Van Gool et al., 2000).

The DIY nature of digital archaeology (Morgan and Eve, 2012) and ever more user-friendly tools means archaeologists are increasingly experimenting with these methods and combinations have now been applied to a range of archaeological sites (De Reu et al., 2014; Doneus et al., 2011; Dell'Unto, 2014; Forte et al., 2012; Opitz and Nowlin, 2012; Wilhelmson and Dell'Unto, 2015; Ducke et al., 2011; De Reu et al., 2013; Forte and Lercari, 2014; Prins and Adams 2012). A standard unsupervised workflow has developed termed SfM-MVS (also "3D Photogrammetry", "Digital Photogrammetry", or "3D Photography"). There are five main steps (Table 6.1; Figs. 6.3–6.6): data capture with a digital camera and supporting equipment (total stations, GCPs), sparse point cloud processing using image correspondence and SfM, dense cloud processing using MVS, creating and rectifying the 3D mesh, and finally analyzing and sharing the model and data. This may be exported to a 3D GIS or published online. Increased quantities of stereoscopic images from different perspectives will improve model quality, and GCPs or survey points included in data collection can enable georeferencing and rectification of the model, which enhances analytical potential.

Studies have attempted to quantify accuracy compared with active techniques like TLS and SLS. At Çatalhöyük, Forte et al. (2012) found SfM-MVS of acceptable accuracy and more flexible compared to TLS. El-Hakim et al. (2008) found negligible differences between the two.

Table 6.1 Steps in the SfM-MVS Workflow

Step		Details
Data capture	Equipment	Capture Equipment: a high-quality digital camera with *. RAW output capability is preferable as higher quality images will provide better results. Tripods, drones or scaffolds, GCPs, and scales can be used to aid capture.
		Processing Equipment: a computer with sufficient storage and processing power is required. Software for photo editing and processing, creating the model, modifying the 3D mesh and illustration is necessary. For processing and creating the model a range of software is available such as Agisoft Photoscan (see comparison in Moraes, 2016).
	Capture	Overlapping or stereoscopic images are required, therefore plan to overlap each image captured by approximately 60%. Ensure capture from different points around the scene, rather than simply turning the camera from a single position. Camera settings should be maintained as uniform. Use of flash is not recommended.
		Apply least three to four GCPs and/or marked total station survey points for georeferencing the final model. Minimize interference from external moving objects, areas of bright light and shadows.
	Image improvements	Preprocessing of *. RAW images by masking problematic areas and moving objects as well as color balancing can improve the final results.
Sparse point cloud	Feature extraction	Extraction of features is completed using algorithms for Feature Correspondence such as Scale Invariant Feature Transform.
	"Structure from Motion"	SfM matches the corresponding features and provides a "sparse point cloud" using multiimage and bundling techniques.
		This can calculate the camera pose and calibration without prior information.
Dense point cloud	Multi-View Stereo	MVS algorithms (Debevec et al., 1996; Grzeszczuk, 2002; Pollefeys et al., 2004) can build the dense point cloud from the known camera positions and points provided by SfM. (Variants include Patch-based Multi-View Stereo PMVS; Furukawa and Ponce, 2007.)
Mesh and texture construction	Mesh construction and texturing	A mesh designed to handle complex geometries is built between the relevant points in the dense cloud to form surfaces. A range of methods are available to complete this task. One of the most common is Poisson Reconstruction.
		The mesh can be "decimated" to reduce the overall file size. Texture may be generated using input from source images to overlay photorealistic colors over the mesh.
	Georeferencing and orthorectification	Models can be linked to absolute coordinates using the references from the GCPs. Matching and assigning the GCPs will allow orthorectification.

(*Continued*)

Table 6.1 (Continued)		
Step		**Details**
Analysis and sharing	Export	Once complete, the mesh and texture file are exported as separate files. They should always be kept together to enable association.
		The rectified model may be exported into GIS software (e.g., ArcScene from ESRI ArcGIS using the 3D Analyst extension) for alignment to the site grid.
		In a 3D GIS polygons, polylines, and points can also be added to the model and data linked.
		Orthophotos can be generated in standard photogrammetric software once the mesh and texture files are available. These prevent the loss of geometry in 2D images of the 3D model, correcting all deformations, and allowing accurate measurements even in 2D.
		The files should be saved in high-quality output file types such as*. tiff for best results in planning. Digitization can also be completed in applications such as ArcMap. Shapefiles (*. mxd) can be preset to allow planning with annotations.
		Models can also be shared online via social platforms such as SketchFab.com or academic repositories such as MorphoSource.org which provide a range of features for metadata and descriptions, as well as licensing and download options. For best practice the data can be referenced with a unique DOI.

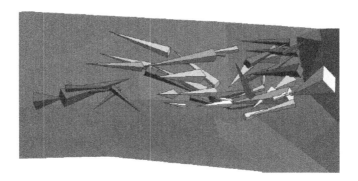

Figure 6.2 Example of 3D model from X-Bones. (Source: Isaksen et al. 2008; Fig. 6.5).

Galeazzi (2015) noted that extreme ambient lighting can negatively influence SfM results, but this also applies to TLS. Koutsoudis et al. (2014) showed that SfM-MVS failed to reconstruct areas of low-frequency color change and areas that lack strong features but can achieve high-quality results with adequate lighting conditions. Green

Figure 6.3 Logging points and collecting photos at Abreu and Garcia. From Juliane Granusso.

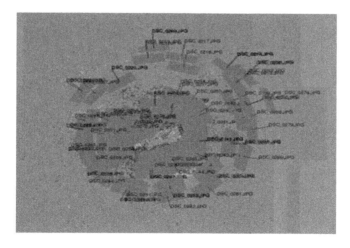

Figure 6.4 Aligned photos with known camera pose and sparse point cloud.

et al. (2014) concluded that point clouds produced using SfM appear to be free of perspective distortion but local conditions and vegetation can impact data quality, and found SfM less accurate than TLS. Nevertheless, a recent review indicated that SfM-MVS can be more accurate than expected results from a mid-range laser scanner and, if implemented correctly, can "outperform all other methods in cost, detail, and accuracy" (Sapirstein, 2016).

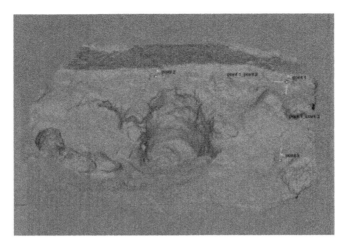

Figure 6.5 Mesh generated over dense point cloud.

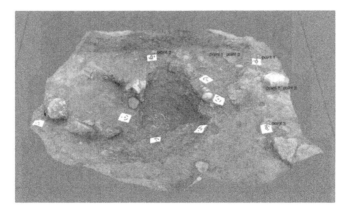

Figure 6.6 Texture overlaid on mesh, with known GCPs marked.

6.3 FUNERARY TAPHONOMY AND THE THIRD DIMENSION

In contrast to general improvements in archaeological recording, the study of human remains and funerary practices "was shackled by…missing methodologies" for years, particularly for detailed in situ contextual recording. This resulted in the "normalization" of the archaeological record, which provided limited means to address funerary taphonomy and questions of "sociocultural variation in ancient deathways" (Knüsel and Robb, 2016). There were some exceptions from the early 20th century where in situ human remains were recorded in three dimensions (Wilder and Whipple, 1917) and in Berlin during the 1960s analogue photogrammetry was applied to in situ human remains in catacombs. It compared favorably to manual planning because, "draughtsmen took up to one and half days to record a single skeleton. With stereometric cameras positioned above the graves, four skeletons could be recorded in a single morning" (Fussell, 1982 in Wölpert, 1964). However, relatively few studies recorded in situ remains in such detail until the 1970s and 1980s (Ubelaker, 1974; Brothwell, 1987; Waldron, 1987). In the 1990s *anthropologie de terrain* or archaeothanatology developed in France, using careful recording of spatial and contextual information to interpret deposition, decomposition, and body treatment (Duday, 2009), and initially relied on traditional planning methods. However, the approach was not broadly adopted beyond the French school until recently. A range of other methods were implemented for complex deposits such as mass graves: manual plans and heights for each bone (Saville, 1990) or digitized composite plans of traced photographs and survey points (Sutherland, 2000), in other cases GIS was applied (Whittle et al., 2006; Galer, 2006; Beckett, 2011; Geiling and Marín-Arroyo, 2015), or specialized programs for survey data visualization like BODROT (Wright, 2003). Some, such as X-bones (Isaksen et al., 2008) and Bodies3D (Wright, 2014), attempted to enhance 3D visualization by building representational polygons from total station points of articulations and the proximal and distal ends of bones (see Fig. 6.2). Other methods applied to funerary structures and in situ human remains include TLS (Shofukuji Burial Chamber: Kanaya et al., 2001; Kadobayashi, 2002; and Sterkfontein "Little Foot" hominin: Subsol et al., 2015), electrical resistivity tomography (burial mounds: Morelli et al., 2004), and CT scanning (unexcavated cremation urns: Harvig et al., 2012). Recently a commercial Artec Eva scanner was used for SLS of in situ *Homo nadeli* remains (Dinaledi Chamber: Kruger et al., 2015). Digital IBM using SfM-MVS for in situ human remains has developed most rapidly since 2009. Published examples fall into two broad categories: firstly, opportunistic applications to archival images, demonstrating the potential for recreating "destroyed" sites in 3D. These appear to have been used solely for visualization, but spatial analyses could be undertaken using the available data. The second category consists of planned implementations within research projects, presenting spatial and temporal analyses and the power of integrated contextual data.

At the Ridgeway Viking mass grave in Dorset, excavated between June and July 2009, Ducke et al. (2011) developed 3D models from existing records to assess the feasibility of "bonus 3D," extracting extra value from existing data at minimal cost. The disused quarry pit was recorded in detail and contained a complex deposit of 51 disarticulated crania and associated skeletons dated between AD 910 and 1030. High-quality image series from the excavation were processed in open source software to generate a 3D mesh. The 3D model was developed for public exhibitions, for which the team originally enabled direct manipulation, but found that users occasionally "got lost," and changed the approach to a predefined "fly-by" of points of interest. The University of Leicester Archaeology Services team took a similar approach in 2016, using archival images to model the in situ remains of Richard III in Agisoft Photoscan Pro (ULAS, 2016). They shared this online via a social platform, generating thousands of hits and significant public interest. In both cases the models have been successfully used for visualization and engagement, but not for specific analyses or interpretation.

Regarding integrated approaches to 3D GIS on funerary sites, from 2010 a team investigated the application of SfM-MVS to provide a "dense time-lapse" (Callieri et al., 2011) of the excavation of a late Neolithic burial mound at Uppåkra, Sweden, which contained the fragmented remains of least two individuals, an adult and a child (Larsson et al., 2015). Initially, photographs were taken following each day of excavation and a model made available for daily review on-site. In 2011, the daily models were used to discuss strategy but were limited by their lack of GIS integration. After 2011 images were reprocessed in Agisoft Photoscan and imported into ArcScene which enabled direct linking of 3D models with field record attribute tables and metadata within—a 3D GIS (Dell'Unto, 2014). The team was also able to export and georeference models in MeshLab and use the tool to highlight, measure, and analyze surfaces and sections. This highlighted the simplicity of data capture potential for rapid processing and review, contributing significantly to the richness of the site records. Similar 3D GIS functionality was implemented at the site of Gabii, Italy, from 2009 onward by Opitz and Nowlin (2012), who recorded some in situ skeletons. Although others have attempted to address the 3D-GIS integration gap (Nigro et al., 2003; Katsianis et al., 2008; Conolly and Lake, 2006; Lock, 2001; Harris and Lock, 1996; Taylor,

2016), these were two of the first attempts to integrate digital IBM outputs for funerary structures. The approach has since been applied to other sites (Dell'Unto et al., 2013, 2015; Landeschi et al., 2015; Fera and Budka, 2016).

In the same period, from 2009, experiments developed at Çatalhöyük as part of "3D Digging." Initially, laser scanning of macro-areas was combined with IBM of excavated surfaces within a Neolithic house (Building 89) (Forte et al., 2012; Forte, 2014; Berggren et al., 2015). From 2012 bioarchaeologists were trained to build 3D models of in situ skeletal remains. They progressed from documenting only fully exposed skeletons to recording multiple excavation phases (Knüsel et al., 2013; Berggren et al., 2015) with an integrated recording workflow using tablets, Microsoft Office and ESRI ArcGIS 10.2 (Issavi and Taylor, 2014, p. 168). Haddow et al. (2016) were able to use these models to virtually analyze the distribution of two skeletal assemblages found within adjacent platforms in one part of the site, Building 52. This enabled the team to simultaneously analyze different phases of excavation and distinguish that crania and other elements within the deposits in the northeast platform were disturbed, removed, retained, and redeposited. This developed on earlier discussions of secondary deposition and commingling in this Building and revealed the power of the "dense time-lapse" in interpreting funerary taphonomy, confirming that specific secondary deposition was occurring in this part of the site.

Elaborating on earlier investigations into 3D GIS in Sweden (Dell'Unto, 2014), Wilhelmson and Dell'Unto (2015) recently published an approach for in situ modeling and interpretation of human remains termed "Virtual Taphonomy." A context containing the skeletal remains of two male individuals at the Sandby ring fort, Oland dated between AD 460 and 490 was recorded in 2012 and 2013. Data were processed in Agisoft Photoscan and imported into ESRI ArcScene 10.1, a 3D GIS. Here, 3D polygons and polylines were used to mark important features and linked to data tables documenting skeletal part representation, fracture patterns, and taphonomic indicators (Wilhelmson and Dell'Unto, 2015). The combination of data supported the conclusion that the individuals suffered traumatic perimortem injuries; the bodies were left intact postmortem as primary depositions; the roof potentially collapsed on them after death due to bilateral symmetry of fracture distribution in the long bones; and postmortem movement of the right foot of one individual appeared to be due to soil movement rather than disturbance (Wilhelmson and Dell'Unto, 2015). Other studies are now applying a similar approach to 3D GIS, for example, mapping entire cemeteries (Van Wessel, 2016), or for more detailed site taphonomic study, such as at the early Bronze Age cemetery of Weiden-am-See, where it has been used in conjunction with other methods to interpret grave reopening (Aspöck and Fera, 2015; Aspöck and Banerjea, 2016).

SfM-MVS workflows have also been applied to cremated deposits during excavations in the southern Brazilian highlands at the Abreu and Garcia mound and enclosure complex. The site revealed a series of secondary deposits of cremated human remains, both scattered and in circular features below a central mound. A workflow for gathering integrated spatial information and 3D data was applied during the 2015 field season (Ulguim, 2016a,b) (see Figs. 6.3−6.6). This was used for detailed postexcavation planning and interpretation. Cremated deposits are often complex and consist of fragmented, fragile, and commingled bone, and this method maximized the information recorded, enabling improved interpretation of the spatial distribution of deposits.

6.4 DISCUSSION

The case studies described indicate that digital IBM can support improved data integration and visualization through rapid, accurate, digital records of excavations using readily available equipment. Prompt data availability may also enable greater reflexivity in fieldwork by concentrating more information "at the moment of excavation" (Berggren et al., 2015), as described in the Uppåkra case study. This data also enriches post-excavation review and provides greater opportunity for future analysis. In addition to the clear benefits there are issues of interpretation and objectivity, contextualization, storage requirements, and ethical questions regarding human remains.

Although the model can enable greater reflexivity, there is a risk that applying these methods without supporting detailed planning could lead to "the 'mass-production' of interchangeable, standardized, and fungible outputs over intellectual engagement" (Kansa, 2015;

Opitz and Johnson, 2016), with reduced engaged in-field interpretation (cf. Perry, 2015). A similar issue can occur where models are used for public engagement with "little specific and clear direction and participation by the public themselves" (Richardson, 2013; Williams and Atkin, 2015). To address these problems part of the growing body of literature on digital archaeological theory aims to understand how we avoid models becoming divorced from context or simple "technical showcases" (Perry and Taylor, 2016; Lock and Brown, 2000; Evans and Daly, 2005; Lock and Molyneaux, 2006). Although post-hoc "bonus 3D" modeling can provide useful visualizations and permit reinterpretation (cf. Falkingham et al., 2014), their strategic value is in analytical and interpretative applications. For these well-planned, integrated, and reflexive approaches are required (see Haddow et al., 2016; Wilhelmson and Dell'Unto, 2015) focused on learning or interpretative requirements (Terras, 1999).

Furthermore, just what "the digitization process is imposing on the data" (Wright, 2011, p. 133) requires attention. The process of documentation is implicitly unobjective: Decisions will be taken about what to record and when. From this perspective excavators and viewers actively "construct" the archaeological record in a "knowledge-saturated process of cognition and action" (Dallas, 2015), rather than simply viewing it passively. This is an important point because digital models present a highly photorealistic virtual experience, which viewers expect to be "reality" (Miller and Richards, 1995) without necessarily appreciating the nuanced imposition of interpretation. One means to counter this is improving data contextualization and access, which includes good metadata and paradata management, and data integration. The idea of contextualization has parallels in the "slow data" approach (Kansa, 2015), which highlights "the value of small and properly contextualized data." This is important as recent studies revealed that the lack of context is also a recurring issue in attempts to reuse publically available archaeological data (Faniel et al., 2013). In this case, models can be better contextualized when applied in conjunction with other methods such as spatial data from total station survey for georectification, or integration with assemblage analysis data in a 3D GIS as described in some of the case studies above. Others have explored customized GUIs to better contextualize data for viewers (Opitz and Johnson, 2016). For metadata and paradata the project strategy should adhere to recognized standards for improved interoperability. One option is a CIDOC-CRM based ontology for metadata representation for which extensions such as CRMdig are available to encode provenance (Felicetti and Lorenzini, 2011). Another option is MayaArch3D which includes the prototype QueryArch3D to integrate 3D models and GIS in virtual environments (Dell'Unto et al., 2015). Access, hosting, and archiving of the digital data can also pose problems. Proprietary formats for 3D data do not promote interoperability, and can cause the loss of information, so open formats should be selected where possible (Felicetti and Lorenzini, 2011; Münster et al., 2015). In addition, the significant size of the source photographs, often large RAW files, and resulting 3D mesh and texture files, need long-term hosting and storage plans.

There are further ethical considerations when curating and sharing models of human remains (Ulguim, 2016c). Current guidelines emphasize the scientific value of remains and encourage communication of analysis, but also stress requirements for consent (WAC, 1989, 2005; BABAO Code of Practice, 2010; Code of Ethics, 2010; Morgan and Boutin, 2009). Yet, obtaining consent may not always be straightforward, for example, where provenance or descendent group is unclear. Again, contextualization is important as the best displays of ethically loaded material are "well-contextualized ...and attempt to trace—or account for the lack of tracing of—consent" (Perry, 2011). The project design can mitigate some of these ethical issues by including an approach or ethical statement on the creation, dissemination, and curation of 3D data which considers relevant local legislation and copyright (Ulguim, 2016c).

6.5 CONCLUSIONS

For the excavation of human remains digital IBM digitalizes the "unrepeatable experiment" of excavation and can contextualize detailed spatial relationships within 3D GIS. Integration with data from other analytical methods can support the study of funerary taphonomy and enable clear insights into funerary practice. There is also great potential for engagement through digital media sharing (Morgan and Eve, 2012). However, even if these methods are seen as more "accurate," they still depend on the skill of the operator and careful, planned recording, without which they lose value. In addition, that which is recorded remains subjective, and so rather than simplifying interpretation, digital methods simply represent "new 'contact zones' for...contestation" of the interpretation of the archaeological record (Dallas, 2015, p. 191). To fulfill the potential of digital IBM, researchers should consider the purpose of the application in project design, and in developing frameworks for digital archaeology we should aim to improve integration with other data sources, safeguard interoperability and standards, and provide high-quality, data-rich, contextualized outputs with critical consideration of their role within archaeology and funerary taphonomy. Finally, as our common heritage, we should share and use the outputs of this process to encourage engagement with and understanding of the archaeological record.

REFERENCES

Anderson, R.C., 1982. Photogrammetry: the pros and cons for archaeology. World Archaeol. 14 (2), 200−205.

Aspöck, E., Banerjea, R.Y., 2016. Formation processes of a reopened early Bronze Age inhumation grave in Austria: the soil thin section analyses. J. Archaeol. Sci. Rep. Available from: http://dx.doi.org/10.1016/j.jasrep.2016.07.003.

Aspöck, E., Fera, M., 2015. 3D-GIS für die taphonomische Auswertung eines wiedergeöffneten Körpergrabes. AGIT—Journal für Angewandte Geoinformatik 1, 2−8.

BABAO, 2010. BABAO Code of Ethics [online]. www.babao.org.uk/assets/Uploads/code-of-ethics.pdf (accessed 28.03.16).

BABAO, 2010. BABAO Code of Practice [online]. http://www.babao.org.uk/assets/Uploads/code-of-practice.pdf (accessed 28.03.16).

Barceló, J.A., de Castro, O., Travet, D., Vicente, O., 2003. A 3D model of an archaeological excavation. In: Doerr, M., Sarris, A. (Eds.), The Digital Heritage of Archaeology. CAA2002. Computer Applications and Quantitative Methods in Archaeology. Proceedings of the 30th CAA Conference. April 2002, Heraklion, Crete. Hellenic Ministry of Culture. Archive of Monuments and Publications, pp. 85−90.

Barker, P., 1982. Techniques of Archaeological Excavation, New Ed. B.T. Batsford, London.

Beckett, J.F., 2011. Interactions with the dead: a taphonomic analysis of burial practices in three megalithic tombs in County Clare, Ireland. Eur. J. Archaeol. 14, 394−418.

Berggren, Å., Dell'Unto, N., Forte, M., Haddow, S., Hodder, I., Issavi, J., et al., 2015. Revisiting reflexive archaeology at Çatalhöyük: integrating digital and 3D technologies at the trowel's edge. Antiquity 89 (344), 433−448. Available from: http://dx.doi.org/10.15184/aqy.2014.43.

Bezerra Mendonça, F.J., 1992. Combination close range photogrammetry and digital processing in archaeology. ISPRS Int. Arch. Photogramm. Remote Sens. 29, 130−133.

Boule, M., 1911. L'homme fossile de la Chapelle-aux-Saints. Annales de Paléontologie I(VI).

Brothwell, D.R., 1987. Decay and disorder in the York Jewbury skeletons. In: Boddington, A., Garland, A.N., Janaway, R.C. (Eds.), Death, Decay, and Reconstruction. Manchester University Press, Manchester, pp. 22−26.

Browman, D.L., Givens, D.R., 1996. Stratigraphic excavation: the first 'new archaeology'. Am. Anthropol. New Ser. 98 (1), 80−95.

Callieri, M., Dell'Unto, N., Dellepiane, M., Scopigno, R., Soderberg, B., Larsson, L., 2011. Documentation and interpretation of an archaeological excavation: an experience with dense stereo reconstruction tools. In: Dellepiane, M., Niccolucci, F., Pena Serna, S., Rushmeier, H., Van Gool, L. (Eds.), The 12th International Symposium on Virtual Reality, Archaeology and Cultural Heritage VAST.

Campana, D.V., 1977. Making stereo-photomacrographs for archaeological studies. J. Field Archaeol. 4, 435–440.

Carbonnell, M. 1968. L'Histoire et la situation presente des applications de la photogrammétrie à l'architecture. 11th Congress of the International Society for Photogrammetry: Commission V. Lausanne, pp. 1–42.

Clouten, N., 1974. The application of photogrammetry to recording rock art, Australian Institute of Aboriginal Studies Newsletter, 1. pp. 33–39.

Conolly, J., Lake, M., 2006. Geographical Information Systems in Archaeology. Cambridge University Press, Cambridge.

Curless, B., 2000. Overview of active vision techniques. Course Notes for SIGGRAPH 2000 Los Angeles, California, July 24, 2000, pp. 1–24.

Curless, B. and Seitz, S., 2000. 3D Photography. Course Notes for SIGGRAPH 2000 Los Angeles, California, July 24, 2000.

Dallas, C., 2015. Curating archaeological knowledge in the digital continuum: from practice to infrastructure. Open Archaeol. 1, 176–207.

Dallas, R.W.A., Kerr, J.B., Lunnon, S., Bryan, P.G., 1995. Windsor Castle: photogrammetric and archaeological recording after the fire. Photogrammetr. Rec. 15 (86), 225–240.

De Reu, J., Verhoeven, G., Plets, G., De Smedt, P., Cherretté, B., 2013. Towards a three-dimensional cost-effective registration of the archaeological heritage. J. Archaeol. Sci. 40 (2), 1108–1121.

De Reu, J., De Clercq, W., De Smedt, P., 2014. On introducing an image-based 3D reconstruction method in archaeological excavation practice. J. Archaeol. Sci. 41, 251–262.

Debevec, P.E. Taylor, C.J. Malik, J., 1996. Modelling and rending architecture from photographs: a hybrid geometry- and image-based approach. Proceedings of SIGGRAPH 96 23rd International Conference on Computer Graphics and Interactive Techniques. 04–09 August 1996, New Orleans, LA, pp. 11–20.

Dell'Unto, N., 2014. The use of 3D models for intra-site investigation in archaeology. In: Remondino, F., Campana, S. (Eds.), 3D Recording and Modelling in Archaeology and Cultural Heritage: Theory and Best Practices. BAR International Series 2598. Archaeopress, Oxford, pp. 151–158.

Dell'Unto, N., Leander, A.N., Dellepiane, M., Callieri, M., Ferdani, D., Lindgren, S., 2013. Digital reconstruction and visualization in archaeology. Case-study drawn from the work of the Swedish Pompeii Project. Digital Heritage International Congress (DigitalHeritage), IEEE 1, 621–628.

Dell'Unto, N., Landeschi, G., Leander Touati, A., Dellepiane, M., Callieri, M., Ferdani, D., 2015. Experiencing ancient buildings from a 3D GIS perspective: a case drawn from the Swedish Pompeii Project. J. Archaeol. Method Theory 23 (1), 73–94.

Doneus, M., Verhoeven, G., Fera, M., Briese, C., Kucera, M., Neubauer, W., 2011. From deposit to point cloud—a study of low-cost computer vision approaches for the straightforward documentation of archaeological excavations. Geoinformatics FCE CTU 6, 81–88.

Ducke, B. Score, D. Reeves, J. 2011. Multiview 3D reconstruction of the archaeological site at Weymouth from image series [online]. https://library.thehumanjourney.net/550/1/Weymouth_3D_CV.pdf (accessed 28.03.16).

Duday, H., 2009. In: Cipriani, A.M., Pearce, J. (Eds.), The Archaeology of the Dead: Lectures in Archaeothanatology. Oxbow Books, Oxford.

Ebert, J.I., 1984. Remote sensing applications in archaeology. Adv. Archaeol. Method Theory 7, 293–362.

Ebert, J.I., Lyons, T.R., Drager, D.L., 1979. Comments on "Application of orthophoto mapping to archaeological problems". Am. Antiq. 44 (2), 341–345.

El-Hakim, S. Remondino, F. Gonzo, L. Voltolini, F., 2008. Effective high resolution 3D geometric reconstruction of heritage and archaeological sites from images. In: Posluschny, A., Lambers, K., Herzog, I. (Eds.), Layers of Perception. Proceedings of the 35th International Conference on Computer Applications and Quantitative Methods in Archaeology (CAA). 2–6 April 2007, Berlin, pp. 43–50.

Evans, T.L., Daly, P., 2005. Digital Archaeology: Bridging Method and Theory. Routledge, London.

Falkingham, P.L., Bates, K.T., Farlow, J.O., 2014. Historical photogrammetry: Bird's Paluxy River dinosaur chase sequence digitally reconstructed as it was prior to excavation 70 years ago. PLoS One 9, e93247.

Faniel, I., Kansa, E., Kansa, S., Barrera-Gomez, J., Yakel, E., 2013. The challenges of digging data: a study of context in archaeological data reuse. JCDL 2013 Proceedings of the 13th ACM/IEEE-CS Joint Conference on Digital Libraries. pp. 295–304.

Felicetti, A., Lorenzini, M., 2011. Metadata and tools for integration and preservation of cultural heritage 3D information. Geoinformatics FCE CTU 6, 18–124.

Fera, M., Budka, J., 2016. Leben und Tod auf der Nilinsel Sai—GIS-gestützte Untersuchungen zu einer pharaonischen Tempelstadt in Obernubien. AGIT—Journal für Angewandte Geoinformatik 2, 18–24. Available from: http://dx.doi.org/10.14627/537622003.

Forte, M. (Ed.), 1997. Virtual Archaeology: Great Discoveries Brought to Life Through Virtual Reality. Thames and Hudson, London.

Forte, M., 2014. 3D Archaeology: new perspectives and challenges—the example of Çatalhöyük. J. East. Mediterr. Archaeol. Herit. Stud. 2 (1).

Forte, M., Lercari, N., 2014: Building 89 3D digging project. In Çatalhöyük Research Project, Çatalhöyük 2014 Archive Report. pp. 186–193.

Forte, M., Dell' Unto, N., Issavi, J., Onsurez, L., Lercari, N., 2012. 3D Archaeology at Çatalhöyük. Int. J. Herit. Digit. Era 1, 351–378.

Frankel, D., 1993. The excavator: creator or destroyer. Antiquity 67, 875–877.

Furukawa, Y. Ponce, J., 2007. Accurate, dense, and robust multi-view stereopsis. IEEE Computer Society Conference on Computer Vision and Pattern Recognition, July 2007.

Furukawa, Y., Curless, B., Seitz, S.M., Szeliski, R., 2010. Towards internet-scale multi-view stereo, computer vision and pattern recognition (CVPR). 2010 IEEE Conference. San Francisco, CA, pp. 1434–1441. http://dx.doi.org/10.1109/CVPR.2010.5539802.

Fussell, A., 1982. Terrestrial photogrammetry in archaeology. World Archaeol. 14 (2), 157–172.

Galeazzi, F., 2015. Towards the definition of best 3D practices in archaeology: assessing 3D documentation techniques for intra-site data recording. J. Cult. Herit. 17, 159–169.

Galer, D., 2006. The human remains. In: Benson, D., Whittle, A. (Eds.), Building Memories: The Neolithic Cotswold Long Barrow at Ascott-under-Wychwood, Oxfordshire. Oxbow, Oxford, pp. 189–220.

Garrison, E.G., 1992. Recent advances in close range photogrammetry for underwater historical archaeology. Hist. Archaeol. 26 (4), 97–104.

Geiling, J.M., Marín-Arroyo, A.B., 2015. Spatial distribution analysis of the Lower Magdalenian human burial in El Mirón Cave (Cantabria, Spain). J. Archaeol. Sci. 60, 47e56.

Green, S., Bevan, A., Shapland, M., 2014. A comparative assessment of structure from motion methods for archaeological research. J. Archaeol. Sci. 46, 173–181.

Grzeszczuk, R., 2002. Course 44: image-based modelling. SIGGRAPH.

Haddow, S.D., Sadvari, J.W., Knüsel, C.J., Hadad, R., 2016. A tale of two platforms: commingled remains and the life-course of houses at Neolithic Çatalhöyük. In: Osterholtz, A.J. (Ed.), Theoretical Approaches to Analysis and Interpretation of Commingled Human Remains, Bioarchaeology and Social Theory. Springer International Publishing, Switzerland.

Harris, E.C., 1979. Principles of Archaeological Stratigraphy. Academic Press, London.

Harris, T.M., Lock, G., 1996. Multidimensional GIS: exploratory approaches to spatial and temporal relationships within archaeological stratigraphy. Analecta Praehistorica Leidensia 28 (2), 207–316.

Harvig, L., Lynnerup, N., Amsgaard Ebsen, J., 2012. Computed tomography and computed radiography of late bronze age cremation urns from Denmark: an interdisciplinary attempt to develop methods applied in bioarchaeological cremation research. Archeometry 54, 369–387.

Hartley, R., Zisserman, A., 2003. Multiple View Geometry in Computer Vision. Cambridge University Press, Cambridge.

Holmes, O.W., 1859. The stereoscope and the stereograph. The Atlantic. June 1859 Issue [online]. http://www.theatlantic.com/magazine/archive/1859/06/thestereoscopeandthestereograph/303361 (accessed 25.09.16).

Isaksen, L. Loe, L. Saunders, M.K., 2008. X-Bones: a new approach to recording skeletons in 3D.

Issavi, J., Taylor, J., 2014. Tablet recording overview. In Çatalhöyük Research Project, Çatalhöyük 2014 Archive Report. pp. 168–172.

Kadobayashi, R., 2002. 3D Digitizing and modeling of Japanese Stone Burial Chamber using two types of 3D laser scanners. ICITA, i–iv.

Kanaya, I., Kadobayashi, R., Chihara, K., 2001. Three-dimensional modelling of Shofukuji Burial Chamber. Proceedings of the Seventh International Conference on Virtual Systems and Multimedia (VSMM'01), i–viii.

Kansa, E., 2015. Click here to save archaeology [online]. https://ekansa-pubs.github.io/click-here-to-save-archaeology/ (accessed 13.08.16).

Katsianis, M., Tsipidis, S., Kotsakis, K., Kousoulakou, A., 2008. A 3D digital workflow for archaeological intra-site research using GIS. J. Archaeol. Sci. 35, 655–667.

Kimata, K., 1980. The rope-way camera system for archaeological sites. Int. Arch. Photogramm. XIV Congr., Hamburg XXIII, 430–436.

Knüsel, C.J., Robb, J., 2016. Funerary taphonomy: an overview of goals and methods. J. Archaeol. Sci. Rep.. Available from: http://dx.doi.org/10.1016/j.jasrep.2016.05.031.

Knusel, C.J. Haddow, S.D. Sadvari, J.W. Dell' Unto, N. Forte, M., 2013. Bioarchaeology in 3D: three-dimensional modeling of human burials at Neolithic Çatalhöyük. Poster presented at the Society for American Archaeology 78th Annual Meeting. Honolulu, Hawaii.

Koch, R., Pollefeys, M., Van Gool, L., 2000. Realistic surface reconstruction of 3D scenes from uncalibrated image sequences. J. Vis. Comput. Animat. 11, 115–127.

Koutsoudis, A., Vidmar, B., Ioannakis, G., Arnaoutoglou, F., Pavlidis, G., Chamzas, C., 2014. Multi-image 3D reconstruction data evaluation. J. Cult. Herit. 15, 73–79.

Kruger, A., Randolph-Quinney, P., Elliott, M., 2015. Multimodal spatial mapping and visualisation of Dinaledi Chamber and Rising Star Cave. South. Afr. J. Sci. 112 (5/6).

Landeschi, G. Dell'Unto, N. Ferdani, D. Leander Touati, A.-M. Lindgren, S., 2015. Enhanced 3D-GIS: documenting Insula VI in Pompeii. Proceedings of the 42nd Annual Conference on Computer Applications and Quantitative Methods in Archaeology. pp. 349–360.

Larsson, L., Trinks, I., Söderberg, B., Gabler, M., Dell'Unto, N., Neubauer, W., et al., 2015. Interdisciplinary archaeological prospection, excavation and 3D documentation exemplified through the investigation of a burial at the Iron Age settlement site of Uppåkra in Sweden. Archaeol. Prospect. 22, 143–156. Available from: http://dx.doi.org/10.1002/arp.1504.

Lock, G., 2001. Theorising the practice or practicing the theory: archaeology and GIS. Archaeologia Polona 39, 153–164.

Lock, G., Brown, K. (Eds.), 2000. On the Theory and Practices in Archaeological Computing. Oxford University Committee for Archaeology Monograph 51. Oxford University, Oxford.

Lock, G., Molyneaux, B. (Eds.), 2006. Confronting Scale in Archaeology: Issues of Theory and Practice. Springer, New York.

Longuet-Higgins, H.C., 1981. A computer algorithm for reconstructing a scene from two projections. Nature 293, 133–135.

Lowe, D.G., 2004. Distinctive image features from scale-invariant keypoints. Int. J. Comput. Vision. 60 (2), 91–110. Available from: http://dx.doi.org/10.1023/B:VISI.0000029664.

May, S.C., Crosby, V., 2010. Holy Grail or Poison Chalice? Challenges in implementing digital excavation recording. In: Nicolucci, F., Hermon, S. (Eds.), Beyond the Artifact. Digital Interpretation of the Past. Proceedings of CAA2004, Prato 13–17 April 2004. Archaeolingua, Budapest, pp. 49–54.

Miller, P., Richards, J., 1995. The good, the bad, and the downright misleading: archaeological adoption of computer visualisation. In: Huggett, J., Ryan, N. (Eds.), CAA94. Computer Applications and Quantitative Methods in Archaeology 1994 (BAR International Series 600). Tempus Reparatum, Oxford, pp. 19–22.

Miyatsuka, Y., 1996. Archaeological real-time photogrammetric system using digital still camera. Asia Air Survey Co. Ltd. Commission V, Working Group 4. Int. Arch. Photogramm. Remote Sens. 31 (B5), 374–377.

MoLAS, 1994. Museum of London Archaeology Service Archaeological Site Manual. MoLAS, London.

Moraes, C. 2016. Comparando 7 sistemas de fotogrametria 3D. Qual se saiu melhor? [online] http://www.ciceromoraes.com.br/blog/?p=2525 (accessed: 30.11.2016).

Morelli, A., Morelli, G., Chiara, P., Pacchini, A., Fischanger, F., 2004. Characterization of complex archaeological sites using 3D electrical resistivity tomography. Symposium on the Application of Geophysics to Engineering and Environmental Problems. 185–192.

Morgan, C., Boutin, A. 2009. The Dilmun Bioarchaeology Ethics Statement [online]. https://middlesavagery.wordpress.com/2013/10/24/the-dilmun-bioarchaeology-ethics-statement/ (accessed 27.03.16).

Morgan, C., Eve, S., 2012. DIY and digital archaeology: what are you doing to participate? World Archaeol. 44 (4), 521–537.

Münster, S. Kuroczyński, P. Pfarr-Harfst, M. Grellert, M. Lengyel, D., 2015. Future research challenges for a computer-based interpretative 3D reconstruction of cultural heritage—a German community's view. ISPRS Annals of the Photogrammetry, Remote Sensing and Spatial Information Sciences, Volume II-5/W3. 25th International CIPA Symposium 2015. 31 August–04 September 2015, Taipei, Taiwan, pp. 207–213.

Nagano, M. Sato, K. Chihara, K., 1997. Shape integration of multi stereo images using surveyed points for an archaeological site. Proceedings of the 1997 International Conference on Shape Modeling and Applications (SMA '97). pp. 140–148.

Nigro, J.D., Ungar, P.S., de Ruiter, D.J., Berger, L.R., 2003. Developing a geographic information system (GIS) for mapping and analysing fossil deposits at Swartkrans, Gauteng Province, South Africa. J. Archaeol. Sci. 30, 317–324. Available from: http://dx.doi.org/10.1006/jasc.2002.0839.

Opitz, R.S., Johnson, T.D., 2016. Interpretation at the controller's edge: designing graphical user interfaces for the digital publication of the excavations at Gabii (Italy). Open Archaeol. 2016 (2), 1–17. Available from: http://dx.doi.org/10.1515/opar-2016-0001.

Opitz, R.S., Nowlin, J., 2012. Photogrammetric modeling + GIS. Esri.com Spring 2012, 46–49.

Perry, S., 2011. Ethics and the display of human and non-human remains [online]. https://saraperry.wordpress.com/2011/12/05/ethics-and-the-display-of-human-and-non-human-remains/ (accessed 27.03.16).

Perry, S., 2015. Why are heritage interpreters voiceless at the trowel's edge? A plea for reframing the archaeological workflow [online]. https://saraperry.wordpress.com/2015/04/02/why-are-heritage-interpreters-voiceless-at-the-trowels-edge-a-plea-for-reframing-the-archaeological-workflow/ [accessed 13.08.16).

Perry, S. Taylor, J., 2016. Theorising the digital turn in archaeology. Paper presented at CAA 2016 OSLO.

Pollefeys, M. Koch, R. Vergauwen, M. Van Gool, L., 1999. An automatic method for acquiring 3D models from photographs: applications to an archaeological site. ISPRS International Workshop on Photogrammetric Measurement, Object Modeling and Documentation in Architecture and Industry, Thessaloniki, International Archive of Photogrammetry and Remote Sensing, Vol. XXXII, Part 5W11, pp. 76–80.

Pollefeys, M., Proesmans, M., Koch, R., Vergauwen, M., Van Gool, L., 2000a. Acquisition of detailed models for virtual reality. In: Barcelo, J.A., Forte, M., Sanders, D.H. (Eds.), Virtual Reality in Archaeology. Oxbow, Oxford, pp. 71–77.

Pollefeys, M., Koch, R., Vergauwen, M., Van Gool, L., 2000b. Automated reconstruction of 3D scenes from sequences of images. ISPRS J. Photogramm. Remote Sens. 55 (4), 251–267.

Pollefeys, M., Van Gool, L., Vergauwen, M., Cornelis, K., Verbiest, F., Tops, J., 2003. 3D Recording for archaeological fieldwork. IEEE Comput. Soc. 2–9.

Pollefeys, M., Van Gool, L., Vergauwen, M., Verbiest, F., Cornelis, K., Tops, J., et al., 2004. Visual modeling with a hand-held camera. Int. J. Comput. Vision 59 (3), 207–232.

Prins, A., Adams, M.J., 2012. Practical uses for photogrammetry on archaeological excavations. JVRP White Papers in Archaeological Technology [online]. http://www.jezreelvalleyregionalproject.com/practical-uses-for-photogrammetry-on-archaeological-excavations.html (accessed 09.02.16).

Reeves, D.M., 1936. Aerial photography and archaeology. Am. Antiq. 2 (2), 102–107.

Reilly, P., 1990. Towards a virtual archaeology. In: Lockyear, K., Rahtz, K. (Eds.), Computer Applications in Archaeology. British Archaeological Reports 565.. Archaeopress, Oxford, pp. 133–139.

Remondino, F., El-Hakim, S., 2006. Image-based 3D modelling: a review. Photogrammetr. Rec. 21 (115), 269–291.

Richardson, L.-J., 2013. A digital public archaeology? Papers from the Institute of Archaeology 23 (1), 1–12.

Rivett, L.J., 1980. The photogrammetric recording of rock art in the Kakadu National Park, Australia. Austr. Archaeol. 10, 38–51.

Roosevelt, C.H., Cobb, P., Moss, E., Olson, B.R., Ünlüsoy, S., 2015. Excavation is destruction digitization: advances in archaeological practice. J. Field Archaeol. 40 (3), 325–346. Available from: http://dx.doi.org/10.1179/2042458215Y.0000000004.

Rosencrantz, D.M., 1975. Underwater photography and photogrammetry. In: Elmer Jr., H. (Ed.), Photography in Archaeological Research.. University of New Mexico Press, Albuquerque, pp. 265–310.

Sapirstein, P., 2016. Accurate measurement with photogrammetry at large sites. J. Archaeol. Sci. 66, 137–145.

Savara, B.S., 1965. Applications of photogrammetry for quantitative study of tooth and face morphology. Am. J. Phys. Anthropol. 23 (4), 427–434.

Saville, A., 1990. Hazelton North. The Excavation of a Neolithic Long Cairn of the Cotswold-Severn Group. Archaeological Report 13. English Heritage, London.

Sjöqvist, E., 1960. Excavations at Morgantina (Serra Orlando) 1959: preliminary report IV. Am. J. Archaeol. 64 (2), 125–135.

Snavely, N., Seitz, S., Szeliski, R., 2007. Modeling the world from internet photo collections. Int. J. Comput. Vision 80 (2), 189–210.

Subsol, G., Moreno, B., Jessel, J.-P., Braga, J., Bruxelles, L., Thackeray, F., et al., 2015. In situ 3D digitization of the "Little Foot" Australopithecus skeleton from Sterkfontein. Paleoanthropology 2015, 44–53.

Sutherland, T., 2000. Recording the grave. In: Fiorato, V., Boylston, A., Knusel, C. (Eds.), Blood Red Roses. The Archaeology of a Mass Grave from the Battle of Towton AD 1461. Oxbow, Oxford, pp. 36–44.

Taylor, J.S., 2016. Making Time for Space at Çatalhöyük: GIS as a Tool for Exploring Intra-Site Spatiotemporality Within Complex Stratigraphic Sequences. University of York, Department of Archaeology, PhD Thesis.

Teaford, M.F., 1982. Differences in molar wear gradient between juvenile macaques and langurs. Am. J. Phys. Anthropol. 57, 323–330.

Terras, M.M., 1999. The Sen-nedjem Project: archaeology, virtual reality and education. Archaeol. Comput. Newslett. 53, 4–10.

Thompson, M., 1977. General Pitt-Rivers: Evolution and Archaeology in the Nineteenth Century. Moonraker, Bradford-on-Avon.

Trigger, B.G., 2006. A History of Archaeological Thought. Cambridge University Press, Cambridge.

Triggs, B., McLauchlan, P., Hartley, R., Fitzgibbon, A., 1999. Bundle adjustment—a modern synthesis. Int. Workshop Vision AlgorithmsSeptember 1999.

Turpin, S.A., Watson, R.P., Dennett, S., Muessig, H., 1979. Stereophotogrammetric documentation of exposed archaeological features. J. Field Archaeol. 6 (3), 329–337.

Ubelaker, D., 1974. Reconstruction of Demographic Profiles from Ossuary Skeletal Samples. Smithsonian Institution, Washington, DC.

ULAS, 2016. King Richard III's grave [online]. https://sketchfab.com/models/00d23c7defd0476d-b1a36c08728fa60f (accessed 04.08.16).

Ulguim, P., 2016a. Report on the 2015 Archaeological Excavations at the Abreu and Garcia Site, Campo Belo do Sul, Santa Catarina, Brazil. Jê Landscapes of Southern Brazil. Middlesbrough.

Ulguim, P., 2016b. Circling the enclosure: documenting cremated deposits in 3D with photogrammetry. Poster Presented at School of Science and Engineering Annual Research Day, May 2016.

Ulguim, P., 2016c. Models and metadata: the ethics of sharing bioarchaeological 3D data on online. Paper Presented at World Archaeological Congress 8. 28 August–2 September 2016, Kyoto.

Ullman, S., 1979. The interpretation of structure from motion. Proc. R. Soc. B 203, 405–426. Available from: http://dx.doi.org/10.1098/rspb.1979.0006.

Van Gool, L., Defoort, F., Hug, J., Kalberer, G., Koch, R., Martens, D., et al., 2000. Image-based 3D modeling: modeling from reality. In: Leonardis, A., Solina, F., Bajcsy, R. (Eds.), Proceedings NATO Advanced Research Workshop on Confluence of Computer Vision and Computer Graphics, August 29-31, 1999, Ljubljana, Slovenia. NATO Science Series 3 Volume 84. Kluwer Academic Publishers, Amsterdam, pp. 161–178.

Van Wessel, J., 2016. Osteo-grammetry—using photographs to model large cemeteries in three dimensions. Paper presented at 18th Annual Conference, British Association for Biological Anthropology and Osteoarchaeology. 9–11 September 2016, University of Kent, Canterbury.

Waldron, T., 1987. The relative survival of the human skeleton: implications for palaeopathology. In: Boddington, A., Garland, A.N., Janaway, R. (Eds.), Death, Decay and Reconstruction: Approaches to Archaeology and Forensic Science. Manchester University Press, Manchester, pp. 149–162.

World Archaeological Congress, 1989. Vermillion accord on human remains [online]. WAC Code of Ethics. http://worldarch.org/code-of-ethics/ (accessed 27.03.16).

World Archaeological Congress, 2005. Tamaki Makau-rau accord on the display of human remains and sacred objects [online]. WAC Code of Ethics. http://worldarch.org/code-of-ethics/ (accessed 27.03.16).

Wheatley, D., Gillings, M., 2002. Spatial Technology and Archaeology: The Archaeological Applications of GIS. Taylor and Francis, New York.

Whittlesey, J.H., 1966. Photogrammetry for the excavator. Archaeology 19 (4), 273–276.

Whittle, A., Galer, D., Benson, D., 2006. The layout, composition and sequence of the human bone deposits. In: Benson, D., Whittle, A. (Eds.), Building Memories: The Neolithic Cotswold Long Barrow at Ascott-under-Wychwood, Oxfordshire. Oxbow, Oxford, pp. 137–188.

Wilder, H.H., Whipple, R.W., 1917. The position of the body in aboriginal interments in western Massachusetts. Am. J. Anthropol. 19, 372–387.

Wilhelmson, H., Dell'Unto, N., 2015. Virtual taphonomy: a new method integrating excavation and postprocessing in an archaeological context. Am. J. Phys. Anthropol. Available from: http://dx.doi.org/10.1002/ajpa.22715.

Williams, H., Atkin, A., 2015. Virtually dead: digital public mortuary archaeology. Internet Archaeol. 40. Available from: http://dx.doi.org/10.11141/ia.40.7.4.

Wölpert, D., 1964. Uber eine Anwendung der Photogrammetrie im archäologischen Ausgrabungswesen. 10th Congress of the International Society for Photogrammetry: Commission V. Lisbon, pp. 1–8.

Wright, H., 2011. Seeing Triple: Archaeology, Field Drawing and the Semantic Web. University of York, Department of Archaeology, PhD Thesis.

Wright, R., 2003. Aids to the display of bodies from mass graves represented in 3D: Program BODROT.

Wright, R. 2014. Bodies3D [Online]. https://osteoware.si.edu/forum/osteoware-communityan-nouncements/bodies3d-richard-wright-0 (accessed 02.08.16).

CHAPTER 7

Shedding Light on Skeletal Remains: The Use of Structured Light Scanning for 3D Archiving

David Errickson
Teesside University, Middlesbrough, United Kingdom

7.1 INTRODUCTION

The use of human skeletal remains for education in anthropology and archaeology is of paramount importance to progress our understanding of the past. To ensure academic enhancement, access to comparative osteological collections with a diverse range of populations, ages, occupational markers, trauma, pathological conditions, and representation of both biological sexes is critical. The importance of such a valuable resource is demonstrated by the fact that educational institutions strive to maintain or increase their own physical in-house archives.

However, even those who have access to skeletal collections still face issues as variability in *in situ* preservation, and archaeological recovery techniques affect skeletal completeness. Furthermore, continued handling of the individuals increases the fragility of remains (Betts et al., 2011). In turn, this impacts on their potential for prolonged

Human Remains: Another Dimension. DOI: http://dx.doi.org/10.1016/B978-0-12-804602-9.00008-4

preservation, which makes it difficult to teach specific methods pertaining to anthropological and osteoarchaeological techniques, especially if the required elements are not present or incomplete. Further to these issues, an increasing amount of human remains are being reburied. For example, guidelines (such as NAGPRA, 1990 and the DCMS, 2005) concern groups of peoples and their rights to the management of their own cultural heritage (Payne, 2012; Sellevold, 2012), contexts involving known or recent individuals (HTA, 2004), and a frequent practice of reburial for most archaeological units (Orr and Bienkowski, 2006). In these cases, any information previously unrecorded is lost in the reburial process and any information that has been documented is limited due to the traditional techniques used.

Unfortunately, some institutions only have access to published data and not individual physical remains. Such data are the result of traditional documentation procedures: photography, radiography, professional drawing, and sketching (Buikstra and Ubelaker, 1994; Brickley and McKinley, 2004). However, these documentation techniques are not as valuable in comparison to accessing the actual physical remains, as they can make interpretation of the remains at a later date difficult. These traditional recording procedures produce a two-dimensional (2D) representation that is typically an individual's interpretation of a three-dimensional (3D) object (Thali et al., 2003). For example, written descriptions form a very important way of capturing data, but are dependent on the interpretation made by the person writing. In addition, these images are often out of context and may not demonstrate the necessary angle or region needed for analysis when diagnosing pathological conditions or taphonomic factors.

To overcome such limitations, the structured light scanning (SLS) technique can be utilized. The SLS documents objects by creating a 3D representation that can be virtually moved, rotated, and magnified on a computer. The SLS instrumentation consists of a camera with a mounted projector and uses patterned light through a form of geometrical calibration to generate its image. This method is an active-light documentation technique which digitizes objects noninvasively, preserving the object that is documented in its entirety (Errickson et al., 2015). It should be noted that there are alternative 3D noncontact techniques including laser scanning and photogrammetry; however, this is not the focus of this chapter.

SLS has successfully been utilized to create comparative 3D faunal, object, and skeletal collections (McPherron et al., 2009; Niven et al., 2009; Betts et al., 2011). These include the Web-based applications "digitized disease" and "VZAP," and the tablet-based app, "dactyl," demonstrating that SLS can be used as an alternative to traditional methods to create an accurate and permanent record of individual skeletal elements, in the form of fully representative 3D digitizations.

A major advantage of 3D documentation is that an accurate to-scale representation for those individuals who are due for reburial can be created. To demonstrate this, SLS was employed on two archaeological skeletal collections that were chosen for reburial: Hazel Grove, Greater Manchester and Fewston, North Yorkshire.

7.2 CONTEXTUAL INFORMATION

Two archaeologically excavated sites at Hazel Grove, Greater Manchester and Fewston, North Yorkshire uncovered a large number of human remains that were commissioned for osteological analysis by York Osteoarchaeology.

7.2.1 Hazel Grove, Greater Manchester

Excavations were undertaken in 2016 at the former Wesleyan Chapel on Chapel Street, Hazel Grove, Greater Manchester. Thirty-nine individuals were recovered in the north-west and south-west of the rear of the church. These individuals were representative of the 18th and early 19th centuries. The osteological analysis revealed evidence of trauma, childhood stresses, one individual with possible mixed ancestry, and an individual with severe osteoporosis who possibly suffered from elder/ spousal abuse (Newman and Holst, 2016).

7.2.2 Fewston, North Yorkshire

Excavations at the Church of St. Michael and St. Lawrence, Fewston, North Yorkshire were undertaken in 2009 and 2010. The assemblage consisted of 154 articulated individuals plus disarticulated remains. The skeletal analysis documented a range of pathological conditions, including childhood stress, trauma, joint disease, neoplastic disease, and evidence for dissection. Some of the lesions recorded are not commonly encountered in skeletal collections. It should be noted that some

of the individuals excavated have living relatives and therefore are not
discussed in detail (Caffell and Holst, forthcoming).

7.2.3 Significance of Skeletal Remains

The individuals recovered from both archaeological sites were important in terms of osteoarchaeological understanding, as the bones displayed a range of unusual pathological and traumatic lesions. These
included neoplastic disease, osteoporosis, health stresses, and evidence
of lifestyle. For example, individual 426's ribs (Fewston, North
Yorkshire) were thinner with an altered morphology indicative of a
continued period of wearing a corset (Fig. 7.1). Also, Skeleton 36
(Hazel Grove, Greater Manchester) had a minimum of 42 rib fractures
at different stages of healing, in addition to a number of healed fractures elsewhere in the skeleton. This is indicative of severe osteoporosis
and/or osteomalacia in an individual of advanced age, but may also
signify elder/spousal abuse.

Unfortunately, both sites were due to be reburied at the same time,
and as a result only 1 week was available to undertake digitization.

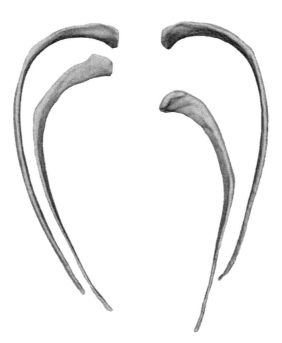

Figure 7.1 Digitization of individual 426's ribs which have been physically altered possibly indicative of wearing a corset.

Reburial provided a great opportunity to assess the effectiveness of the rapid digitization process. Therefore, it was agreed that due to the number of complex individuals, particular elements from each site that had significant merit for future analysis, and the majority of one specific individual from Hazel Grove (SK 15), would be documented using the SLS. As a result, 141 individual bones were captured within the 1 week scanning period.

7.2.4 The Scanning Process

For digitization, the PicoScan (4DDynamics, Belgium) was utilized. This scanner consists of a Canon EOS 1100 D camera with a Pico Projector vertically mounted onto it. Accurate active surface scanning techniques have often been classed as expensive and not portable (Evin et al., 2016). The initial cost of the PicoScan used to undertake documentation was £1995.00. This is low in comparison to some laser-based surface scanning modalities such as the FARO arm. In addition, the SLS technique is becoming more and more portable. For example, the PicoScan is a normal SLR camera with a projector mounted to the top. This sits on top of a gorilla grip tripod and can be transported in a 26 L bag. To demonstrate the technique's portability, McPherron et al. (2009) used the structured light technique on *in situ* archaeological finds, only experiencing positioning and light issues.

The PicoScan projector has a resolution of 800×600 pixels with an average point accuracy of 0.1 mm. All the scanning took place within a light tent to produce an accurate texture and eliminate shadows in accordance with Niven et al. (2009), in order to reduce the lighting issues discussed by McPherron et al. (2009). For capture, the bone was placed on a turntable and in this setup, a single bone scan was obtained in two successive rotations, each with 12 30° stops. Each bone was rotated in a horizontal and vertical position to ensure full capture. The 24 individual scans were then merged together using the software Process (4DDynamics, Belgium) creating a uniform digitization. The final renders were saved as .ply, .obj, and .stl file formats.

7.3 RESULTS AND DISCUSSION

All 141 individual bones were successfully captured and reconstructed in both color and greyscale using the SLS approach (Fig. 7.2). In this study the issues experienced by McPherron et al. (2009) were not encountered. This is because it was possible to control the variables

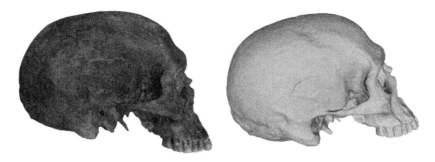

Figure 7.2 The 3D reconstruction of the cranium from skeleton 21 (Hazel Grove) in color and grey scale.

within the environment due to scanning in a laboratory. For a comprehensive study into the importance of this refer to Errickson et al. (2015). Therefore, the documentation process accurately captured all trauma and pathological lesions in 3D and was presented as a scalable accurate virtual representation of the actual object.

One of the main advantages of using a noncontact technique is the reduction of invasiveness. As the method does not need physical touch to document an object the integrity and completeness of the bone can be maintained. Likewise, using the 3D data for teaching as an alternative to physically handling individual bones can limit the wear-and-tear on the actual human remains.

The actual human remains from Fewston were used by Durham University for teaching and research, ensuring Masters students (future academics and osteologists) could learn from the variable skeletal traits and unique pathological conditions contained within that collection. Capturing such an extensive collection of individuals in 3D prior to reburial ensures a permanent record is created, free from an individual's interpretation. In turn, unlike physical skeletal collections, these virtual objects can be accessed at any time and by anyone (Weber, 2014). Likewise, for institutions that do not have access to skeletal remains, they can literally "fill in the gaps" of physical teaching with these representations and maintain an understanding of the complex 3D human structure that cannot be conveyed in traditional literature-based resources. The use of this digital resource is currently planned for teaching undergraduate students at Durham University in the upcoming academic year.

Similarly, diagnosing pathological conditions can often be challenging. Also, sometimes original diagnoses are reevaluated when new evidence becomes available (Rogers et al., 1985). If the actual skeletons are available, these can be revisited in the light of new understanding, however if they have been reburied, reevaluation relies entirely on the original records. These are not always suitable, but having a 3D digitization will allow the best chance to properly reevaluate diagnosis in the future.

Therefore, these scans now lend to a body of data that can be drawn upon at a later date. Such information can be accessed by osteoarchaeologists around the world to increase their sample size and comparative data. This can be achieved because statistical analysis can be conducted; something that was not possible with 2D imaging. Complex quantitative shape analysis through the use of geometric morphometrics, which was only previously achieved using contact digitizers (Lycett and von Cramon-Taubadel, 2013), can now be accomplished.

For example, Sholts et al. (2010) used surface scan data to assess variability in measurements for cranial volume and surface area. Similarly, Shearer et al. (2012) used a digital morphometric approach to analyze sexual dimorphism in 3D digitizations of the human brow ridge. Hence, with accurate scans of the pelvis (Fig. 7.3), future studies investigating biological traits such as age and sex will allow for more accurate estimation methods and smaller margins of error. Other examples of statistical studies include the analysis of variation in shape; with regards to skeleton 426's ribs (Fig. 7.1), a shape analysis test would provide numerical data on the deformation allowing direct numerical comparison to nondeformed ribs.

Finally, it is hoped that the surface scanning approach may improve international collaboration. For example, unlike physical human remains, the data can be shared internationally using e-mail or external

Figure 7.3 A 3D scan of the right os coxa for SK 15 (Hazel Grove) showing biological traits of a male.

storage devices. In turn, this will reduce expenses for travelling from one institution to another to access skeletal remains, or alternatively, mean the human remains will not get damaged in transit.

7.4 CONCLUSIONS

3D digitizations will never replace the need to study an actual individual's skeleton. However, imaged-based techniques have grown significantly offering new possibilities for documenting objects (Evin et al., 2016). 3D scanners provide a way to produce permanent replications of human remains that can be rotated, enlarged, and measured in 3D (Niven et al., 2009). The resulting 3D data can be shared worldwide using computer technology.

It is demonstrated that SLS can help build on osteological research by creating a virtual database that includes skeletal variation and population differences. This is beneficial to teaching and research if the skeleton is no longer available to study, particularly if the individual has uncommon traits. For example, 3D images mean that students can access and learn about unusual pathological conditions that they may not otherwise have an opportunity to see, thus broadening and deepening their knowledge and understanding. In turn, building digital osteological databases will allow for scientific progress through collaboration, enhance our potential to reevaluate diagnosis of pathological lesions in the future, and open up further avenues for sharing data.

ACKNOWLEDGMENTS

I am grateful to Malin Holst and Sophie Newman of York Osteoarcheology, Becky Gowland of Durham University, Anwen Caffell of both York Osteoarchaeology and Durham University, and Tim Thompson of Teesside University. I would also like to thank CFA Archaeology and Wigget Construction for access to the individuals from Hazel Grove, Greater Manchester. Likewise, I would like to thank Washburn Heritage Centre and the living descendants for access to the individuals from Fewston, North Yorkshire.

REFERENCES

Betts, M.W., Maschner, H.D.G., Schou, C.D., Schlader, R., Holmes, J., Clement, N., et al., 2011. Virtual zooarchaeology: building a web-based reference collection of northern vertebrates for archaeofaunal research and education. J. Archaeol. Sci. 755–762.

Brickley, M., McKinley, J., 2004. Guidelines to the Standard for Recording Human Remains. IFA/BABAO.

Buikstra, J.E., Ubelaker, D.H., 1994. Standards for Data Collection from Human Skeletal Remains. Arkansas Archaeological Survey, Fayetteville, Research Series, no. 44.

Caffell, A., Holst, M., forthcoming. Osteological analysis, The Church of St Michael and St Lawrence, Fewston, North Yorkshire. York Osteoarchaeology, Unpublished Osteological Report.

Dactyl, http://www.anthronomics.com/?page_id=16 (accessed 03.08.16).

DCMS, 2005. Guidance for the Care of Human Remains in Museums. Department for Culture, Media and Sport, London, UK, Digitised Diseases, http://www.digitiseddiseases.org/mrn.php?mrn=xx (accessed 03.08.16).

Errickson, D., Thompson, T.J.U., Rankin, B., 2015. An optimum guide for the reduction of noise using a surface scanner for digitising human osteological remains. Guides to Good Practice. Archaeological Data Service. University of York, UK.

Evin, A., Souter, T., Hulme-Beaman, A., Ameen, C., Allen, R., Viacava, P., et al., 2016. The use of close-range photogrammetry in zooarchaeology: creating accurate 3D models of wolf crania to study dog domestication. J. Archaeol. Sci. 87–93.

Human Tissue Act 2004, http://www.legislation.gov.uk/ukpga/2004/30/contents (accessed 07.09.16).

Lycett, S.J., von Cramon-Taubadel, N., 2013. Understanding the comparative catarrhine context of human pelvic form: a 3D geometric morphometric analysis. J. Hum. Evol. 64 (4), 300–310.

McPherron, S.P., Gernat, T., Hublin, J.J., 2009. Structured light scanning for high resolution documentation of in situ archaeological finds. J. Archaeol. Sci. 19–24.

Native American Graves Protection and Repatriation Act, 1990. Public Law 101–601; 25 U.S.C. 3001–3013.

Newman, S., Holst, M., 2016. Osteological analysis, Chapel Street, Hazel Grove, Greater Manchester. York Osteoarchaeology, Unpublished Osteological Report 2116.

Niven, L., Steele, T.E., Finke, H., Gernat, T., Hublin, J.J., 2009. Virtual skeletons: using a structured light scanner to create a 3D faunal comparative collection. J. Archaeol. Sci. 2018–2023.

Orr, E.R., & Bienkowski, P. 2006. Respectful treatment and reburial: a practical guide. Paper presented to the Respect for Ancient British Human Remains: Philosophy and Practice conference. 17 November 2006, Manchester Museum. http://www.museum.manchester.ac.uk/medialibrary/documents/respect/respect_practical_guide.pdf (accessed 18.09.16).

Payne, S., 2012. Archaeology and human remains. In: Fossheim, H. (Ed.), More Than Just Bones: Ethics and Research on Human Remains. The Norwegian National Research Committee, Oslo, pp. 49–64.

Rogers, J., Wait, I., Dieppe, P., 1985. Palaeopathology of spinal osteophytosis, vertebral ankylosis, ankylosing spondylitis, and vertebral hyperostosis. Ann. Rheum. Dis. 44, 113–120.

Sellevold, B., 2012. Ancient skeletons and ethical dilemmas. In: Fossheim, H. (Ed.), More Than Just Bones: Ethics and Research on Human Remains. The Norwegian National Research Committee, Oslo, pp. 139–160.

Shearer, B.M., Sholts, S.B., Garvin, H.M., Warmlander, S.K.T.S., 2012. Sexual dimorphism in human browridge volume measured from 3D models of dry crania: a new digital morphometrics approach. Forensic Sci. Int. 222, 400.e1–400.e5.

Sholts, S.B., Wärmländer, S.K.T.S., Flores, L.M., Miller, K.W.P., Walker, P.L., 2010. Variation in the measurement of cranial volume and surface area using 3D laser scanning technology. J. Forensic Sci. 55 (4), 871–876.

Thali, M.J., Braun, W., Brueschweiler, W., Dirnhofer, R., 2003. 'Morphological imprint': determination of the injury-causing weapon from the wound morphology using forensic 3D/CAD supported photogrammetry. Forensic Sci. Int. 132 (3), 177–181.

VZAP, 2016. http://vzap.iri.isu.edu/ViewPage.aspx?id=230 (accessed 03.08.16).

Weber, G.W., 2014. Another link between archaeology and anthropology: virtual anthropology. Digit. Appl. Archaeol. Cult. Herit. 3–11.

CHAPTER 8

The Use of Laser Scanning for Visualization and Quantification of Abrasion on Water-Submerged Bone

Samuel J. Griffith and Charlotte E.L. Thompson
University of Southampton, Southampton, United Kingdom

8.1 INTRODUCTION

This chapter discusses the potential of laser scanning for quantitatively recording sediment abrasion on bone in experimental and actualistic taphonomy studies. Recording physical diagenetic change on the surface of bone, such as abrasion, can be a useful tool for understanding the depositional histories of remains (Fisher, 1995; Haglund and Sorg, 2002; Lyman, 1994). With this intention, bone taphonomy studies attempt to correlate diagnostic features of change with specific modifying agents. This reconciliation of cause and effect facilitates an assessment of the types of environments and processes osseous material has been exposed to. Of equal importance in such studies is the ability to ascertain both predictability and rate of diagenetic change as they relate to different environmental and spatial parameters: Establishing the uniformity of change to bone allows an evaluation of how reliable

Human Remains: Another Dimension. DOI: http://dx.doi.org/10.1016/B978-0-12-804602-9.00009-6

such modifications are for making inferences about the occurrence and temporality of different taphonomic processes.

A major issue to overcome in such analyses is that of equifinality, where alterations caused by different taphonomic processes or durations produce seemingly indistinguishable features of change on bone (Cook, 1995; Lyman, 1994, 2004). As a result, the etiology of modifications, such as abrasion, may be hard to determine (Madgwick, 2014). The inability to correlate modifications with specific taphonomic agents and durations can be attributed to four potential factors: Firstly, the complexity of taphonomic systems at work is such that they confound analysis; second, there is not sufficient variability in the way bone responds to different processes, hence restricting differential determinations; in contrast, variations in the physicochemical properties of bone may cause it to react differently to the same taphonomic stimuli; and finally, the resolution of analysis used to interpret these changes is inadequate. The latter leads to the question: Can improved methodologies help to decode taphonomic pathways where before this was not possible?

Traditional methods for recording taphonomic alterations on bone's surface often utilize qualitative, point-based scoring of gross morphological change. For example, Behrensmeyer's now classic study on the interpretation of taphonomic and ecologic information from bone weathering relates surface modifications to durations of exposure to specific environmental processes (Behrensmeyer, 1978). Behrensmeyer's research resulted in the now widely used six-point weathering scale of bone and provides invaluable information regarding the interpretation of taphonomic pathways. However, while facilitating a rapid assessment of bone tissue modification using easily recordable criteria, qualitative, gross morphological measures do have inherent caveats; most notably they may lack a degree of temporal specificity and the ability to record small-scale surface details. Arguably more accurate measures of material change allow for an improved assessment of both cause and frequency of bone tissue modification by removing a degree of ambiguity inherent in more traditional measures. Such methodology, as we discuss herein using an example of quantitatively recording abrasion on submerged bone, may therefore help to limit the aforementioned issue of the chosen analysis being a factor which inhibits the successful reconciliation of taphonomic effect, cause, and duration.

8.1.1 Abrasion on Submerged Bone

A common modification to submerged bone is abrasion caused by mobile sediment impacts when the bone is suspended in a flow or transported along the sediment–water interface (Cook, 1995; Thompson et al., 2011). Numerous studies have attempted to accurately link degrees of abrasion (rounding, polishing, and smoothing) on bone surfaces with useful taphonomic information: namely, research aims to elucidate transport distances, submersion times; and to classify the impacting sediment (Cook, 1995; Nawrocki et al., 1997; Thompson et al., 2011). Such methods are often based on the principals of mobile sediment grain modification, where transport in aquatic systems results in incremental rounding of sediment particles; which facilitates correlations between hydrological processes, resultant sediment grain morphology, and duration of exposure to bombardment. However, in large it has proven difficult to definitively relate degrees of abrasion recorded on bone at a gross morphological level to environmental processes operating within defined spatio-temporal parameters (Evans, 2014). Resultantly, there is a limited understanding of whether sediment-induced abrasion can be used to accurately interpret the aquatic taphonomic pathways of bone.

It should be noted that a degree of this ambiguity is attributable to the potential complexity of taphonomic pathways in marine, lacustrine, and fluvial systems and variations in the morphology and physiochemical properties of bone itself (Griffith et al., 2016). For example, periods of bone floatation or burial in bottom sediment can disrupt linear wear progression, hence confounding predictable rates of erosion (Evans, 2014; Griffith et al., 2016; Thompson et al., 2011). Similarly, different extents of bone soft tissue cover and weathering at the point of submersion or transport result in variable erosion rates under the same hydrological conditions (Fernandez-Jalvo and Andrews, 2003; Thompson et al., 2011). However, discrepancies are also derived from the limited resolution of qualitative measures of material change, as at a gross morphological level small-scale abrasive changes are hard to distinguish and assign temporal specificity (Cook, 1995). Furthermore, smoothing, polishing, and rounding are often subjective judgements and not direct measures of material removal (Griffith et al., 2016).

To thoroughly assess whether abrasion can be used to elucidate bones' submersion times and transport pathways, more quantitative methodologies which afford sequential measures of material change are needed. For example, using scanning electron microscopy Thompson et al. (2011) and Griffith et al. (2016) have shown success in quantitatively linking micro-abrasion propagation to water-based taphonomic processes. Here we investigate the potential of quantitative imaging, through laser scanning, for improving taphonomic interpretations of water-submerged bone in experimental studies.

8.2 EXPERIMENTAL FLUME STUDIES

A series of flume-based experiments were conducted to allow incremental abrasion on bone to be recorded. Fresh adult sheep (*Ovis aries*) bones ($n = 17$) were bombarded by gravel ranging from 3.35 to 13.2 mm in diameter. An enzyme maceration method (Simonsen et al., 2011) was used in sample preparation to remove any adherent soft tissue. After maceration bone samples were classified at stage 0 of the Behrensmeyer weathering scale (Behrensmeyer, 1978), and pre-abrasion laser scans recorded (see Section 8.2.1).

The full experimental setup for the abrasion of water-submerged bone can be found in the work of Thompson et al. (2011). In brief, samples were fixed to the floor of an annular flume to simulate bone being trapped and eroded in bottom sediments under unidirectional flow conditions. Experimental bone samples were bombarded by saltating gravel grains, so as to induce maximum wear (Thompson et al., 2011) and were removed from the experimental conditions at set time intervals of 24, 48, 72, and 120 h and rescanned. To facilitate an energy-based assessment of wear, the abrasive forces of the different sediment sizes used were calculated by recording the number of impacts of sediment on the bone surface per second, and their impact on trajectory and velocity (Table 8.1) using a Casio's Exilim Pro EX-F1 high-speed video camera. Recorded variables were then used in the impact wear equation given below (Amos et al., 2000):

$$T = \left(N M_g \left[\sqrt{U_y^2 + W_s^2} \right] / \varepsilon A_r \right) \mathrm{Pa},$$

where T is an expression of the abrasive force of the sediment (the Ballistic Momentum Flux) measures in Pascals (Pa), N is number of impacts per unit area per second, M_g is sediment grain mass, $\sqrt{U_y^2 + W_s^2}$ is speed of impact, and εA_r is an efficiency term dependent on the transfer of momentum from the grain to the bone (ε), and the area of impact (A_r). In addition, variations in sediment grain morphology were recorded, with angularity and sphericity being determined

Table 8.1 Summary of Sediment Grain's Physical and Hydrodynamic Properties				
Median Grain Size (mm)	4.475	7.350	9.600	12.000
Median grain mass (g)	0.3087	1.3925	5.0164	8.3096
Mean impacts per second	1.9250	1.5190	1.1822	0.7720
Mean impact velocity (cm/s)	0.4891	0.4632	0.7572	0.5646
Mean impact trajectory (degrees from vertical)	88.8300	90.8098	90.7198	90.3326
T (Pa)	6166.6518	8921.6312	28,815.9620	20,425.5920
Grain sphericity	0.6	0.7	0.6	0.6
Grain angularity	0.7	0.4	0.6	0.7

using the Krumbein roundness chart (Krumbein and Sloss, 1951) (Table 8.1).

8.2.1 Quantitative Measures of Abrasion

A FARO Arm Fusion laser scanner, capable of 36 μm repeatability, was used to digitize the pre- and post-abrasion surfaces of bone. Pre-abrasion volumes of bone were computed using an automated function in Geomagic software: Meshed scans were made watertight using the fill holes tool allowing polygon models of bone to become closed cylindrical objects with their internal portions representing their volumes (Fig. 8.1). Similar approaches adopted by Kuzminsky and Gardiner (2012), Shearera et al. (2012), and Sholts et al. (2010) have successfully acquired volumetric data from bone. However, it should be noted that these methods do not record any internal structural properties. Surface scanning therefore cannot provide a definitive measure of bone's internal volume due to the medullary cavity and porous areas not being recoded. However, when assessing the removal of small quantities of compact tissue from the surface of bone, such methodology provides a suitable approximate pre-abrasion volumetric measure. An attempt was made to compare pre- and post-abrasion volumes of bone using this closed surface approach. However, this was challenging as unwanted artefacts (minor undulations or depressions not present on the bone surface) were sometimes generated in the filled areas when closing holes in the polygon models, causing volumetric differences between meshes that were potentially greater than those caused by abrasion. Resultantly, while this approach provided a good approximation of pre-abrasion volume, to which volume change calculated using an additional method (discussed below) could be compared, it could not be used to compare pre- and post-abrasion volumes directly.

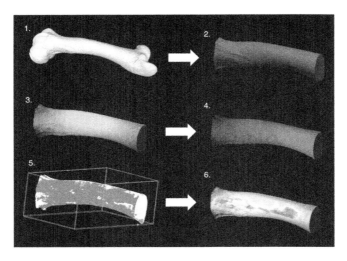

Figure 8.1 Laser scanning workflow: (1) bone sample point cloud captured using FARO Arm scanner; (2) epiphyses cropped to reduce noise; scans are then meshed and made watertight, allowing pre-abrasion volumes to be computed in Geomagic software; (3) pre-abrasion point cloud manually aligned with; (4) the post-abrasion point cloud using CloudCompare software; (5) fine alignment preformed between point clouds; (6) M3C2 measure applied to calculated surface displacement between pre- and post-abrasion point clouds, producing a heat map of measured abrasions (warm areas indicate abrasion).

A Multiscale Model to Model Cloud Comparison (M3C2) (Lague et al., 2013) was used to measure erosion depths and volumetric changes by detecting surface displacements between pre- and post-abrasion point clouds. The M3C2 algorithm was initially developed to record differences in large-scale point cloud data collected by terrestrial laser scanning (TSL), so as to quantify topographic changes to complex landforms (Barnhart and Crosby, 2013). Recently, this algorithm has been applied in other contexts: Majcherczyk et al. (2015) used this method to monitor morphological changes to roadways; while Troisi et al. (2015) used the distance measure at a smaller scale, assessing error between point clouds of a Charonia Tritonis shell, which was digitized in an underwater and dry environment using photogrammetry. Although the primary focus of Troisi et al. (2015) was a determination of 3D image capture accuracy under different environmental conditions, the authors also show that M3C2 can be used to record material removal from the surface of a small, complex object: A small amount of material was lost from the surface of the shell during removal from the submerged context, which was effectively recorded using the M3C2 distance measure (Troisi et al., 2015, p. 221).

Scans were saved in point cloud format and imported into the public domain software CloudCompare for analysis. Prior to analysis, point clouds were manually cleaned to remove any extraneous points. The articular ends of the bone scans displayed moderate levels of noise due to areas with occluded light, such the trochanteric and intercondylar fossae, being difficult to record. Therefore, to limit the effects of noise, the epiphyseal areas were cropped, meaning comparisons were only conducted on the bone diaphyses (Fig. 8.1).

The M3C2 algorithm allows signed distances to be calculated between two point clouds and has some distinct analytical advantages over Cloud to Cloud and Cloud to Mesh comparisons, which are discussed in depth by Lague et al. (2013) and Barnhart and Crosby (2013). M3C2 incorporates a spatially variable confidence interval and limits sources of uncertainty (noise, surface roughness, scan registration error, and surface orientation) which are problematic in the analysis of irregular point cloud surfaces (Barnhart and Crosby, 2013). The algorithm makes use of core points by calculating the average positions and surface orientations of total points within a surface area specified by the user (Lague et al., 2013) (Fig. 8.2); this can allow for a reduction in computational intensity by limiting the number of points used in analysis while still utilizing the entire density of the reference model (in this case the pre-abrasion point cloud) (Barnhart and Crosby, 2013). Importantly, M3C2 has been found to have good application in the analysis of surfaces which display transitions between more uniform and irregular topographies, with composite surface orientations (Barnhart and Crosby, 2013).

Outputs from M3C2 comparisons were analyzed in two ways. Firstly, measured distances between pre- and post-abrasion point clouds allowed for a quantification of the depth of erosion across the bone surface. Distances between point clouds were plotted using a colored scalar field; allowing abrasion to be visualized as heat maps, with erosion depths being assigned specific colors and hues. An automated function in CloudCompare allows raw numerical data of the range of recorded displacements (erosion depths), and the number of points which display these displacements, to be exported as a histogram plot and in ASCII or CSV file format (Table 8.2). For this study an equation was employed which allowed volume change to be calculated using the raw data. The principals behind these volumetric calculations

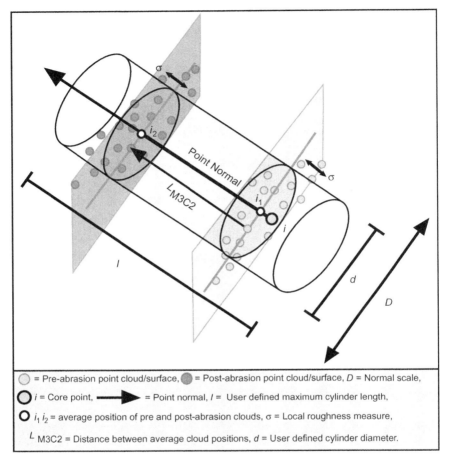

Figure 8.2 The point normal (normal direction/orientation) for a core point i, *is calculated at a user-defined scale of* D. *A projection cylinder with user-defined diameter (*d*) and length (*l*) denotes the area over which points in the pre- and post-abrasion clouds are selected. Selected points are used to calculate the average position of the two point clouds (*i$_1$ *and* i$_2$*). The* L$_{M3C2}$ *is the distance between these average positions, along the point normal. The shaded blue (shaded light gray in print version) cylindrical area (which we will refer to as the displacement cylinder) is the space between point cloud surfaces, in this case it represents volume loss due to abrasion. The distances between every point in the pre-abrasion cloud and the post-abrasion surface can be computed by specifying all points in the reference cloud as core points when running the M3C2 algorithm. A local roughness measure is used to calculate a spatially variable confidence interval for* i. *Image adapted from Lague, D., Brodu, N., Leroux, J., 2013. Accurate 3D comparison of complex topography with terrestrial laser scanner: application to the Rangitikei canyon (N-Z). ISPRS J. Photogramm. Remote Sens. 82, 10—26; Barnhart T.B., Crosby B.T., 2013. Comparing two methods of surface change detection on an evolving thermokarst using high-temporal-frequency terrestrial laser scanning, Selawik River, Alaska. Remote Sens. 5, 2813—2837.*

are originally discussed in the CloudCompare online forum (CloudCompare, 2016a). In addition, Stumpf et al. (2015) use a more complex approach involving M3C2 distances and a plane fitting algorithm to calculate sediment volume differences after landslide events. While Olsen et al. (2010) adopted a comparable cross sectional and point averaging approach to calculate volume change in scans collected using TSL.

The principals behind volume change computation are given below; all calculations can be carried out using CloudCompare and the formula provided herein. Cloudcompare.org should be consulted for further details on input parameters and settings when using the M3C2 plugin (CloudCompare, 2016a,b). Initially, raw point cloud data must undergo some straightforward postprocessing: The clouds must be subsampled at a known density by applying universal point spacing, resulting in a model with a fixed number of points across any given surface area. This is important as when using handheld scanners the user may capture an area of the scanned object multiple times resulting in a point cloud that is not uniformly dense. After subsampling, to allow for volume calculations, all evenly spaced points within the cloud must be specified as core points when running the M3C2 plugin (CloudCompare, 2016a) (note as show in Fig. 8.2, M3C2 utilizes cylinders with a user-defined diameter and maximum height to denote the area over which signed distances calculations between core points are conducted; applying uniform point spacing therefore results in a set number of points being contained within the cylinder base areas).

Table 8.2 Raw M3C2 Output Data

A

Class	No. of Core Points	Distance Range (mm)	
		Lower	Upper
1	10,523	0.211261	0.237224
2	8369	0.237224	0.263186
3	7419	0.263186	0.289149

B

No. of Core Points in Output Cloud	M3C2 Distance (mm)
33	0.402960
37	0.418763

A: Example of M3C2 output bins from plotted histogram. In Class 1 there are 10,523 core points showing displacements between pre- and post-abrasion clouds of 0.211261–0.237224 mm; the median distance value of the lower/upper range in each class is used to define displacement cylinder lengths (L_{M3C2}) for volume change calculations. B: Alternatively, exact distances for each core point can be exported in ASCII format, where the M3C2 distance is used to define the displacement cylinder length.

If the user were to specify parameters to allow one core point to be contained within its base, then the total approximate volume difference between clouds could be calculated as follows:

$$\text{Vol} = \left(\sum [(AL_{M3C2})N_{pts}] \right) \text{mm}^3,$$

The cylinder base area A (a user-defined constant) is multiplied by a recorded L_{M3C2} value (displacement cylinder length (Fig. 8.2)). Looking at Table 8.2A for example, the Class 1 bin has a displacement range of between 0.211261 and 0.237224 mm; the median displacement value (L_{M3C2} value), in this case 0.22422 mm, is multiplied by A to calculate a displacement cylinder volume. This displacement cylinder volume value (AL_{M3C2}) is then multiplied by the variable N_{pts}, which is the number of core points that display a specific L_{M3C2} distance range. For the example given in Table 8.2A, Class 1, there are ($N_{pts} = $)10523 core points that have displacement values of between 0.211261 and 0.237224 mm. In the above formula we consider parameters where only one core point is contained within the cylinder base area. Therefore, the variable N_{pts} is equivalent to the total number of times a cylinder with a distinct volume occurs. It is the sum of the values from all Classes or specific M3C2 distances (Table 8.2), and hence the sum of all distinct cylinder volumes that allows for an approximate quantitation of total volume change. Put simply, all distinct cylinder volume values are multiplied by the number of times they occur across the point cloud surface. Exporting exact M3C2 distances for each core point in ASCII file format (Fig. 8.2B), rather that utilizing median displacement values, is also possible and is the more favorable approach as this will provide more accurate displacement values. This will however also result in larger file sizes, so the user must decide which approach to adopt based on the size of the point clouds being analyzed.

It should be noted that specifying all points in the cloud as core points allows for more confident estimations of surface displacements, as the distance between every point is being computed (Fig. 8.3). It is also advisable to specify a high number of points to be contained within a cylindrical base area, and a sufficiently large scale D to account for surface roughness (CloudCompare, 2016b). As distances between all points are being measured when taking this approach (Fig. 8.3), N_{pts} must be divided by the number of points occupying

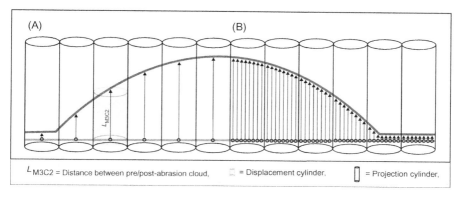

Figure 8.3 2D representation of projection and displacement cylinders used to measure distances between pre-(green (light gray in print version)) and post-abrasion (red (black in print version)) surfaces. (A) This shows parameters where one core point is contained within the displacement cylinder base area; hence number of core points is equivalent to the number of cylinders. (B) This shows parameters where multiple core points occupy a cylinder base area, allowing for more confident displacement measures. Note it is not shown in (B) that each core point still uses its own projection cylinder and set of neighboring points to calculate displacements. Neighboring points also function as core points in this scenario; therefore, over each area of the point cloud surface that is equivalent to the cylinder projection base area, multiple distance measures are computed.

each cylinder base area (CB_{pts}). For example, in the case of this study, approximately 30 points covered one cylinder base area, which was ca. 0.5 mm in diameter; resultantly each core point displaying a specific L_{M3C2} distance value only occupies ca. 1/30 of a cylinder's base. Therefore, the number of times a displacement cylinder with a specific L_{M3C2} value occurs across the point cloud surface is equal to the number of times 30 core points with the same L_{M3C2} value occur; hence the division by CB_{pts} is necessary to allow the variable, N_{pts} to again be equivalent to the total number of times a cylinder with a distinct volume occurs across the point cloud surface area. This leads to a slight revision of the above equation:

$$\text{Vol} = \left(\sum \left[(AL_{M3C2}) \left(\frac{N_{pts}}{CB_{pts}} \right) \right] \right) \text{mm}^3,$$

Calculated surface displacements were then subtracted from the initial volumes computed in Geomagic using the closed surface approach. As samples were morphologically distinct, showing different starting volumes, abrasion is represented as percentage volume loss from the original pre-abrasion scan rather than total material loss; this approach facilitates a better understanding of abrasion rate as volume loss is being presented relative to the size of the bone sample.

It should be noted that during the process of M3C2, distance computation pre- and post-abrasion point clouds are aligned in a common coordinate system. There is inevitably a minor degree of error during point cloud alignment; therefore, this distance error between scans was used as a change detection threshold. Resultantly, if surface displacement was detected within the misalignment range, it was not used for the quantitation of volumetric differences. In addition, as the M3C2 measure allows the user to define a maximum cylinder height; an upper limit of 4 mm was selected to exclude measuring any unrealistic surface displacement attributable to noise rather than real topographic change. Typically, abrasion depths did not exceed 1.5 mm; however, the limit of 4 mm ensured that any larger chipping of the bone surface (pockmarks) would also be recordable.

To allow for a preliminary assessment of M3C2 volume calculation accuracy, a custom 225 kV Nikon/Metris HMX ST Computed Tomography (CT) scanner operating at 15 μm resolution was used to record a single bone sample. CT scanning is known to provide the most accurate measures of bone volume and density (Lam et al., 2003) and therefore acts as a good benchmark for comparison. Pre- and post-abrasion volumes of the CT scanned bone were rendered using Avizo software. While CT scanning has distinct analytical advantages, such as the ability to image bones' internal structures at high resolutions, laser scanning is in general more cost-effective. In addition, many laser scanners are portable, which facilitates the recording of in situ deposits in the field.

8.3 RESULTS AND DISCUSSION

It should be noted that the method adopted in this study does not currently have application in quantifying changes to bone recovered from natural settings; this is because the methodology relies on pre-abrasion scans of bone for comparison. In addition, the abrasion rates shown here represent idealized conditions of maximum wear, which are unlikely to occur in a natural setting over the same timescales. However, importantly this method has direct application in experimental and actualistic studies, which generate data to better understand the etiology, principal modifying agents, and temporality of diagenetic change to bone.

8.3.1 Quantitative Imaging

Point spacing after subsampling varied between scans, but was approximately 0.1 mm; this cloud density allowed small-scale surface displacements to be effectively captured, with the smallest abrasive change recorded outside the error range being 0.08 mm in depth. While the resolution of change detection using M3C2 is also dependent on instrument capabilities and calibration, in this study it provided a measure of surface modification which affords far greater detail than visual, gross morphological assessment. While such detail can be captured using microscopy for example (Fernandez-Jalvo and Andrews, 2003; Shipman and Rose, 1988; Thompson et al., 2011) laser scanning allowed abrasion to be viewed across a much larger area (the entirety of the bone's surface) and did not require any destructive sectioning of the samples.

Calculated volumetric differences provided a good approximation of surface changes. When using this method involving the summation of multiple cylinder volumes, some error may occur due to either cylindrical projection shapes not fully tessellating on the point cloud surface, hence resulting in missing mass; or overlap of cylinders due to the orientation of points across a curved surface (CloudCompare, 2016a). CT scanning allowed for a preliminary assessment of this potential error; M3C2 recorded a 264.34 mm^3 volume loss and CT a 273.78 mm^3 loss on the same sample, a 3.44% error between methods. Currently the source of this error is unknown. The discrepancy may be attributable to the higher sampling resolution of CT scanning, the conservative nature of M3C2 change detection (see Barnhart and Crosby, 2013, p. 2852 for further detail), potential overlap or missing data between cylinders, or any point cloud alignment error. Despite this uncertain source of error, volumetric differences were minor; indicating that volume calculation using M3C2 has good potential application in measuring small-scale topographic changes to bone. It is reasonable to suggest, given the limited sample size used, that error between these methods should be considered as approximately 5%. However, this approximate error range may increase when multiple samples, or surfaces with more complex and widely distributed changes are analyzed.

Heat maps of the geometric distances between point clouds were generated allowing an assessment of spatial differentiation of wear

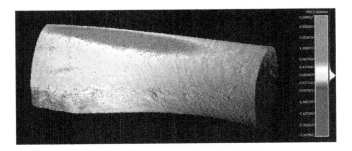

Figure 8.4 Colored scalar field map of abrasion on bone's surface; wear (warm regions) is focused on the top and upstream side of the bone where impacts are most frequent. M3C2 distances are given in millimeters.

across the bone surface (Fig. 8.4). Abrasion was concentrated on the upstream side of the bone where impacts were most frequent due to the bone being bombarded in a fixed position. In addition to providing a superior assessment of depth and location of wear than is possible through gross morphological assessment, an improved understanding of the spatial distribution of abrasion may provide additional tapho-nomic insights. For example, during deposition and transport in water, while there is some variation, different skeletal elements tend to orien-tate and move nonrandomly due to their distinct morphologies (Coard and Dennell, 1995; Voorhies, 1969). Similarly, different degrees of skel-etal completeness cause variation in orientation and transport potential of bone (Coard and Dennell, 1995); theoretically, such variability leaves different areas of bone's surface exposed to impacting sediments. Therefore, differentiation of abrasion across a bone's surface may aid in determining whether erosion occurred in transit or in situ and may help to elucidate differences in skeletal completeness and soft tissue cover upon deposition in water.

8.3.2 Abrasion Rates

Bombardment produced unique extents of wear, with abrasion rates being relatable to different hydrodynamic and morphological proper-ties of the sediment grains. Between 0 and 48 h a distinct wear trend, other than that of abrasion increasing with time, is hard to establish. This is most probably due to natural variability in the pre-abrasion surfaces of bone: It has been observed microscopically that abrasion on bone's surface initially proceeds through the removal of loosely bound surface material (Griffith et al., 2016; Thompson et al., 2011). While samples were prepared in a way so as to ensure they were as structurally homogenous as possible, variation in the presence of this loosely bound material between samples may confound abrasion rates. After 72 h, presumably when a more uniformly compact surface was being abraded, a general trend emerges of abrasion progressing as a function of increasing time and sediment size (Fig. 8.5).

The dominant wear trend is broken by the 7.35 mm gravel size causing the highest degree of abrasion over earlier time intervals (Fig. 8.5). Previous studies, using macro- and microscopic observations of abrasion, have found that sediment particles with increased angularity may cause higher degrees of wear (see, e.g., Griffith et al., 2016 and Shipman and Rose, 1988); this is likely due to the increased ability of an angular abrasive to penetrate the bone's surface (Griffith et al., 2016). The 7.35 mm grains used in this study were angular/sub-angular with medium−low sphericity, whereas the other grains used were either sub-angular or sub-rounded grains of medium sphericity (Table 8.1). This morphological difference explains the increased abrasive capabilities displayed by this sediment size.

While there is a general linear trend of abrasive force increasing in conjunction with changes in sediment size, the apparent discrepancies between these measures (Fig. 8.6) are also attributable to variations in grain morphology which were not accounted for sufficiently in the calculation of T values: In addition to the 7.35 mm grain showing a lower T value but inducing higher wear rates due to increased angularity, the calculated value for 12 mm gravel was lower than that of the 9 mm grains due to fewer number of impacts per second and a lower impact velocity being recorded (Table 8.1). However, the 12 mm grains caused higher degrees of abrasion. These two grain sizes had similar angularity and sphericity, meaning that relative to particle size the concentration of their impact across the bone surface was approximately equal; therefore, it is likely that the larger size of the 12 mm particles allowed them to impact a wider surface area, resulting in higher degrees of wear. These preliminary results identify variations in particle morphology, the potential effects of changing structure as surface layers of bone are worn; and the area over which impacts are concentrated as being important variables influencing wear rate; holding more weight of influence than number of impacts per second and impact velocity. While these relationships are as of yet imperfectly understood, future empirical work can now investigate and incorporate these variables into taphonomic models.

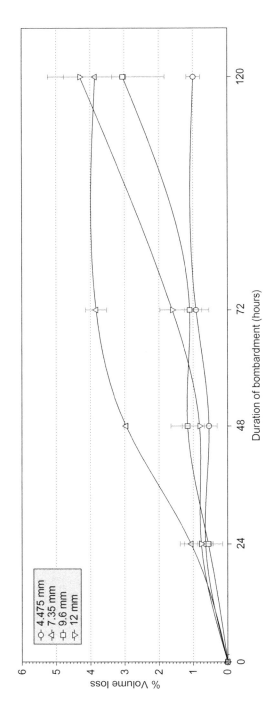

Figure 8.5 Percentage volume loss from bone samples between 0 and 120 h of bombardment by mobile sediments. Error bars show values for when any scan alignment error is included in total volume calculation.

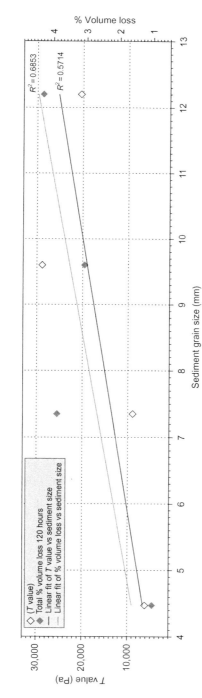

Figure 8.6 The relationship between recorded abrasive force (T value), measure in pascals, sediment grain size, and % volume loss after 120 h of bombardment. Note there is not a clear increase in recorded abrasion when T value increase, indicating that more experimental work is needed to understand this relationship.

It is apparent that a more sequential understanding of abrasion provides insight into taphonomic variables influencing wear rate. If this methodology were adopted in actualistic experimental studies, in natural aquatic systems, it would allow for an improved understanding of the relationship between abrasion rates and hydrodynamic processes. By removing the ambiguity of more qualitative measures of material change, one can fully assess whether precise correlations can be made between bone tissue modifications and useful taphonomic information such as submersion times and transport pathways. This quantitative approach allows influences which confound correlations between taphonomic effect and cause to be attributed to environmental variability or changes in bone tissue quality, rather than the resolution of the chosen analysis. While we use an example of abrasion on water-submerged bone here, the discussed methodology also has good potential applications in recording small-scale topographic changes to bone, and other artifacts of archaeological interest, which may undergo similar forms of surface alteration.

8.4 CONCLUSIONS

This preliminary study has shown that laser scanning can be used to accurately record abrasion on submerged bone at a resolution not possible through gross morphological assessment. Using a M3C2 plugin for CloudCompare software, erosion depths and locations as well as incremental volume changes were measured. Through this approach it was possible to understand differences in bone abrasion rates as they relate to specific taphonomic variables; with duration of bombardment (time), sediment grain morphology and size being identified as having notable influences. While the application of this quantitative imaging methodology in bone taphonomy studies is still developing, it has some clear analytical advantages over more qualitative approaches. In experimental studies the acquisition of quantitative data facilitates a better fundamental understanding of modifying processes by allowing more accurate correlations between taphonomic effect, cause, and duration. Such quantitation enables subtle variations in abrasion extents to be differentiated which may help to overcome certain issues of equifinality, particularly when attempting to establish the temporality of changes. In summation, a more detailed and sequential understanding of material change, which is afforded by laser scanning, may lead to an improved assessment of the accuracy, and hence the propriety, of using abrasion recorded on bone for decoding aquatic taphonomic pathways.

ACKNOWLEDGMENTS

The authors acknowledge the μ-VIS X-ray Imaging Centre at the University of Southampton for provision of tomographic imaging facilities, supported by EPSRC grant EP-H01506X. We also thank the Natural Environment Research Council (NERC) for funding this research. Thanks are extended to Tim Thompson and David Errickson for use of the FARO Arm scanner at Teesside University. We would also like to thank the anonymous reviewers of this chapter for their helpful and insightful suggestions. Finally we would like to thank the creators of CloudCompare for developing and maintaining this great open source program.

REFERENCES

Amos, C., Sutherland, T.F., Cloutier, D., Patterson, S., 2000. Corrasion of a remoulded cohesive bed by saltating littorinid shells. Cont. Shelf Res. 20, 1291–1315.

Barnhart, T.B., Crosby, B.T., 2013. Comparing two methods of surface change detection on an evolving thermokarst using high-temporal-frequency terrestrial laser scanning, Selawik River, Alaska. Remote Sens. 5, 2813–2837.

Behrensmeyer, A.K., 1978. Taphonomic and ecologic information from bone weathering. Paleobiology 4 (2), 150–162.

Coard, R., Dennell, R.W., 1995. Taphonomy of some articulated skeletal remains: transport potential in an artificial environment. J. Archaeol. Sci. 22, 441–448.

Cook, E., 1995. Sedimentology and Taphonomy of Wealden (Lower Cretaceous) Bone Accumulations. University of Bristol, PhD Thesis.

Evans, T., 2014. Fluvial taphonomy. In: Pokines, T.J., Symes, S.A. (Eds.), Manual of Forensic Taphonomy. CRC Press, 2014.

Fernandez-Jalvo, Y., Andrews, P., 2003. Experimental effects of water abrasion on bone fragments. J. Taphonomy 3, 147–163.

Fisher, J.W., 1995. Bone surface modifications in zooarchaeology. J. Archaeol. Method Theory 2 (1), 7–68.

Griffith, S.J., Thompson, C.E.L., Thompson, T.J.U., Gowland, R.L., 2016. Experimental abrasion of water submerged bone: the influence of bombardment by different sediment classes on microabrasion rate. J. Archaeol. Sci. Rep. 10, 15–29.

Haglund, W.D., Sorg, M., 2002. Human remains in water environments. In: Haglund, W.D., Sorg, M. (Eds.), Advances in Forensic Taphonomy: Methods, Theory, and Archaeological Perspectives. CRC Press, Boca Raton, FL, pp. 219–243, 2002.

Krumbein, W.C., Sloss, L.L., 1951. Stratigraphy and Sedimentation. W. H. Freeman & Co., San Francisco, CA, 1951.

Kuzminsky, S.C., Gardiner, M.S., 2012. Three-dimensional laser scanning: potential uses for museum conservation and scientific research. J. Archaeol. Sci. 39 (8), 2744–2751.

Lague, D., Brodu, N., Leroux, J., 2013. Accurate 3D comparison of complex topography with terrestrial laser scanner: application to the Rangitikei canyon (N-Z). ISPRS J. Photogramm. Remote Sens. 82, 10–26.

Lam, Y.M., Pearsonc, O.M., Mareand, C.W., Chene, X., 2003. Bone density studies in zooarchaeology. J. Archaeol. Sci. 30 (12), 1701–1708.

Lyman, R.L., 1994. Vertebrate Taphonomy. Cambridge Manuals in Archaeology. Cambridge University Press.

Lyman, R.L., 2004. The concept of equifinality in taphonomy. J. Taphonomy 2 (1), 15–26.

Madgwick, R., 2014. What makes bones shiny? Investigating trampling as a cause of bone abrasion. Archaeol. Anthropol. Sci. 6 (2), 163–173.

Majcherczyk, T., Niedbalski, Z., Ulaszek, A., 2015. Roadway stability evaluation on the basis of modern monitoring of displacement. Studia Geotechnica et Mechanica 37 (1), 45–52.

Nawrocki, S.P., Pless, J.E., Hawley, D.A., Wagner, S.A., 1997. Fluvial transport of human crania. In: Haglund, W.D., Sorg, M.H. (Eds.), Forensic Taphonomy: The Postmortem Fate of Human Remains. CRC Press, 1996.

Olsen, M.J., Kuester, F., Chang, B.J., Hutchinson, T.C., 2010. Terrestrial laser scanning-based structural damage assessment. J. Comput. Civil Eng. 24, 264–272.

Simonsen, K.P., Rasmussen, A.R., Mathisen, P., Petersen, H., Borup, F., 2011. A Fast Preparation of skeletal materials using enzyme maceration. J. Forensic Sci. 56 (2), 480–484.

Shearera, B.M., Sholts, S.B., Garvind, H.M., Wärmländerb, S.K.T., 2012. Sexual dimorphism in human browridge volume measured from 3D models of dry crania: a new digital morphometrics approach. Forensic Sci. Int. 222 (1–3), 400.e1–400.e5.

Shipman, P., Rose, J., 1988. Bone tools and experimental approach. In: Olson, S. (Ed.), Scanning Electron Microscopy in Archaeology, British Archaeological Reports National Series, vol. 452. pp. 303–335.

Sholts, S.B., Wärmländer, S.K.T., Flores, L.M., Miller, K.W.P., Walker, P.L., 2010. Variation in the measurement of cranial volume and surface area using 3D laser scanning technology. Am. J. Phys. Anthropol. 55 (4), 871–876.

Stumpf, A., Malet, J.P., Alleand, P., Pierrot-Deseilligny, M., Skupinski, G., 2015. Ground-based multi-view photogrammetry for the monitoring of landslide deformation and erosion. Geomorphology 231, 130–145.

Thompson, C.E.L., Ball, S., Thompson, T.J.U., Gowland, R., 2011. The abrasion of modern and archaeological bones by mobile sediments: the importance of transport modes. J. Archaeol. Sci. 38 (4), 784–793.

Troisi, S., Del Pizzo, S., Gaglione, S., Miccio, A., Testa, R.L., 2015. 3D model comparisons of complex shell in underwater and dry environment. Int. Arch. Photogramm. Remote Sens. Spatial Inf. Sci. 5, 215–222.

Voorhies, M.R., 1969. Taphonomy and Population Dynamics of an Early Pliocene Vertebrate Fauna. Knox County, Nebraska, University of Wyoming Contributions to Geology Special Paper 1, pp. 1–69.

WEBSITES
CloudCompare, 2016a. http://www.cloudcompare.org/forum/ (last accessed 02.04.16).

CloudCompare, 2016b. http://www.cloudcompare.org/doc/wiki/index.php?title=M3C2_(plugin) (last accessed 02.04.16).

CHAPTER *9*

Laser Scanning of Skeletal Pathological Conditions

Andrew S. Wilson, Andrew D. Holland and Tom Sparrow
University of Bradford, Bradford, United Kingdom

9.1 INTRODUCTION

Digital Bioarchaeology and Virtual Anthropology (Weber and Bookstein, 2011; Weber, 2015) are complementary fields that are evolving fast as new digital innovations offer increased research potential. For instance many osteological studies have made use of 3D laser scanning technology—ranging from low-cost solutions such as the NextEngine device which for a cranium requires roughly 20 scans over the course of an hour (Boutin et al., 2012), through handheld devices to high-fidelity engineering instruments such as Laserarm devices (Kuzminsky and Gardiner, 2012). Of course laser scanning is also multiscalar and standards produced for 3D laser scanning have largely concentrated on airborne and terrestrial scanning, with object-scale scanning a more recent focus (Jones, 2011).

Human Remains: Another Dimension. DOI: http://dx.doi.org/10.1016/B978-0-12-804602-9.00010-2

3D capture methods vary in their applicability to osteological collections for various conservation and practical reasons concerned with safeguarding what are often fragile bone elements. It is recognized that some osteological collections are heavily called upon for teaching and by researchers (Caffell et al., 2001). Of these collections it is often the individuals manifesting pathological lesions that are most commonly sought after. Yet the bones of these individuals may be among the most fragile.

Many of the handheld devices make use of range-finding optics that calculate the distance from the object to the scanner and record the position as a point in 3D-space. These optics further help to track movement by establishing these points relative to the transmitter, or datum (Allard et al., 2005). Handheld scanners often require targets to facilitate accurate positioning and in the past this has often required targets to be physically placed on the bone, with some using adhesive tabs to hold these in place.

When working with fragile osteological material such as bones exhibiting pathological lesions it is important to minimize movement. However, some devices use a turntable or vice for holding specimens. The ability to limit movement of a specimen and explore the complex physical geometry of a 3D specimen without the need for a vice makes the use of a Laserarm particularly suitable for fragile specimens. A laserarm approach was used for the *Digitised Diseases* project (www.digitiseddiseases.org) to help with capturing complex surface geometry of these pathological conditions. A more static scanning approach would not have been practical, since surface detail could not be captured from a fixed orientation or turntable, without additional handling—causing risk to these fragile specimens.

Just as there are many variables involved in taking a good photograph, there are similarly many things to take account of when using 3D imaging techniques—again a further reason why researchers should consider a range of imaging approaches when selecting the most appropriate for the application. Complexities include: (1) color—too dark and the laser is heavily absorbed, as with material from waterlogged peat soils (Little et al., 2016); (2) reflectivity—too shiny and there is specular reflectance that introduces considerable noise to the scanned data that the scanner may filter leaving holes in the scan; and (3) opacity/translucency—partially translucent material (fresh bone and dental enamel are a particular difficulty) reflects the scanners light

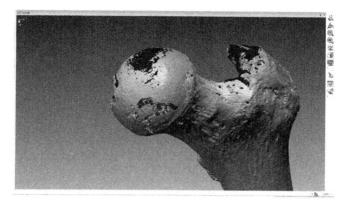

Figure 9.1 High reflectance produces holes in the scan data. From A Holland.

at different depths below the surface dependent on the wavelength and angle of incidence of the light, producing noise artefacts and poor dimensional accuracy (Fig. 9.1). (4) All 3D imaging methods need to be able "to see" intricate detail, otherwise holes appear in the data.

Despite color being a potential obstacle to effective digital documentation, we often use color as a guide to understanding taphonomic change and in interpreting pathological lesions. Yet, many of the 3D capture methods in use, either produce greyscale models or have only rudimentary "texture" information. In order to create photo-realistic models it is necessary to augment the scan data with high-resolution texture photography which is then matched and overlaid on the hole-filled scan data.

The limitations of 3D imaging include: (1) creation of surface artefacts (in particular alignment artefacts brought about by thin/sharp edges); (2) difficulty in scanning trabecular bone; (3) problems with shiny surfaces, including eburnation and highly reflective dental enamel; (4) difficulties with contrasting staining resulting from the depositional environment or conservation methods—too dark or too light/bleached; (5) the size of the laser line and resolution of the capture system which also define the speed and efficacy of the system.

9.2 USE OF MULTISCALAR TECHNIQUES

Laser scanning is used at a variety of scales in relation to funerary contexts. For example, airborne LiDAR has been used to map burial mounds (Artz et al., 2013). Whereas terrestrial laser scanning is often employed at a site scale (Opitz and Limp, 2015). The value of integrating complementary methods at a variety of scales, using both 3D laser scanning and photogrammetry, is seen in the 3D-Digging at Çatalöyük Project where graves are considered in relation to wider contextual information (Forte, 2014; Forte et al., 2015). At the other end of the scale, confocal laser scanning microscopy has been used on archaeological bone to study bone microstructure and bone pathology where precise visualization and quantification are critical (Papageorgopoulou et al., 2010).

Other multiscalar approaches complement surface scanning, many of which are discussed elsewhere in this volume. These complementary methods include z-stack imagery, structure from motion or close-range photogrammetry (Falkingham, 2012; Evin et al., 2016), reflectance transformation imagery (Duffy et al., 2013), structured light scanning (Niven et al., 2009; Schmalz et al., 2012), computed tomography (CT), and micro-CT, given increased emphasis on virtual anatomy and virtopsy (Franklin et al., 2016).

9.3 DEVELOPING RESEARCH BEYOND TRADITIONAL LANDMARKS

The laserarm method is a logical progression from 3D digitizer methods such as the Microscribe (Kuzminsky and Gardiner, 2012) previously in common usage for obtaining 3D coordinate data. In fact, the laserarm can be used in the same way as a Microscribe to define 3D points using the same principles of trigonometry to position the device in 3D space and is used in this way in engineering applications. The choice of landmarks is often fundamental. Within dental anthropology the peculiar conformation of each single tooth makes identification of the landmarks difficult. As such, digital approaches help to reduce errors due to subjective choices (Benazzi et al., 2009).

Increasingly, the use of 3D imaging is helping to take research beyond the use of traditional fixed landmarks to analyze, understand, and interpret patterns of facial recognition/configuration or volumetric data that is more favorable than that provided by a set of inter-land-mark distances (Sforza et al., 2013) and as part of morphometric analysis (Rein and Harvati, 2014; Friess et al., 2002; Selden et al., 2014).

Research projects are utilizing 3D imaging in more defined and targeted ways, e.g., tibial plateau morphology (Macintosh et al., 2015) and cross-sectional data (Davies et al., 2012) and in studies to verify the accuracy of shape measurements (Villa et al., 2015).

9.3.1 Digitised Diseases and From Cemetery to Clinic

Our 3D imaging work at the University of Bradford began in December 2010 with the submission of our proposal for a pilot 3D imaging project *From Cemetery to Clinic* which was focused on leprous individuals from the Medieval leprosarium of St. James and St. Mary Magdalen, Chichester curated at the University of Bradford. This particular project concentrated on the following skeletal changes involving pathological changes to the upper jaw (rhino-maxillary syndrome—defining evidence for lepromatous leprosy), resorption of bones of the hands and feet (including knife-edge remodeling of metatarsals and concentric remodeling of phalanges), secondary infectious involvement of the tibiae and fibulae (periostitis), and remodeling of the hand phalanges caused by fixed flexion of the fingers (e.g., volar grooves due to claw-hand deformity)—see http://www.barc.brad.ac.uk/FromCemeterytoClinic/.

The success of this pilot project led to the establishment of the *Digitised Diseases* project which secured almost £1 million from Jisc and the University of Bradford (Wilson, 2014). The legacy of these digital bioarchaeology projects is continued within Bradford Visualisation (www.bradford-visualisation.com).

9.4 WORKFLOWS

The use of a stable surface is important for any scanning task. The need for two custom designed, scan tables as a stable scanning platform was identified for work at Bradford and in London during *Digitised Diseases*. The tables were designed to enable fixation of a FARO QuantumArm with V3 laser to the same surface as the bones were resting on. Previously, laser scanning during the pilot project had been undertaken with the bone element positioned on a benchtop that was independent of the scanning tripod. The need for this type of solution was designed to limit scan artefacts generated through vibration, thus also speeding up the registration process. For mobile applications it is still possible to use a scan tripod that also anchors to the surface being used as a platform for bone elements, to limit independent movement. Since the surface of our scan table was engineered from steel it was possible to use small soft rubber mounts that are magnetic to support and raise the bone element above the surface of the scan bench to image beneath the specimen and help the process of registering scans while also limiting the contact points on fragile osteological material (Fig. 9.2).

Typically the scan parameters were adjusted according to the nature of the bone surface. This was defined by whether the bone element in question was derived from an archaeological deposit (the majority of the bone scanned), or had previously been macerated as in the case of clinically derived specimens in the collections of the Royal College

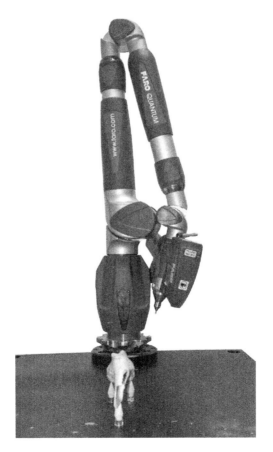

Figure 9.2 Support method used on custom-built scan bench. From A Holland.

of Surgeons. This saw bone manifest from bleached/white appearance through to dark and sometimes variable staining, the result of the conditions in the depositional environment. Archaeologically derived material is rarely intact and so broken elements and exposed trabecular bone was often evident. The most fragile conditions were best represented in the material scanned from the collections of the Royal College of Surgeons.

9.5 POSTPROCESSING

Initial registration steps in any 3D imaging workflow, progress from independent scan passes to full alignment of these using a variety of software packages to create a 3D polygonal model. Prior to registration it is possible to remove portions of the scan data that relate to the supports, or scan bench. The length of time required for registration is defined by the data size (size, shape, and complexity of bone element which in turn dictates the number of scan passes needed) and by the degree of overlap between scan passes and the quality of the scan data.

All 3D capture methods require considerable effort in postprocessing, although this can be reduced by choosing the most appropriate scanning methodology and recognizing the limits of the 3D digitization methodology chosen. Furthermore, the constraints of bone taphonomy and need to optimize capture should also be recognized at the outset.

The overlap between scan passes required for good alignment results in duplication of data and the models were decimated to reduce the size of the final point cloud before creating a surface mesh. These models were then subject to hole-filling, and the removal of artefacts created during scanning. Some of these steps can be automated, although commonly this can introduce further artefacts, without a degree of manual checking.

The data handling requirements involved in a large throughput workflow such as was faced with the *Digitised Diseases* project are substantial. A key guiding principle was to ensure that data was future-proofed—both through use of open access and archival formats for output and storage.

9.6 CONTEXTUALIZING OUTPUTS FROM DIGITAL BIOARCHAEOLOGY

Increasingly museums are utilizing 3D visualization work to represent their collections (Mathys et al., 2013). These outputs are made accessible through a variety of means, with some being less restrictive than others. 3D models in themselves have only limited use. The value of digital bioarchaeology described in this chapter shows that detailed 3D imaging methods offer an objective approach to researching and interpreting human skeletal remains in context (Mahfouz et al., 2016). Furthermore, the outputs can be used in a contextualized way to work alongside other interpretive frameworks such as the Bioarchaeology of Care methodology (Tilley, 2015; Wilson et al., 2017) and as a scalar approach to the study of taphonomy (Mitchell and Booher, 2015; Wilhelmson and Dell'Unto, 2015; Knusel and Robb, 2016) and archaeothanatology (Dufton and Fenwick, 2012; Duday, 2009), and with interpretation and presentation methods used in virtopsy (Antoine and Ambers, 2014; Nather et al., 2009).

While many consider the ability to 3D-print bones to be a logical next step in working with scan data, there are some considerations that should be borne in mind when assessing use for output and display. In a UK context pathological collections are frequently subject to the requirements of HTA licensing because of the relatively recent nature of their holdings, many of which are less than 100 years old. This helps to strengthen the protection of these collections for their intended use within education and research, limiting the risk of inappropriate usage. Of course the need for ethical treatment governs the use of all human remains and is covered in more detail elsewhere in this volume. An important consideration here is to ensure that human remains are studied in context as emphasized in the recent WAC Kyoto accord on Digital Bioarchaeology data (WAC, 2016) and as evidenced in the contextualized display discussed by Allard et al. (2005).

As a born-digital resource the *Digitised Diseases* Web site promotes these principles of context by offering open access use via a bespoke WebGL viewer launched in 2013 (Fig. 9.3), but requesting that users do not 3D-print content, since translation from the digital format has the potential to divorce that content from the specimen descriptions and clinical synopses provided. A further reason behind this is that digital data needs to be quality checked to ensure that it is printable—

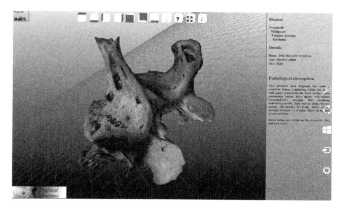

Figure 9.3 Bespoke WebGL viewer created for Digitised Diseases.

requiring additional checks to remove alignment errors such as inverted triangles that would otherwise cause print artefacts or other printing errors. We will in due course introduce a library of printable models on the *Digitised Diseases* resource that have clear attributes on source, permission, and context, containing models that have been processed and checked to ensure that they are printable.

9.7 SUMMARY

Digital bioarchaeology has the potential to reach many more people than traditionally study human remains, including those from related disciplines such as medicine, physiology, and the history of medicine. Digital bioarchaeology can be integrated alongside new interpretative frameworks such as Index of Care and Archaeothanatology. Many different approaches exist for 3D capture and no single method should be relied on completely. It is important to see these methods as complementary tools that should be matched to the task.

The particular constraints of working with fragile pathological bones require a minimum of handling and movement for reasons of conservation to limit damage. Furthermore, the 3D nature of many of these pathological conditions required the greatest possible freedom of access and coverage. For these reasons we adopted the laserarm approach when working with pathological bone. 3D laser scanning offers an objective and measurable solution that provides good geometric accuracy. While helping to limit issues of subjectivity it offers the potential to explore surface characteristics in detail.

The field is open to further advances with detailed and objective shape analysis using 3D morphometrics and the potential of 3D printing and haptic technologies offer considerable scope for representing the touch and feel of otherwise fragile elements. However, models should have clear attribution and should never be divorced from their context.

ACKNOWLEDGMENTS

The authors would like to thank Jisc and the University of Bradford for funding the following projects—Digitised Diseases and From Cemetery to Clinic. The success of these projects was dependent on a highly skilled team of researchers and interns based at the University of Bradford (including Jo Buckberry, Chris Gaffney, Hassan Ugail, Keith Manchester, Maryann Hardy, Rebecca Storm, Emma Brown, Alan Ogden, Chris Watkins, David Connah, David Keenan, Pawel Eliasz), Museum of London Archaeology (Natasha Powers, Don Walker, Michael Henderson), The Royal College of Surgeons of London (Sam Alberti, Carina Phillips, Martyn Cooke, Emmy Bocage), and The Museum of London (Jelena Bekvalac and Rebecca Redfern). We also thank the following organizations for allowing access to their collections—The Novium, York Archaeological Trust, York Museum, and York Minster. The following also contributed valuable advice as part of the advisory panel—Don Ortner, Niels Lynnerup, Simon Mays, Charlotte Roberts, Anthea Boylston, and Piers Mitchell.

REFERENCES

Allard, T.T., Sitchon, M.L., Sawatzky, R., Hoppa, R.D., 2005. Use of hand-held laser scanning and 3D printing for creation of a museum exhibit. In: M. Mudge, N. Ryan, R. Scopigno (Eds.), The 6th International Symposium on Virtual Reality, Archaeology and Cultural Heritage VAST.

Antoine, D., Ambers, J., 2014. The scientific analysis of human remains from the British museum collection research potential and examples from the Nile valley. In: Fletcher, A., Antoine, D. & Hill, J.D. (Eds.), Regarding the Dead: Human Remains in the British Museum. pp. 20–30.

Artz, J.A., Bristow, E.L.D., Whittaker, W.E., 2013. Mapping precontact burial mounds in sixteen Minnesota counties using Light Detection and Ranging (LiDAR). Contract Completion Report 1976, Office of the State Archaeologist, The University of Iowa, Iowa City.

Benazzi, S., Fantini, M., De Crescenzio, F., Persiani, F., Gruppioni, G., 2009. Improving the spatial orientation of human teeth using a virtual 3D approach. J. Hum. Evol. 56, 286–293.

Boutin, A.T., Nusse, G.L., Sholts, S.B., Porter, B.W., 2012. Face to face with the past: reconstructing a teenage boy from early Dilmun. Near E. Archaeol. 75 (2), 68–79.

Caffell, A.C., Roberts, C.A., Janaway, R.C., Wilson, A.S., 2001. Pressures on osteological collections—the importance of damage limitation. In: Williams, E. (Ed.), Human Remains: Conservation, Retrieval and Analysis. British Archaeological Reports, International Series, Oxford, pp. 187–197.

Cowley, D.C., Opitz, R.S., 2013. Interpreting Archaeological Topography: Lasers, 3D Data, Observation, Visualisation and Applications. Oxbow, Oxford.

Davies, T.G., Shaw, C.N., Stock, J.T., 2012. A test of a new method and software for the rapid estimation of cross-sectional geometric properties of long bone diaphysis from 3D laser surface scans. Archaeol. Anthropol. Sci. 4, 277e290.

Duday, H., 2009. The Archaeology of the Dead: Lectures in Archaeothanatology. Oxbow Books, Oxford.

Duffy, S., Bryan, P., Earl, G., Beale, G., Pagi, H., Kotouala, E., 2013. Multi-light Imaging for Heritage Applications. Historic England.

Dufton, A., Fenwick, C., 2012. Beyond the grave: developing new tools for medieval cemetery analysis at Villamagna, Italy. In: Chrysanthi, A., Flores, P.M., Papadopoulos, C. (Eds.), Thinking Beyond the Tool: Archaeological Computing & the Interpretive Process, BAR Int Series 2344.

Evin, A., Souter, T., Hulme-Beaman, A., Ameen, C., Allen, R., Viacava, P., et al., 2016. The use of close-range photogrammetry in zooarchaeology: creating accurate 3D models of wolf crania to study dog domestication. J. Archaeol. Sci. Rep. 9, 87–93.

Falkingham, P.L., 2012. Acquisition of high resolution three-dimensional models using free, open-source, photogrammetric software. Palaeontologia Electronica 15 (1), 1T:15p.

Forte, M., 2014. New perspectives and challenges—the example of Çatalhöyük. J. East. Mediterr. Archaeol. Herit. Stud. 2 (1).

Forte, M., Dell'Unto, N., Jonsson, K., Lercari, N., 2015. Interpretation process at Çatalhöyük using 3D. In: Hodder, I., Marciniak, A. (Eds.), Assembling Çatalhöyük—EAA—Themes in Contemporary Archaeology, Chapter: 4. Maney Publishing.

Franklin, D., Swift, L., Flavel, A., 2016. Virtual anthropology' and radiographic imaging in the Forensic Medical Sciences. Egypt. J. Forensic Sci. 6 (2), 31–43.

Friess, M., Marcus, L.F., Reddy, D.P., Delson E., 2002. The use of 3D laser scanning techniques for the morphometric analysis of human facial shape variation. In: Bertrand Mafart, Hervé Delingette (Eds.), Three-Dimensional Imaging in Paleoanthropology and Prehistoric Archaeology, BAR S1049.

Jones, D.M. (Ed.), 2011. 3D Laser Scanning for Heritage: Advice and Guidance to Users on Laser Scanning in Archaeology and Architecture. 2nd ed. Historic England.

Knusel, C.J., Robb, J., 2016. Funerary taphonomy: an overview of goals and methods. J. Archaeol. Sci. Rep.. Available from: http://dx.doi.org/10.1016/j.jasrep.2016.05.031.

Kuzminsky, S.C., Gardiner, M.S., 2012. Three-dimensional laser scanning: potential uses for museum conservation and scientific research. J. Archaeol. Sci. 39, 2744–2751.

Little, A., Elliott, B., Conneller, C., Pomstra, D., Evans, A.A., Fitton, L.C., et al., 2016. Technological analysis of the world's earliest shamanic costume: a multi-scalar, experimental study of a red deer headdress from the early Holocene site of Star Carr, North Yorkshire, UK. PLoS One. Available from: http://dx.doi.org/10.1371/journal.pone.0152136.

Macintosh, A.A., Davies, T.G., Pinhasi, R., Stock, J.T., 2015. Declining tibial curvature parallels ~6150 years of decreasing mobility in central European agriculturalists. Am. J. Phys. Anthropol. 157, 260–275.

Mahfouz, M.R., Langley, N.R., Herrmann, N., ElHak, E., Fatah, A., 2016. Computerized Reconstruction of Fragmentary Skeletal Remains for Purposes of Extracting Osteometric Measurements and Estimating MNI. US Department of Justice Award 2011-DN-BX-K537 (report no. 249948).

Mathys, A., Lemaitre, S., Brecko, J., Semal, P., 2013. Agora 3D: evaluating 3D imaging technology for the research, conservation and display of museum collections. Antiquity 87 (336), Project gallery: http://antiquity.ac.uk/projgall/mathys336/.

Mitchell, S., Booher, A., 2015. Digitization to realization: the utilization of structure from motion, ESRI ArcScene, and 3D printing to identify taphonomic processes and digitally preserve Burial CC-B14. In: Houk, B. A. (Ed.), The 2015 Season of the Chan Chich Archaeological Project. pp. 163–174. Papers of the Chan Chich Archaeological Project, Number 10. Department of Sociology, Anthropology, and Social Work, Texas Tech University, Lubbock.

Nather, S.M., Buck, U., Thali, M.J., 2009. The virtopsy approach: 3D optical and radiological scanning. In: Thali, M., Dirnhofer, R., Vock, P. (Eds.), The Virtopsy Approach: 3D Optical and Radiological Scanning and Reconstruction in Forensic Medicine. CRC Press, Boca Raton, FL.

Niven, L., Steele, T.E., Finke, H., Gernat, T., Hublin, J.-J., 2009. Virtual skeletons: using a structured light scanner to create a 3D faunal comparative collection. J. Archaeol. Sci. 36 (9), 2018–2023.

Opitz, R., Limp, W.F., 2015. Recent developments in high-density survey and measurement (HDSM) for archaeology: implications for practice and theory. Annu. Rev. Anthropol. 44, 347–364.

Papageorgopoulou, C., Kuhn, G., Ziegler, U., Ru, F.J., 2010. Diagnostic morphometric applicability of confocal laser scanning microscopy in osteoarchaeology. Int. J. Osteoarchaeol. 20, 708–718.

Rein, T.R., Harvati, K., 2014. Geometric morphometrics and virtual anthropology: advances in human evolutionary studies. Anthropol. Anz. 71 (1–2), 41–55.

Schmalz, C., Forster, F., Schick, A., Angelopoulou, E., 2012. An endoscopic 3D scanner based on structured light. Med. Image Anal. 16 (5), 1063–1072.

Selden Jr., R.Z., Perttula, T.K., O'Brien, M.J., 2014. Advances in documentation, digital curation, virtual exhibition, and a test of 3D geometric morphometrics: a case study of the Vanderpool vessels from the ancestral Caddo territory. Adv. Archaeol. Pract. 2 (2), 64–79.

Sforza, C., de Menezes, M., Ferrario, V.F., 2013. Soft- and hard-tissue facial anthropometry in three dimensions: what's new. J. Anthropol. Sci. 91, 159–184.

Tilley, L., 2015. Theory and Practice in the Bioarchaeology of Care. Springer International Publishing, Switzerland.

Villa, C., Gaudio, D., Cattaneo, C., Buckberry, J., Wilson, A.S., Lynnerup, N., 2015. Surface curvature of pelvic joints from three laser scanners: separating anatomy from measurement error. J. Forensic Sci. 60, 374–381.

WAC, 2016. Resolution on the creation, dissemination, and curation of digital bioarchaeological data accepted at the World Archaeology Congress, Kyoto Friday 2 September 2016.

Weber, G.W., 2015. Virtual Anthropology. Am. J. Phys. Anthropol. 156 (Suppl. 59), 22–42.

Weber, G.W., Bookstein, F.L., 2011. Virtual Anthropology: A Guide to a New Interdisciplinary Field. Springer-Verlag, Vienna.

Wilhelmson, H., Dell'Unto, N., 2015. Virtual taphonomy: a new method integrating excavation and postprocessing in an archaeological context. Am. J. Phys. Anthropol. 157, 305–321.

Wilson, A.S., 2014. Digitised diseases: preserving precious remains.. Br. Archaeol. 136, 36–41.

Wilson, A.S., Manchester, K., Buckberry, J., Storm, R., Croucher, K., 2017. Digitised diseases: seeing beyond the specimen to understand disease and disability in the past. In: Tilley, L., Schrenk, A.A. (Eds.), New Developments in the Bioarchaeology of Care, Part of the Series Bioarchaeology and Social Theory. Springer International Publishing, Switzerland, pp. 301–315.

CHAPTER 10

Virtual Reconstruction of Cranial Remains: The *H. Heidelbergensis*, Kabwe 1 Fossil

Ricardo M. Godinho[1,2] and Paul O'Higgins[1]
[1]University of York, York, United Kingdom [2]University of Coimbra, Coimbra, Portugal

10.1 INTRODUCTION

Archaeological human skeletal remains are typically recovered during excavations of funerary contexts. Such remains provide considerable paleobiological information about past populations (Katzenberg and Saunders, 2011), however they are frequently fragmented due to taphonomical factors, which limits research (Stodder, 2007; Waldron, 1987). Similarly, fossil specimens (which are the focus of this manuscript) are usually fragmented, distorted, and invaded by sedimentary matrix, thus limiting subsequent research on morphological evolution and disparity (Arbour and Brown, 2014; Neeser et al., 2009). This has led researchers to physically reconstruct fragmented hominin crania, such as OH 5 (Leakey, 1959; Tobias, 1967) or Zhoukoudian (Tattersall and Sawyer, 1996; Weidenreich, 1937). However, physical reconstruction is heavily based on anatomical expertise and involves multiple assumptions, making it a subjective process with limited reproducibility (Benazzi et al., 2009c). Moreover, the Le Moustier Neanderthal cranium is an unfortunate example showing that physical reconstruction using original specimens may be detrimental to the preservation of fossils (Weber and Bookstein, 2011).

Ready access to computing power and new specialist software have enabled limitations to reconstructing specimens using computer-based

Human Remains: Another Dimension. DOI: http://dx.doi.org/10.1016/B978-0-12-804602-9.00011-4

approaches to be overcome. Virtual reconstruction is now a common procedure that has been applied not only to hominin fossils (Amano et al., 2015; Benazzi et al., 2011a, 2014; Grine et al., 2010; Gunz et al., 2009; Kalvin et al., 1995; Kranioti et al., 2011; Neubauer et al., 2004; Ponce De León and Zollikofer, 1999; Watson et al., 2011; Zollikofer et al., 1995, 2005), but also in the context of biological and forensic anthropology (Benazzi et al., 2009a–c) and cranial surgery (Benazzi et al., 2011b; Benazzi and Senck, 2011). Such reconstructions are commonly based on CT scans, which provide detailed imaging of bone and capture external and internal anatomy. Once completed, such reconstructions can be used in several ways, to make a physical model using 3D printing, submitted to morphometric analyses, or used in studies of biomechanics including finite element analysis (FEA) (Strait et al., 2005).

CT scan based reconstructions begin with segmentation, during which the relevant structures are identified and labeled within the scanned volume based on differences in density, and thus on gray level Hounsfield Units (Weber, 2015; Weber and Bookstein, 2011). Segmentation choices depend on the intended further use of the model. If used only for visualization purposes in which detailed internal anatomical reconstruction is of no concern, single thresholds (set values of Hounsfield Units) that segment most of the structure can be used. Such thresholds may be set manually or calculated using a variety of approaches (Coleman and Colbert, 2007; Spoor et al., 1993), but will either exclude bones that are too thin to be selected or overestimate bone thickness. Thus, if detailed anatomy is important, complex approaches that combine global, regional, and manual thresholding are necessary (Weber and Bookstein, 2011). In such cases one may set a global threshold and subsequently apply thresholds to specific anatomical regions that were not selected by previous thresholding. Finally, manual segmentation is usually necessary for fine details that were not picked up by the previous approaches.

Once the segmentation process is finished, reconstruction of missing anatomical regions begins. This process usually combines imaging software (e.g., Avizo/Amira) and geometric morphometrics (GM) to approximately restore the original geometry of an incomplete/distorted specimen (Weber, 2015; Weber and Bookstein, 2011). In specimens that preserve one side intact the most straightforward approach is to use bilateral symmetry (Gunz et al., 2009) to reconstruct the damaged side. In such cases it is possible to reflect the preserved regions onto the incomplete side and use them to replace the missing areas (Gunz et al., 2009). However, no skeletal structures are completely symmetric and crania present different magnitudes of asymmetry (Quinto-Sánchez et al., 2015). Thus, reflected regions will not perfectly fit the remaining preserved anatomy. To overcome this mismatch, and account for asymmetry, it is possible to warp the reflected structure onto the remaining preserved anatomy (Gunz et al., 2009). This warping uses a mathematical function based on shared landmarks to deform the landmarks and regions between landmarks from one specimen (usually referred to as the reference) into the space of a second specimen (usually referred to as the target) such that landmarks coincide and the material between them is smoothly interpolated between reference and target forms. The most commonly used function in virtual anthropology, for good statistical and mathematical reasons (minimization of deformation), is the thin-plate spline (TPS; Bookstein, 1989).

Even though this is a desirable approach, fossils often lack preserved structures on both sides or along the midline, thus precluding reflection. In these cases reference-based reconstruction (Gunz et al., 2004, 2009) should be used. The choice of reference specimen should be considered carefully so as to not bias the reconstruction and it has been suggested that references should be species specific (Gunz et al., 2009; Senck et al., 2015; Zollikofer and Ponce de León, 2005). Such reconstructions may be statistical or geometric (Gunz et al., 2004, 2009; Neeser et al., 2009). Statistical reconstruction uses patterns of covariance in a given sample to predict the locations of missing landmarks via multivariate regression (Gunz et al., 2009; Neeser et al., 2009). Geometric reconstruction uses the TPS function to estimate the positions of missing landmarks based on known ones (Gunz et al., 2004, 2009). The latter has the advantage of requiring only one specimen, which may be a particular individual or a mean specimen calculated from a given sample using GM (Gunz et al., 2009) but it omits information on intraspecific covariations. However, Senck and Coquerelle (2015) show that using mean specimens yields good results when reconstructing large portions of incomplete specimens. Furthermore, where sample sizes are limited to one or a few specimens, as with fossils, TPS-based warping can be applied, whereas statistical approaches cannot.

Reconstruction choices impact the final result, hence they have to be considered carefully (Gunz et al., 2009; Senck et al., 2015). One option is to exclude fragmentary or damaged specimens from analysis, however when dealing with fossil remains, the number of specimens is commonly very low and their exclusion may be detrimental to the study. In fact, in a study that examines the impact of different reconstruction approaches and of exclusion of incomplete specimens on morphological analysis, Arbour and Brown (2014) show that it is better to estimate missing landmarks, and thus reconstruct missing anatomy, than to exclude incomplete specimens. This is because the inclusion of incomplete specimens with estimated missing landmarks may better reflect the morphological variance of a sample than excluding incomplete specimens, especially when the available sample is small, as is often the case with fossils.

In this manuscript the steps are presented that were used to make a full reconstruction of Kabwe 1, a middle Pleistocene hominin cranium (dating from 150 to 250 thousand years before present) that has been classified as *Homo heidelbergensis* (Stringer, 2012). Despite missing some parts of the right side of the cranium and other localized bony structures (e.g., ethmoidal cells, orbital region of the maxilla and ethmoid) it is one of the best preserved crania in the hominin fossil record (Schwartz and Tattersall, 2003). The reconstruction is intended for use as the basis of FEA studies in which the functional performance of this specimen will be compared to that of other hominins. Biomechanical studies using FEA are increasingly common (e.g., Benazzi et al., 2015; Ledogar et al., 2016; Smith et al., 2015; Strait et al., 2007, 2009, 2010; Wroe et al., 2010) but for the results to be meaningful detailed and accurate anatomical restoration is necessary. Thus, in this reconstruction, internal and external anatomy was carefully restored. For morphometric studies of external morphology, less effort is required to reconstruct internal anatomical detail. Although the methodology for reconstruction is described in the context of a fossil, it is equally applicable to modern human skeletal remains.

10.2 MATERIALS AND METHODS

The cranium of Kabwe 1 is remarkably well preserved but is missing some anatomy due to taphonomic and pathological processes (Schwartz and Tattersall, 2003). Missing areas include a large portion of the right side of the cranial vault and base (parts of the right tempo-ral, right parietal and occipital), right zygomatic, maxilla, teeth, and small portions of the orbital cavities (Fig. 10.1). Reconstruction was based on a CT scan (courtesy of *Robert Kruszynski, Natural History Museum, London*) performed with a Siemens Somatom Plus 4 CT scanner, with voxel size of $0.47 \times 0.47 \times 0.50$ mm and 140 kVp, and was divided in four main phases (Fig. 10.2). In the first phase, the existing anatomy was segmented from the scanned volume. This was followed by reconstruction of the left side of the vault, which was then used to reconstruct the large missing region on the right side of the cranium. Lastly, all remaining missing features were reconstructed.

Segmentation was performed in Avizo 7.0 and used a combination of approaches. First, the half maximum height value (HMHV; Spoor et al., 1993) was calculated and applied to the whole volume for threshold segmentation. This inevitably excluded thin bones, requiring the use of regional thresholds as a second step, applied to specific ana-tomical regions, such as parts of the ethmoid bone. This allowed semi-automated segmentation of more, but not all, of the bony anatomy without overestimating bone thickness. Thus, manual segmentation was required for fine details of thin bones. Teeth were segmented sepa-rately, which required calculation of specific thresholds to avoid

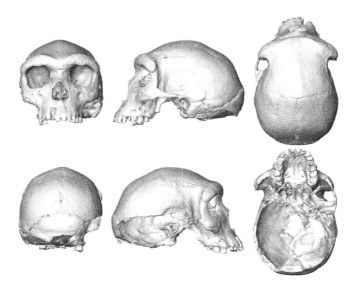

Figure 10.1 Standardized views showing missing bony structures of the cranium of Kabwe 1. Note that, despite some missing portions, the cranium is extremely well preserved and presents no distortion.

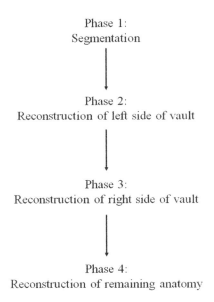

Phase 1:
Segmentation

Phase 2:
Reconstruction of left side of vault

Phase 3:
Reconstruction of right side of vault

Phase 4:
Reconstruction of remaining anatomy

Figure 10.2 Workflow of the reconstruction of Kabwe 1.

overestimating their dimensions. Last, it was necessary to remove sedimentary matrix that had invaded the cranium. This required a manual approach due to overlap of gray values between matrix and bone.

Once segmentation was complete, the left half of the cranium was mirrored to reconstruct the missing large right portion of the cranium that includes parts of the parietal, temporal, occipital, and zygomatic bone. Because of asymmetry, the reflected region did not fit the remaining preserved anatomy perfectly. Thus it was necessary to warp it to the preserved structures. TPS-based warping was performed using Avizo 7.0 using 20 existing landmarks (bregma, nasion, rhinion, anterior nasal spine, zygomaxillare, lambda, jugale, infraorbital foramen, prosthion, orale, incisive foramen, staphylion, hormion, foramen lacerum, inferiormost point of lateral pterygoid plate, inferiormost point of medial pterygoid plate, pterygoid fossa, basion, opistion, staphanion) and resulted in an almost perfect fit between reconstructed and preserved anatomy that required minimal manual editing. After warping, only the reconstructed regions were preserved and the remaining reflected hemi-cranium was discarded. The alveolar process of the right hemi-maxilla was also restored by reflecting the preserved contralateral region. Regions that presented gaps (orbital surfaces of the maxilla and ethmoid, periapical regions of the maxilla, left temporal bone, occipital bone, nasal cavity walls, ethmoid bone, and vomer) were reconstructed using a combination of manual editing and the software Geomagic 2011 to interpolate between existing bone edges. The missing portion of the occipital bone, affecting the superior nuchal line, was reconstructed using the occipital of a modern human cranium, manually editing it to adjust its morphology. Editing was performed in Geomagic 2011. Teeth were restored by reflecting existing antimeres. When this was not possible portions of teeth from a modern human were used to reconstruct incomplete teeth.

10.3 RESULTS AND DISCUSSION

The reconstruction of Kabwe 1 allowed restoration of missing anatomical regions (Figs. 10.3 and 10.4) and, in our particular application, creation of a model for further use in FEA. While it was carried out as objectively as possible, any reconstruction, physical or virtual, requires assumptions and a certain degree of subjectivity (Gunz et al., 2009). Thus other reconstructions will likely yield different results, but disparities are likely very small in most regions because segmentation was mainly based on global and regional HMHVs and restoration was highly constrained by existing structures which provided good local

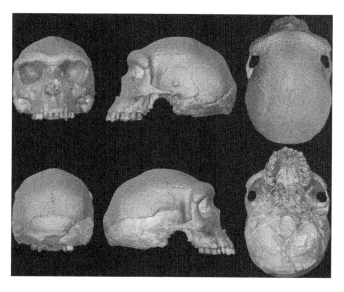

Figure 10.3 Standardized views showing the original (dark gray) and the reconstructed (translucent gray) crania of Kabwe 1.

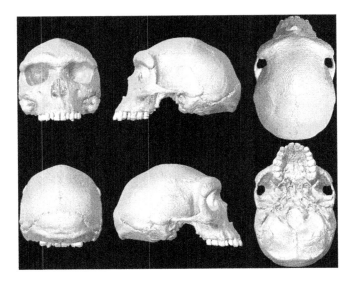

Figure 10.4 Standardized views showing the reconstructed cranium of Kabwe 1.

information on general contours and proportions. Additionally the use of objective GM-based approaches reduced guesswork.

The segmentation process relied mainly on global and regional thresholds that were selected using HMHVs. This provides a generally objective approach but depends on the sites at which the values are measured and it does not segment the whole cranium without further manual intervention if bone thickness is not to be overestimated. Thus, while this process is generally reproducible, minor differences relative to other possible segmentations are to be expected due to differences in sites where gray levels are measured and subjective decisions during manual segmentation.

Reconstruction of the large missing portion on the right side of the vault and base used the reflected left side, which was then warped based on the TPS function to account for asymmetry. This procedure is expected to yield good results and to outperform statistical reconstruction based on multivariate regression because it used the same individual and the reflected region was warped to the existing anatomy. The TPS warping used classical landmarks and no sliding semi-landmarks. While these potentially improve warping, only minor differences are to be expected because the reference is individual specific (reflected left hemi-cranium), TPS warping used several landmarks in the vicinity of the restored region and the reflected warped portion fitted the target region almost perfectly.

While it would be preferable to use species-specific homologous structures to restore teeth and the occipital we did not have access to other *H. heidelbergensis* specimens. As such, a modern human was used and its morphology was manually edited after warping to account for morphological differences in the nuchal line region of the occipital. Furthermore, reconstruction was only performed as far as the midline and the contra-lateral side was reconstructed using the reflection/ TPS-based warping procedure. Visual assessment of the smoothness of the reconstruction provides confidence that the original morphology is likely closely approximated and that the results of using other approaches may differ only slightly.

The use of mesh editing software such as Geomagic to fill small gaps (in the occipital bone, alveolar region of the maxilla, orbital cavities, and temporal bone) is very efficient and visual assessment shows smooth reconstructions. The region in which reconstruction was most subjective was in defining the cells of the ethmoid bone, and this was performed manually. An alternative approach would have been to use the ethmoid bone of a modern human (to the best of our knowledge no other closely related fossil hominin has this bone fully preserved), warping its ethmoid to replace the existing incomplete bone. While this would have been more objective, the bone forming the ethmoid sinus is extremely thin and has limited load bearing significance during biting (Ross, 2001). Moreover, because it is so thin, warping would likely have required further manual editing. Thus, while results would have been different they would probably have had minor, if any, impact on subsequent work based on this reconstruction.

As mentioned above, any reconstruction is subjective (Gunz et al., 2009). Thus, several studies have assessed the impact of reconstruction approaches and compared the impact of using TPS-based estimation of missing landmarks versus multivariate regression versus mean specimen (Arbour and Brown, 2014; Gunz et al., 2009; Neeser et al., 2009), reference specimen selection (Gunz et al., 2009; Neeser et al., 2009), sample size of reference sample (Neeser et al., 2009), and number of missing landmarks (Arbour and Brown, 2014). Based on these studies we are confident that the present reconstruction reasonably approximates the original morphology.

Nonetheless, it is feasible, and in many circumstances desirable, to carry out studies assessing the impact of different reconstruction approaches on the eventual virtual model and on results of subsequent analyses using the model. Thus, morphometric comparison of different variants of the same reconstruction can inform with regard to the nature and magnitude of any differences in size and shape. The significance of such differences in relation to the results of comparative morphometric studies can be assessed by incorporating different versions of the reconstruction, assessing within reconstruction (specimen) variation relative to among specimen variation. Similarly, the impact of morphological reconstruction choices on predicted stresses and strains from FEA can be assessed through sensitivity analyses that compare results among variant reconstructions (Fitton et al., 2015; Parr et al., 2012, 2013; Toro-Ibacache and O'Higgins, 2016).

Virtual reconstruction of damaged skeletal material from CT scans has opened up new possibilities in virtual anthropology and archaeology. We are at the beginning of this virtual revolution, although even at this stage the power of these approaches is evident, with rapidly increasing rates of publication of studies employing them to gain new insights into old material. As technologies for imaging and segmentation improve and as workers add new tools to the virtual anthropology toolkit we can anticipate continued growth of interest and an exciting future for the field in which hitherto inaccessible remains may yield important and occasionally surprising new morphological information.

ACKNOWLEDGMENTS

RMG is funded by the Portuguese Foundation for Science and Technology (reference SFRH/BD/76375/2011). We thank Dr. W Sellers, University of Manchester, for access to Geomagic. Karen Swan for discussions about procedures with Geomagic.

REFERENCES

Amano, H., Kikuchi, T., Morita, Y., Kondo, O., Suzuki, H., Ponce de León, M.S., et al., 2015. Virtual reconstruction of the Neanderthal Amud 1 cranium. Am. J. Phys. Anthropol. 158, 185–197.

Arbour, J.H., Brown, C.M., 2014. Incomplete specimens in geometric morphometric analyses. Methods Ecol. Evol. 5, 16–26.

Benazzi, S., Senck, S., 2011. Comparing 3-dimensional virtual methods for reconstruction in craniomaxillofacial surgery. J. Oral Maxillofac. Surg. 69, 1184–1194.

Benazzi, S., Fantini, M., De Crescenzio, F., Mallegni, G., Mallegni, F., Persiani, F., et al., 2009a. The face of the poet Dante Alighieri reconstructed by virtual modelling and forensic anthropology techniques. J. Archaeol. Sci. 36, 278–283.

Benazzi, S., Stansfield, E., Kullmer, O., Fiorenza, L., Gruppioni, G., 2009b. Geometric morphometric methods for bone reconstruction: the mandibular condylar process of Pico della Mirandola. Anat. Rec. 292, 1088–1097.

Benazzi, S., Stansfield, E., Milani, C., Gruppioni, G., 2009c. Geometric morphometric methods for three-dimensional virtual reconstruction of a fragmented cranium: the case of Angelo Poliziano. Int. J. Legal Med. 123, 333–344.

Benazzi, S., Bookstein, F.L., Strait, D.S., Weber, G.W., 2011a. A new OH5 reconstruction with an assessment of its uncertainty. J. Hum. Evol. 61, 75–88.

Benazzi, S., Fiorenza, L., Kozakowski, S., Kullmer, O., 2011b. Comparing 3D virtual methods for hemimandibular body reconstruction. Anat. Rec. 294, 1116–1125.

Benazzi, S., Gruppioni, G., Strait, D.S., Hublin, J.-J., 2014. Technical note: virtual reconstruction of KNM-ER 1813 *Homo habilis* cranium. Am. J. Phys. Anthropol. 153, 154–160.

Benazzi, S., Nguyen, H.N., Kullmer, O., Hublin, J.-J., 2015. Exploring the biomechanics of taurodontism. J. Anat. 226, 180–188.

Bookstein, F.L., 1989. Principal warps: thin-plate splines and the decomposition of deformations. IEEE Trans. Pattern Anal. Mach. Intell. 567–585.

Coleman, M.N., Colbert, M.W., 2007. Technical note: CT thresholding protocols for taking measurements on three-dimensional models. Am. J. Phys. Anthropol. 133, 723–725.

Fitton, L.C., PrôA, M., Rowland, C., Toro-ibacache, V., O'Higgins, P., 2015. The impact of simplifications on the performance of a finite element model of a *Macaca fascicularis* cranium. Anat. Rec. 298, 107–121.

Grine, F.E., Gunz, P., Betti-Nash, L., Neubauer, S., Morris, A.G., 2010. Reconstruction of the late Pleistocene human skull from Hofmeyr, South Africa. J. Hum. Evol. 59, 1–15.

Gunz, P., Mitteroecker, P., Bookstein, F., Weber, G., 2004. Computer-aided reconstruction of incomplete human crania using statistical and geometrical estimation methods. Computer Applications and Quantitative Methods in Archaeology. Archaeopress, pp. 92–94.

Gunz, P., Mitteroecker, P., Neubauer, S., Weber, G.W., Bookstein, F.L., 2009. Principles for the virtual reconstruction of hominin crania. J. Hum. Evol. 57, 48–62.

Kalvin, A.D., Dean, D., Hublin, J.J., 1995. Reconstruction of human fossils. IEEE Comput. Graph. Appl. 15, 12–15.

Katzenberg, M.A., Saunders, S.R., 2011. Biological Anthropology of the Human Skeleton. John Wiley & Sons.

Kranioti, E.F., Holloway, R., Senck, S., Ciprut, T., Grigorescu, D., Harvati, K., 2011. Virtual assessment of the endocranial morphology of the early modern European fossil Calvaria from Cioclovina, Romania. Anat. Rec. 294, 1083–1092.

Leakey, L.S., 1959. A new fossil skull from Olduvai. Nature 184, 491–493.

Ledogar, J.A., Smith, A.L., Benazzi, S., Weber, G.W., Spencer, M.A., Carlson, K.B., et al., 2016. Mechanical evidence that *Australopithecus sediba* was limited in its ability to eat hard foods. Nat. Commun. 7.

Neeser, R., Ackermann, R.R., Gain, J., 2009. Comparing the accuracy and precision of three techniques used for estimating missing landmarks when reconstructing fossil hominin crania. Am. J. Phys. Anthropol. 140, 1–18.

Neubauer, S., Gunz, P., Mitteroecker, P., Weber, G.W., 2004. Three-dimensional digital imaging of the partial *Australopithecus africanus* endocranium MLD 37/38. Can. Assoc. Radiol. J. 55, 271–278.

Parr, W.C.H., Wroe, S., Chamoli, U., Richards, H.S., McCurry, M.R., Clausen, P.D., et al., 2012. Toward integration of geometric morphometrics and computational biomechanics: new methods for 3D virtual reconstruction and quantitative analysis of finite element models. J. Theor. Biol. 301, 1−14.

Parr, W.C.H., Chamoli, U., Jones, A., Walsh, W.R., Wroe, S., 2013. Finite element micro-modelling of a human ankle bone reveals the importance of the trabecular network to mechanical performance: new methods for the generation and comparison of 3D models. J. Biomech. 46, 200−205.

Ponce De León, M.S., Zollikofer, C.P.E., 1999. New evidence from Le Moustier 1: computer-assisted reconstruction and morphometry of the skull. Anat. Rec. 254, 474−489.

Quinto-Sánchez, M., Adhikari, K., Acuña-Alonzo, V., Cintas, C., Silva de Cerqueira, C.C., Ramallo, V., et al., 2015. Facial asymmetry and genetic ancestry in Latin American admixed populations. Am. J. Phys. Anthropol. 157, 58−70.

Ross, C.F., 2001. In vivo function of the craniofacial haft: the interorbital "pillar". Am. J. Phys. Anthropol. 116, 108−139.

Schwartz, J.H., Tattersall, I., 2003. The Human Fossil Record—Craniodental Morphology of Genus *Homo*. Wiley-Liss, New York.

Senck, S., Coquerelle, M., 2015. Morphological integration and variation in facial orientation in *Pongo pygmaeus pygmaeus*: a geometric morphometric approach via partial least squares. Int. J. Primatol. 36, 489−512.

Senck, S., Bookstein, F.L., Benazzi, S., Kastner, J., Weber, G.W., 2015. Virtual reconstruction of modern and fossil hominoid crania: consequences of reference sample choice. Anat. Rec. 298, 827−841.

Smith, A.L., Benazzi, S., Ledogar, J.A., Tamvada, K., Pryor Smith, L.C., Weber, G.W., et al., 2015. The feeding biomechanics and dietary ecology of *Paranthropus boisei*. Anat. Rec. 298, 145−167.

Spoor, C.F., Zonneveld, F.W., Macho, G.A., 1993. Linear measurements of cortical bone and dental enamel by computed-tomography—applications and problems. Am. J. Phys. Anthropol. 91, 469−484.

Stodder, A.L.W., 2007. Taphonomy and the nature of archaeological assemblages. Biological Anthropology of the Human Skeleton. John Wiley & Sons, Inc, pp. 71−114.

Strait, D.S., Wang, Q., Dechow, P.C., Ross, C.F., Richmond, B.G., Spencer, M.A., et al., 2005. Modeling elastic properties in finite element analysis: how much precision is needed to produce an accurate model? Anat. Rec. A Discov. Mol. Cell. Evol. Biol. 283A, 275−287.

Strait, D.S., Richmond, B.G., Spencer, M.A., Ross, C.F., Dechow, P.C., Wood, B.A., 2007. Masticatory biomechanics and its relevance to early hominid phylogeny: an examination of palatal thickness using finite-element analysis. J. Hum. Evol. 52, 585−599.

Strait, D.S., Weber, G.W., Neubauer, S., Chalk, J., Richmond, B.G., Lucas, P.W., et al., 2009. The feeding biomechanics and dietary ecology of *Australopithecus africanus*. Proc. Natl. Acad. Sci. U. S. A. 106, 2124−2129.

Strait, D.S., Grosse, I.R., Dechow, P.C., Smith, A.L., Wang, Q., Weber, G.W., et al., 2010. The structural rigidity of the cranium of *Australopithecus africanus*: implications for diet, dietary adaptations, and the allometry of feeding biomechanics. Anat. Rec. 293, 583−593.

Stringer, C., 2012. The status of *Homo heidelbergensis* (Schoetensack 1908). Evol. Anthropol. 21, 101−107.

Tattersall, I., Sawyer, G.J., 1996. The skull of "Sinanthropus" from Zhoukoudian, China: a new reconstruction. J. Hum. Evol. 31, 311−314.

Tobias, P.V., 1967. Olduvai Gorge Vol. 2: The Cranium and Maxillary Dentition of *Australopithecus* (*Zinjanthropus*) *boisei*. Cambridge University Press, Cambridge.

Toro-Ibacache, V., O'Higgins, P., 2016. The effect of varying jaw-elevator muscle forces on a finite element model of a human cranium. Anat. Rec. 299, 828–839.

Waldron, T., 1987. The relative survival of the human skeleton: implications for palaeopathology. In: Boddington, A., Garland, A.N., Janaway, R.C. (Eds.), Death, Decay and Reconstruction: Approaches to Archaeology and Forensic Science. Manchester University Press, Manchester, pp. 55–64.

Watson, P.J., O'Higgins, P., Fagan, M.J., Dobson, C.A., 2011. Validation of a morphometric reconstruction technique applied to a juvenile pelvis. Proc. Inst. Mech. Eng. H 225, 48–57.

Weber, G.W., 2015. Virtual anthropology. Am. J. Phys. Anthropol. 156, 22–42.

Weber, G.W., Bookstein, F.L., 2011. Virtual Anthropology—A Guide for a New Interdisciplinary Field. Springer-Verlag, Wien.

Weidenreich, F., 1937. Reconstruction of the entire skull of an adult female individual of *Sinanthropus pekinensi*. Nature. 140, 1010.

Wroe, S., Ferrara, T.L., McHenry, C.R., Curnoe, D., Chamoli, U., 2010. The craniomandibular mechanics of being human. Proc. R. Soc. B Biol. Sci. 277, 3579–3586.

Zollikofer, C.P., Ponce de León, M.S., 2005. Virtual Reconstruction: A Primer in Computer-Assisted Paleontology and Biomedicine. Wiley-Interscience, New Jersey.

Zollikofer, C.P.E., Ponce de Leon, M.S., Martin, R.D., Stucki, P., 1995. Neanderthal computer skulls. Nature 375, 283–285.

Zollikofer, C.P.E., de Leon, M.S.P., Lieberman, D.E., Guy, F., Pilbeam, D., Likius, A., et al., 2005. Virtual cranial reconstruction of *Sahelanthropus tchadensis*. Nature 434, 755–759.

CHAPTER *11*

Pediatric Medicine—Postmortem Imaging in Suspected Child Abuse

Mayonne van Wijk[1], Marloes E.M. Vester[1,2,3], Owen J. Arthurs[4,5] and Rick R. van Rijn[1,2,3]

[1]Netherlands Forensic Institute, The Hague, the Netherlands [2]Academic Medical Centre Amsterdam, Amsterdam, the Netherlands [3]Amsterdam Centre for Forensic Science and Medicine, Amsterdam, the Netherlands [4]Great Ormond Street Hospital for Children NHS Foundation Trust, London, United Kingdom [5]UCL Great Ormond Street Institute of Child Health, London, United Kingdom

11.1 INTRODUCTION

Child abuse and neglect is a global issue with serious consequences for the victim, not only at the time of abuse, but also with the

Human Remains: Another Dimension. DOI: http://dx.doi.org/10.1016/B978-0-12-804602-9.00012-6

ramifications of the abuse continuing through adolescence and into adulthood (Felitti et al., 1998). Child abuse and neglect is defined by the World Health Organization as "all forms of physical and emotional ill-treatment, sexual abuse, neglect, and exploitation that results in actual or potential harm to the child's health, development or dignity. Within this broad definition, five subtypes can be distinguished: physical abuse; sexual abuse; neglect and negligent treatment; emotional abuse; and exploitation" (World Health Organization, 2016).

In 2012 there were an estimated 3.4 million referrals to child protective services in the United States for neglect or abuse (U.S. Department of Health and Human Services Administration for Children and Families et al., 2013). Of these, 686,000 children (or 9.2 per 1000) were abused, with a rate of 18% for physical abuse. This resulted in an estimated 1640 fatal cases. In Europe, based on a meta-analysis of self-reporting studies, an incidence of 22.9% for physical abuse has been reported (Sethi et al., 2013). Although differences between countries exist, partly true and partly based on a difference in definitions, these figures clearly show that child abuse is a significant and ubiquitous problem worldwide. Child abuse has serious and significantly long-term consequences, as was shown by Felitti et al. (1998) in the Adverse Childhood Experience study. Among these long-term consequences of abuse survivors are risk-related behavior, e.g., drug/alcohol abuse, depression, increased smoking, increased risk for sexual transmitted diseases, but also a relative increased risk for disease, e.g., ischemic heart disease, cancer, chronic lung disease, and liver disease. Besides the long-term outcomes there are also short-term adverse outcomes, the most severe of these is death of the victim as a result of trauma and/or neglect. A special category of fatal child abuse is neonaticide, defined as the killing of a child during the first 24 h of life. In many of these relatively rare cases, the remains are discovered several years later, making gestational age estimation an important aspect of the forensic workup.

In light of the subject of this book we will only deal with fatal physical child abuse and the imaging thereof in this chapter. This chapter is aimed to give a general overview; pertinent references are added to refer the interested reader to more in-depth literature.

11.2 CONVENTIONAL RADIOGRAPHY

11.2.1 Technique and Protocol

In 1946 Caffey was the first to describe a relationship between the presence of multiple long bone fractures and subdural hematoma using conventional radiographs (Caffey, 1946). At present, conventional radiography is still the most commonly used and often most readily available type of imaging technique in the investigation of nonincidental injuries in children as most death investigators will have access to conventional radiography either at their own facilities or through external facilities such as hospitals and clinics (Mendelson, 2004). A 2011 survey among members of the European Society of Paediatric Radiology revealed that 102 (76%) respondents from 134 individual institutions represented by 24 European countries undertook pediatric postmortem (PM) studies (Hulson et al., 2014). Both the Royal College of Radiology, Royal College of Paediatrics and Child Health (RCR/RCPCH) and the American College of Radiology have compiled specific guidelines for radiological imaging in cases of suspected child abuse (Meyer et al., 2011; The Royal College of Radiologists and Royal College of Paediatrics and Child Health, 2008). Many institutions have based their protocol for radiological imaging in cases of suspected child abuse on either of these sets of guidelines (Hulson et al., 2014). In both sets of guidelines the main focus is the skeletal survey. The skeletal survey may provide information about the presence of fresh and healing fractures, both obvious (e.g., transverse fracture) and subtle (e.g., classical metaphyseal lesion (CML)). These radiographs will also give insight to the presence of certain pathologies (e.g., skeletal dysplasia or bone mineralization disorders) and signs of growth arrest (e.g., Harris lines). The skeletal survey consists of a standard series of conventional radiographs (Table 11.1). When an abnormality is suspected on the skeletal survey, additional views should be obtained. It is advised to obtain coned views of the joints, in order to increase the detection of subtle fractures. It should be noted that the skeletal survey in deceased children should be performed before removing breathing or feeding tubes and other medical devices.

11.2.2 Fractures

11.2.2.1 Neonates

During the pregnancy fetuses are, in most cases, being examined regularly with antenatal ultrasound at 12 weeks and 20 weeks of gestation.

Table 11.1 Protocol for the Skeletal Survey (The Royal College of Radiologists and Royal College of Paediatrics and Child Health, 2008)

Skull
• Anterior–posterior, lateral, and Townes view (the latter if indicated).[a]

Chest
• Anterior–posterior including the clavicles. • Oblique views of both sides of the chest (left and right oblique).

Abdomen
• Anterior–posterior of abdomen including pelvis and hips.

Spine
• Lateral, this may consist of separate exposures of the cervical, thoracic, and lumbar spine. • Anterior–posterior only if not visualized on chest and abdomen radiograph. • Anterior–posterior of the cervical spine are not indicated in living children but in deceased children they should be obtained.[b]

Limbs
• Anterior–posterior of both upper arms. • Anterior–posterior of both forearms. • Anterior–posterior of both femurs. • Anterior–posterior of both lower legs. • Posterior–anterior of both hands. • Anterior–posterior of both feet.

[a]*The skull radiograph should be obtained even if a CT of the skull will be or has been done.*
[b]*This is different from the RCR guideline for the skeletal survey.*

Most dysmorphologies are therefore known before the baby is even born. Nonetheless, (hereditary) congenital disorders are not known in advance in all cases and can sometimes mimic child abuse. In these cases differentiation between a congenital disorder, birth trauma, and abuse must be made very carefully. Congenital disorders such as metabolic bone disease of prematurity, osteogenesis imperfecta (Fig. 11.1), Menkes syndrome, Bruck syndrome, neuromuscular diseases, rickets, liver diseases, malabsorption, osteoporosis, CMV infection, and medication and intoxications of the mother during pregnancy, increase the risk of obtaining fractures early in life (Altman and Smith, 1960; Mendelson, 2005; O'Neill et al., 1973). Although these disorders can be accurately diagnosed with a good clinical history in combination with blood or DNA tests, the process of accurate child abuse diagnosis can be complex in these cases.

Birth trauma, especially in living children, can also be an important point of debate between forensic medical experts in cases of child abuse. During birth several known injuries can occur, due to, e.g., cephalo-pelvic disproportion, too rapid or delayed delivery, an

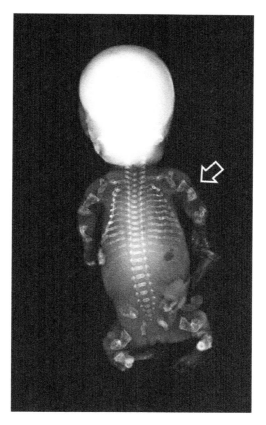

Figure 11.1 Babygram of a newborn showing multiple fractures, resulting in beading of the ribs and bending and shortening of the long bones (arrow). Based on the imaging findings the diagnosis Osteogenesis Imperfecta type 2a can be made.

abnormal position of the baby, or a forceps or vacuum-assisted delivery. This can result in brain damage and bleeding, which cannot be visualized with conventional radiography. The most commonly birth related trauma (90%) is a clavicle fracture (Fig. 11.2), which is seen in up to 13% (1.7–3.5%) of cases (Joseph and Rosenfeld, 1990). Conventional births seldom result in rib fractures, but complicated births can sometimes lead to rib fractures (van Rijn et al., 2009). Skull fractures can also occur but are rare in uncomplicated births. If present, it usually is an uncomplicated linear fracture in the parietal bone, which may be missed by the pediatrician during physical examination (Heise et al., 1996; Nadas et al., 1993; Simonson et al., 2007). These fractures can also result from a fall on the head and need to be differentiated from skull sutures. Impression fractures of the skull can also

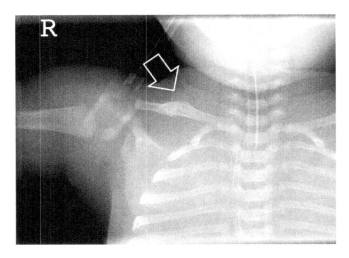

Figure 11.2 Healing clavicular fracture in a newborn after a shoulder dystocia during birth.

occur during birth, but are more easily detected. Birth-related fractures of the extremities are seen in the humeral bone (Fig. 11.3), especially breech deliveries, and in the femur (Camus et al., 1986; Gagnaire et al., 1975; Reed et al., 1994). These fractures are sometimes only noticed several days after the birth (Kendall and Woloshin, 1952; Rizzolo and Coleman, 1989). In such cases a thorough examination of the patient chart, with special attention to the nursing notes is mandatory.

11.2.2.2 Infants and Toddlers
Up to 55% of physically abused children have fractures. Conventional radiography can be used to differentiate them from nonabusive fractures, dating of the fractures, and to see whether the fractures fit the clinical presentation (Kogutt et al., 1974; Loder and Bookout, 1991). Nevertheless, most fractures are not the result of child abuse, since approximately every child has a 1.6–2.1% chance per year of having a fracture (Fig. 11.4) (Landin, 1983, 1997; Worlock and Stower, 1986).

Before the age of 1 year, accidental fractures are rare, with approximately 50–70% being attributed to child abuse (King et al., 1988; Leventhal et al., 1993). Between the ages of 1 and 4 years, accidental fractures most commonly occur in the upper extremities and head after falls, especially bowing, buckle and greenstick fractures of the

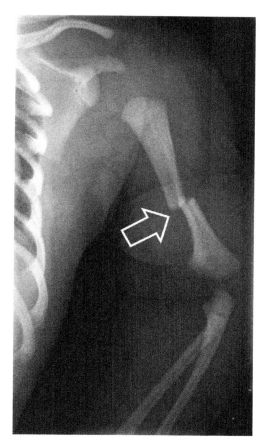

Figure 11.3 Fresh humeral fracture in a newborn girl after a shoulder dystocia during birth.

long bones. In infants and toddlers there are several fractures which have a high specificity for child abuse, using the classification proposed by Kleinman (2015) (Table 11.2).

In children, long bones consist of a diaphysis, metaphyses (growth plates), and epiphyses. Metaphyses are relatively weak in the growing skeleton and may be the first site to fracture. This can either result in a Salter—Harris (SH) fracture (Fig. 11.5), which in case of a SH-I or SH-IV can be hard to visualize, or a metaphyseal corner fracture also known as a CML (Fig. 11.6). CML can be associated with abusive head trauma, formerly referred to as shaken baby syndrome. Another fracture with a high specificity for abuse trauma is posterior or lateral rib fracture, which is the result of compressive forces applied to the

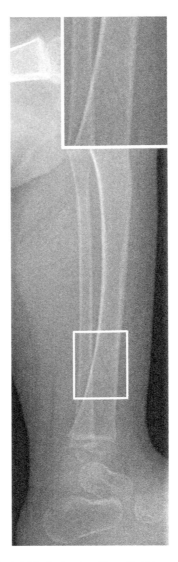

Figure 11.4 Childhood accidental spiral tibia fracture in a 16-month-old boy.

chest, typically by an adult (Kemp et al., 2008). Several studies have shown that in children below the age of 2 years, the predictive value of posterior rib fractures for abuse is well above 80% (Bulloch et al., 2000; Carty and Pierce, 2002). Rib fractures in children are uncommon following resuscitation, but when they do occur, they are usually located on the costochondral junction or in the midclavicular line

Table 11.2 Specificity of Skeletal Findings for Child Abuse (Kleinman, 2015)

High Specificity

- Metaphyseal corner fractures
- Rib fractures, especially posterior
- Scapular fractures
- Spinous process fractures
- Sternal fractures

Moderate Specificity

- Multiple, especially bilateral, fractures
- Fractures of different ages
- SH type-I fractures
- Vertebral fractures
- Digital fractures
- Complex skull fractures
- Pelvic fractures

Low Specificity

- Sub-periosteal new bone formation
- Clavicular fractures
- Long bone diaphysis fractures
- Linear skull fractures

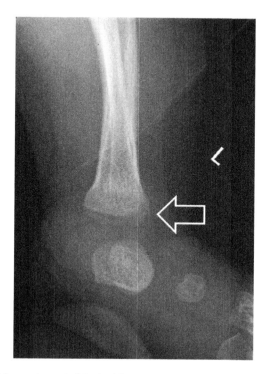

Figure 11.5 SH type 2 fracture (arrow) of the distal femur in an 8-month-old girl.

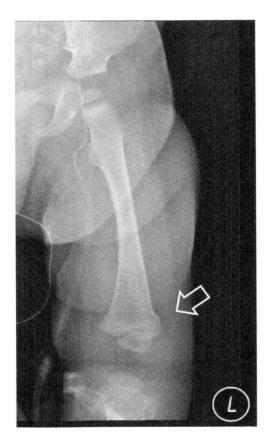

Figure 11.6 CML of the distal tibia in a 2-month-old boy.

(Betz and Liebhardt, 1994; Bush et al., 1996). A proper skeletal survey, performed according to the international guidelines, is essential to image all the bones in nonverbal children, as otherwise subtle fractures may be missed.

11.2.2.3 Older Children

Above the age of 10, children more often present with fractures attributed to injuries sustained while playing sports or in a traffic accident. In this age category fractures resulting from child abuse are less frequently seen. In contrast to young infants and toddlers there are no fractures which are specific for child abuse. Here the clinical history and context is key to the diagnosis.

11.2.2.4 Radiological Dating of Fractures

Multiple fractures and/or fractures of different ages are more suspect of child abuse, since multiple traumatic events must have occurred (Hobbs, 1997; Kleinman, 2015; Kleinman et al., 2015). Furthermore, the age of a fracture must comply with the caregivers' explanation. Therefore dating of the fractures is important, but its accuracy is limited. Moreover in children fractures heal faster compared to adults due to periosteal reactions and remodeling. The dating of fractures used to be based on Kleinman's textbook, however this was largely based on personal experience (Kleinman, 2015). A large systematic review in 2005 showed that dating of fractures in children is imprecise with few studies available, especially in children under 5 years of age (Prosser et al., 2005). A subsequent retrospective cross-sectional study which included 63 children younger than 5 years, with in total 82 fractures, showed that the first sign of healing, periosteal reaction, was visible after 5 days and was present in 62% of cases between days 15 and 35 after fracture (Prosser et al., 2005). Soft callus was first visible 12 days after the fracture and hard callus after 19 days. Remodeling can be seen from day 45 onward. Based on this, relatively small retrospective cohort study the authors concluded that "fractures in young children may be dated as acute (<1 week), recent (8–35 days), or old (≥36 days) on the basis of the presence of six key radiologic features in combination."

11.2.2.5 Specimen Radiography

PM conventional radiography in suspected child abuse cases can be performed both before and after autopsy. When a fracture is observed on the preautopsy imaging, the autopsy typically confirms features of acute fresh fractures such as internal hematomas. Fractured bones or sections of it can be removed and reimaged with a high-resolution mammography system or dedicated specimen radiography system. The more detailed radiographs can help clarify subtle abnormalities including fractures (Figs. 11.7A–C and 11.8A and B) (Kleinman et al., 1992, 1996).

11.2.3 Age Assessment

In a forensic context, establishing the degree of development of a fetus/neonate is important as it impacts on the legal consequences in a case. Although legislation may vary among legal systems, most have incorporated a definition of the beginning of human life. Clinically, normal

(A)   (B)

(C)

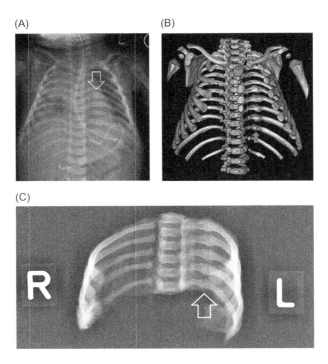

Figure 11.7 (A) PM conventional chest radiograph of a 4-month-old boy showing healing posterior fractures of ribs 6–10 on the left side (arrow). (B) 3D reconstructions of the same boy showing the rib fractures as well. (C) Specimen radiograph of fractured ribs (arrow) improves interpretability by eliminating over projection by other structures.

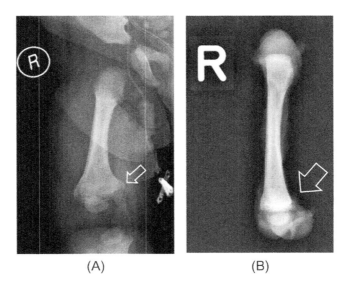

(A)   (B)

Figure 11.8 (A and B) CML (arrows) of the distal right femur with periosteal reaction, in the same 4-month-old boy with the rib fractures (Fig. 11.7A−C).

term is calculated as 40 gestational weeks (280 days) with a range of 37–42 weeks (Scheuer and Black, 2000). For example, according to the Dutch Burial and Cremation Act a stillborn fetus of a gestational age of less than 24 weeks is not considered a legal person, and thus the Burial and Cremation Act does not apply.

In forensic practice, the examination of defleshed bones remains the "golden standard" (Robinson et al., 2008). However, the removal of soft tissue from bone is an invasive procedure. It can damage underlying bone and lead to the loss of potentially vital evidence. Noninvasive alternative approaches that use medical imaging for identification offer considerable practical and aesthetic benefits (Brough et al., 2012).

There are numerous publications on the relation between skeletal and dental development and age (AlQahtani et al., 2010; Fazekas and Kósa, 1978; Maresh and Deming, 1939; Scheuer and Black, 2000). When estimating the age of a fetus or neonate long bone development, presence of ossification nuclei and dental development are recommended to be assessed (Cunha et al., 2009). To date, there is no standardized approach to radiological age assessment of juveniles (Brough et al., 2012). However, several studies have been published on the use of different imaging techniques for age assessment of the growing skeleton (Dedouit et al., 2015). Dental radiographs and orthopantomograms could provide insight in the degree of dental development and eruption. Even though dental radiographic imaging is widely used for age assessment purposes in juveniles and adolescents, to the best of the authors knowledge no data has been published on the use of dental radiographic imaging for the purpose of age estimation of fetuses and neonates.

11.3 COMPUTED TOMOGRAPHY

11.3.1 Technique and Protocol

Because of radiation, total body computed tomography (CT) is, compared to adult radiology, less often performed in children. In deceased children, the clinically limiting radiation exposure is not of importance. Postmortem CT (PMCT) is a fast, noninvasive, and relatively cheap method to investigate the whole body.

Currently most CT scanners are single energy scanners, that is, a scanner using a single energy source and a detector rotating around the body, with an energy level between 80 and 120 kV. As PMCT is mostly performed without the use of intravenous contrast, the distinction between different tissues and within tissues can be very difficult or inconclusive.

However, a relatively new CT technique, called dual energy CT scanning, uses two detectors and two energy sources. One source is set at a high energy level and the other source is set at a low energy level, for instance 80 and 140 kV. Using these two energy sources, the software can present a higher contrast between tissues enabling radiologists to better differentiate between tissues. To date only a few papers have been published referring to the use of dual energy CT in the PM setting (Leth, 2009; Persson et al., 2008). From a forensic point of view, one of the major downsides of the use of PMCT is the fact that CT scanners are not available in most forensic centers. This often means that PMCT scanners available in medical centers have to be employed, thus necessitating transportation of the body.

PMCT can be used to give direction to autopsies, e.g., in case of fractures, massive or minor hemorrhages, and the presence of foreign bodies. It also gives the option of minimal invasive autopsies and may be even make an autopsy redundant (Roberts et al., 2012; Scholing et al., 2009). PMCT is especially important to detect fractures of, e.g., the skull, ribs, or long bones beforehand so they will not be missed. Moreover, PMCT has a higher specificity and sensitivity for fractures, such as posterior rib fractures compared to conventional radiography (Scholing et al., 2009). Like in conventional radiography, the scans should be assessed by a pediatric radiologist, with experience in PM imaging.

From a practical point of view, and with respect to trace evidence also from a forensic point of view, another advantage of CT over conventional radiography is that the body can remain in the body bag during scanning. This minimizes the risk of contamination, spreading of foul odors, and destruction of tissues.

Once scanned, reconstructions in all possible directions and 3D reconstructions can be made if necessary. This can be important for scene reconstructions and bullet trajectories (van Kan et al., 2014). More and more total body PMCT prior to autopsy is advised in all cases, though it has to be kept in mind that, except for specific cases, it cannot replace an autopsy (Rutty et al., 2013; Sieswerda-Hoogendoorn et al., 2013).

Up till now PMCT is mainly used as a diagnostic tool in the forensic autopsy process. Nevertheless, PMCT is becoming increasingly used in court cases, for example, the alleged shaking of a baby may sound relatively innocent to a layman or judge, but actually showing images of subdural hemorrhages, CML's and other fractures can have a very great impact on understanding the injuries present. Given the increasing use of 3D printed models based on the imaging data set, these models can also be used in courts to help explain the anatomy and events. Even with use of such advanced imaging tools the expert testimony of a pediatric radiologist will be of indispensable value.

11.3.2 Age Assessment

The improved CT technology, increased resolution and the capability to create reconstructions in any direction, improves the accuracy of skeletal measurements. Whereas conventional radiographs are projectional images and therefore are subject to magnification factors, which can be unknown, CT images are calibrated and do not suffer from magnification. This enables more accurate measurements used for instance in age assessment (Fig. 11.9) (Robinson et al., 2008). Another key feature of the use of CT images for age assessment is the opportunity to virtually slice up a 3D structure, e.g., to show the development of for instance ossification centers (Weber et al., 2001).

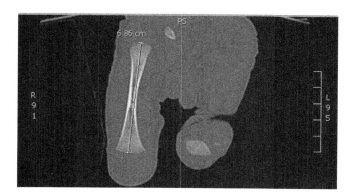

Figure 11.9 Femur length measurement on PMCT for age assessment. The femoral length of 6.9 cm corresponds, according to Scheuer et al., with the clinical gestational age of approximately 36 weeks (Scheuer et al., 1980).

11.3.3 PMCT in Minimally Invasive Autopsy

PMCT is widely used in forensic casework, given the availability of scanners and the speed of scanning more so than PM magnetic resonance imaging (PMMR). The strength of PMCT over PMMR (see Section 11.4) lies in the detection of osseous lesions. It is well known that acute undisplaced rib fractures are difficult to detect on radiography, particularly in the absence of any callus formation. Almost twice as many rib fractures may be seen on PMCT than on radiographs, particularly subtle rib fractures, however rib fracture detection rates using either technique are dependent on observer experience (Hong et al., 2011; Schulze et al., 2013). PMCT may be particularly useful for fractures near the manubrium and sternum, and near the costovertebral junctions, which are particularly difficult to assess on radiographs. Compared to the antemortem situation PMCT is less suitable for the detection of soft tissue lesions, as PMCT angiography (PMCTA) most often will not be performed. Even in case of PMCTA dynamic enhancement patterns, such as seen in hemangioma, will not be present.

In the PM setting, there is little disadvantage to performing more detailed cross-sectional imaging, and thus using a relatively high radiation dose, such as PMCT. An argument could be made that any imaging modality that could possibly increase the detection of injuries should be employed.

In the interpretation of these studies the reporting radiologist/pathologist should however be aware of normal PM findings. There have been some excellent publications describing these normal PMCT findings in children (Klein et al., 2015; Offiah and Dean, 2016). Some salient examples of normal PMCT findings, which would be considered to be pathological in life, are a decreased or absent white–gray matter differentiation of the brain, diffuse opacification of the lungs and air in the portal system (Fig. 11.10), and other vascular structures.

11.3.4 Signs of Life

Differentiation between live birth and stillbirth is of major importance in suspected neonaticide cases. In forensic pathology the flotation test for lungs and the gastrointestinal (GI) tract performed as part of the PM examination is the main method used to assess this difference (Rao, 2013). Aerated lungs and upper GI tract of a neonate who had

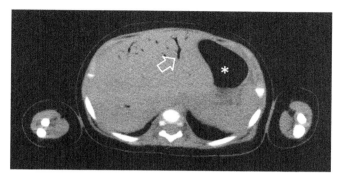

Figure 11.10 PMCT scan of a 4-month-old boy showing air in the stomach (asterisk) and normal PM gas development in the liver vascular structures.

breathed at birth typically float in water. However, putrefaction, Cardiopulmonary resuscitation (CPR), and freezing/thawing may also introduce gas and cause lungs to float (Hartmann and Mueller, 1975). It is possible to identify air within the lungs and GI tract using PMCT. Besides being noninvasive, this technique may allow the differentiation between partially and fully expanded lungs, artificially aerated (mouth-to-mouth resuscitation) and naturally aerated lungs (respiration), and between putrefaction gasses in the hepatic vessels and natural aeration of the lungs and GI tract (Guddat et al., 2013).

11.4 MAGNETIC RESONANCE IMAGING

11.4.1 Technique and Protocol

The introduction of PMMR has helped to advance less-invasive perinatal autopsy in the United Kingdom. Magnetic resonance imaging uses the differences in body tissue water content to give highly detailed 3D imaging of almost all of the body organs, without needed intravenous contrast to be given. MRI does not use ionizing radiation, and is therefore inherently preferable to using CT, but the imaging is typically more expensive and images take longer to acquire. The main advantages of PMCT over PMMR are speed of acquisition, availability in most hospitals, and the better bone detail that is achieved using unenhanced CT. Both have advantages over conventional radiographs, as a permanent 3D record of detailed anatomical features can be stored, for teaching and training purposes, which is not achievable by radiographs nor current histopathological dissection. Detailed 3D imaging also lends itself to 3D printed model, making it easier to learn normal and abnormal anatomy, improving understanding of 3D relationships of complex abnormalities (Schievano et al., 2010).

However, in children, PMCT has several disadvantages, including reduced soft tissue contrast due to reduced abdominal and subcutaneous fat, poor soft tissue contrast in the brain, and assessment of the chest and abdomen is particularly challenging. The advantages of PMMR setting is that it allows highly detailed imaging of the brain and internal body structures without the need for dissection at autopsy, using specific scanning techniques (Norman et al., 2016). Newer developments may also allow us to infer additional useful information in the forensic setting, such as lung inflation (aeration) and PM interval.

11.4.2 PMMR in Minimally Invasive Autopsy

PMMR is the technique for which there is greatest evidence that it can detect abnormalities with very high diagnostic accuracy, compared to conventional autopsy procedures. For example, in a recent study of over 400 stillbirth and childhood cases, 90% of all diagnoses made at autopsy were able to be made at PMMR together with other noninvasive investigations (such as placental examinations or skin microbiology) (Thayyil et al., 2013). PMMR is particularly useful in identifying brain, heart, and solid abdominal organ abnormalities, as would be expected from clinical experience in live children (Arthurs et al., 2014b, 2015a–d, 2016). This has led to PMMR being proposed as a key part of a "less-invasive" autopsy examination, whereby PMMR is used as a first-line investigation to detect or exclude major pathology, particularly where parents are reluctant to proceed to conventional autopsy (Arthurs et al., 2015d).

In the child abuse setting, PMMR can be particularly useful to delineate traumatic injuries, including intracranial injury such as skull fractures or intracranial hemorrhage. Any additional information that PMMR can provide in a child abuse setting regarding the extent of intracranial injury (skull fracture or intracranial hemorrhage), or chest and/or abdominal trauma in association with rib fractures can be useful to guide the forensic pathologist in conducting their detailed examination (Fig. 11.11A–D). Long bone fractures can also be identified using PMMR, although these are often best identified on standard radiographs, as subtle abnormalities may be missed on PMMR

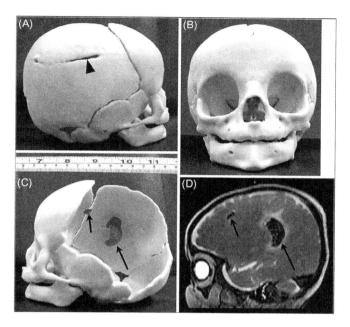

Figure 11.11 3D model of a fracture skull and underlying brain hemorrhage in an infant brain. The PMCT data-set (to provide the 3D skull structure) was coregistered with the PMMR image (to identify the bleed volume and position) to give a composite image (D). This was printed into a skull (B), to demonstrate the fracture (black arrowhead, A) and internal hemorrhage (black arrows, C). These findings were confirmed at autopsy. Reproduced with permission from Schievano, S., Sebire, N.J., Robertson, N.J., Taylor, A.M., Thayyil, S., 2010. Reconstruction of fetal and infant anatomy using rapid prototyping of post-mortem MR images. Insights Imaging 1, 281–286.

(Arthurs et al., 2014a). PMMR can also be used to reassure investigators that no trauma has taken place.

Overall, PMMR performs better than PMCT in most children, largely because PMCT is nondiagnostic in small cases (Arthurs et al., 2016), and PMMR does not need intravenous contrast nor lung ventilation to reach the same diagnoses identified on PMCT (Arthurs et al., 2015b). While PMMR can also be used to perform other activities usually performed during autopsy, such as organ weight or volume estimation, accurate detailed reporting of PMMR needs to be learned by skilled radiologists (Arthurs et al., 2015e). In particular, recognizing normal PM changes which occur such as fluid redistribution (subcutaneous edema, pleural and pericardial effusions, and ascites) can be challenging to radiologists unfamiliar with autopsy work (Fig. 11.12). Small fetuses are also difficult to image using PMMR, but these are unlikely to be the subject of a forensic examination.

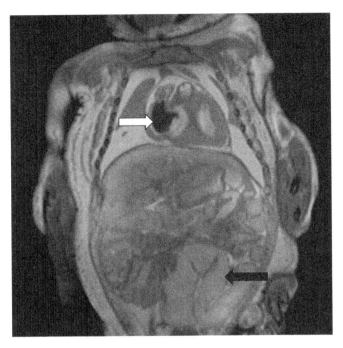

Figure 11.12 Coronal T2-weighted PMMR in a late gestation stillbirth, demonstrating normal physiological PM imaging appearances. There is intracardiac gas, pleural and pericardial effusions in the chest (black arrow), bowel dilatation, and widespread subcutaneous edema (white arrow), all of which can be misinterpreted as pathological to radiologists unfamiliar with autopsy imaging. Adapted with permission from Arthurs, O.J., Taylor, A.M., Sebire, N.J., 2015d. Indications, advantages and limitations of perinatal postmortem imaging in clinical practice. Pediatr. Radiol. 45, 491–500.

11.4.3 Signs of Life and PM interval

Like PMCT, PMMR can also be used to address specific questions. PMMR has recently been shown to be a good indicator of spontaneous breathing, with similar diagnostic accuracy to the lung flotation test and air in the GI tract, but with the clear advantage of being non-invasive (Fig. 11.13A and B) (Barber et al., 2015b). Gas in other parts of the body are seen at PMCT and PMMR and may be attributed to resuscitation, rather than putrefaction or decomposition (Barber et al., 2015a).

With improving PMMR techniques and the ability to quantify some indices such as lung volumes or fluid redistribution, PM imaging may now begin to provide information on PM interval (the time from death to imaging), which will be useful where the time of death is unknown. For example, the accumulation of pleural fluid around the

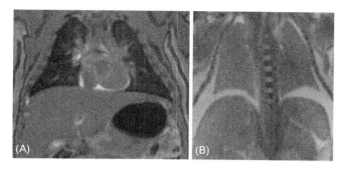

Figure 11.13 Signal intensity differences in the lungs on PMMR may be used to differentiate between a baby who has breathed (dark airways and lungs on coronal T2-weighted PMMR image in a 2-week-old baby; A) versus one that has not (light lungs in a 30-week gestation fetus with no signs of life at delivery; B). Reproduced under Open Access agreement with permission from Barber, J.L., Sebire, N.J., Chitty, L.S., Taylor, A.M., Arthurs, O.J., 2015b. Lung aeration on post-mortem magnetic resonance imaging is a useful marker of live birth versus stillbirth. Int. J. Legal Med. 129, 531–536.

lungs following death corresponds with the PM interval in neonates (Barber et al., 2016), and lung fluid redistribution can be quantified using diffusion-weighted imaging, and also correlates with PM interval (Arthurs et al., 2015c). Together with signal changes in the brain, such as basal ganglia hypoxia-related signal changes, all of these parameters together may give a more accurate retrospective estimation of the time of death.

11.5 CONCLUSIONS

In this chapter, we have shown that PM imaging, using a wide variety of techniques, plays an important role in the workup of children who died as a result of potential child abuse. Moreover, it not only aids in assessing the presence or absence of signs of physical abuse, but also in age assessment in case of a fetus/neonate.

PM radiography, due to availability, in most instances remains the main radiological imaging modality following childhood death. CT should be performed prior to autopsy whenever available, as is able to achieve higher bone detail and allows for a 3D representation. MRI generates better imaging findings concerning soft tissue, especially with respect to the central nervous system, but is not as widely available in a forensic setting. Depending on the forensic question at hand one or more of the modalities should be used in order to come to a differential diagnosis. Interpreting the imaging results requires an in-depth knowledge of pediatric radiology in combination with knowledge of physiological PM changes (Arthurs et al., 2015e). The PM imaging findings, in combination with other clinical results, should be placed in a forensic context. It is important to keep in mind that PM radiology, although in our view of great significance, is only part of the entire PM workup. The diagnosis of death due to child abuse can only be the result of multidisciplinary teamwork in which multiple disciplines participate.

ACKNOWLEDGMENTS

OJA is funded by a National Institute for Health Research Clinician Scientist Fellowship award NIHR-CS-012-002. This chapter presents independent research part-funded by the National Institute for Health Research (NIHR) and supported by the Great Ormond Street Hospital Biomedical Research Centre. The views expressed are those of the author(s) and not necessarily those of the NHS, the NIHR, or the Department of Health.

REFERENCES

AlQahtani, S.J., Hector, M.P., Liversidge, H.M., 2010. Brief communication: The London Atlas of human tooth development and eruption. Am. J. Phys. Anthropol. 142, 481–490.

Altman, D.H., Smith, R.L., 1960. Unrecognized trauma in infants and children. J. Bone Joint Surg. 42-a, 407–413.

Arthurs, O.J., Thayyil, S., Addison, S., Wade, A., Jones, R., Norman, W., et al., 2014a. Diagnostic accuracy of postmortem MRI for musculoskeletal abnormalities in fetuses and children. Prenat. Diagn. 34, 1254–1261.

Arthurs, O.J., Thayyil, S., Olsen, O.E., Addison, S., Wade, A., Jones, R., et al., 2014b. Diagnostic accuracy of post-mortem MRI for thoracic abnormalities in fetuses and children. Eur. Radiol. 24, 2876–2884.

Arthurs, O.J., Barber, J.L., Taylor, A.M., Sebire, N.J., 2015a. Normal perinatal and paediatric postmortem magnetic resonance imaging appearances. Pediatr. Radiol. 45, 527–535.

Arthurs, O.J., Guy, A., Kiho, L., Sebire, N.J., 2015b. Ventilated postmortem computed tomography in children: feasibility and initial experience. Int. J. Legal Med. 129, 1113–1120.

Arthurs, O.J., Price, G.C., Carmichael, D.W., Jones, R., Norman, W., Taylor, A.M., et al., 2015c. Diffusion-weighted perinatal postmortem magnetic resonance imaging as a marker of postmortem interval. Eur. Radiol. 25, 1399–1406.

Arthurs, O.J., Taylor, A.M., Sebire, N.J., 2015d. Indications, advantages and limitations of perinatal postmortem imaging in clinical practice. Pediatr. Radiol. 45, 491–500.

Arthurs, O.J., van Rijn, R.R., Taylor, A.M., Sebire, N.J., 2015e. Paediatric and perinatal postmortem imaging: the need for a subspecialty approach. Pediatr. Radiol. 45, 483–490.

Arthurs, O.J., Guy, A., Thayyil, S., Wade, A., Jones, R., Norman, W., et al., 2016. Comparison of diagnostic performance for perinatal and paediatric post-mortem imaging: CT versus MRI. Eur. Radiol. 26, 2327–2336.

Barber, J.L., Kiho, L., Sebire, N.J., Arthurs, O.J., 2015a. Interpretation of intravascular gas on postmortem CT in children. J. Forensic Radiol. Imaging 3, 174–179.

Barber, J.L., Sebire, N.J., Chitty, L.S., Taylor, A.M., Arthurs, O.J., 2015b. Lung aeration on post-mortem magnetic resonance imaging is a useful marker of live birth versus stillbirth. Int. J. Legal Med. 129, 531–536.

Barber, J.L., Hutchinson, J.C., Sebire, N.J., Arthurs, O.J., 2016. Pleural fluid accumulation detectable on paediatric post-mortem imaging: a possible marker of interval since death? Int. J. Legal Med. 130, 1003–1010.

Betz, P., Liebhardt, E., 1994. Rib fractures in children—resuscitation or child abuse? Int. J. Legal Med. 106, 215–218.

Brough, A.L., Rutty, G.N., Black, S., Morgan, B., 2012. Post-mortem computed tomography and 3D imaging: anthropological applications for juvenile remains. Forensic Sci. Med. Pathol. 8, 270–279.

Bulloch, B., Schubert, C.J., Brophy, P.D., Johnson, N., Reed, M.H., Shapiro, R.A., 2000. Cause and clinical characteristics of rib fractures in infants. Pediatrics 105, E48.

Bush, C.M., Jones, J.S., Cohle, S.D., Johnson, H., 1996. Pediatric injuries from cardiopulmonary resuscitation. Ann. Emerg. Med. 28, 40–44.

Caffey, J., 1946. Multiple fractures in the long bones of infants suffering from chronic subdural hematoma. Am. J. Roentgenol. 56, 163–173.

Camus, M., Lefebvre, G., Darbois, Y., 1986. Obstetrical paralysis of the brachial plexus in breech presentation. J. Gynecol. Obstet. Biol. Reprod. (Paris) 15, 1104–1106.

Carty, H., Pierce, A., 2002. Non-accidental injury: a retrospective analysis of a large cohort. Eur. Radiol. 12, 2919–2925.

Cunha, E., Baccino, E., Martrille, L., Ramsthaler, F., Prieto, J., Schuliar, Y., et al., 2009. The problem of aging human remains and living individuals: a review. Forensic Sci. Int. 193, 1–13.

Dedouit, F., Saint-Martin, P., Mokrane, F.Z., Savall, F., Rousseau, H., Crubezy, E., et al., 2015. Virtual anthropology: useful radiological tools for age assessment in clinical forensic medicine and thanatology. Radiol. Med. 120, 874–886.

Fazekas, I.G., Kósa, F., 1978. Forensic Fetal Osteology. Akadémiai Kiadó.

Felitti, V.J., Anda, R.F., Nordenberg, D., Williamson, D.F., Spitz, A.M., Edwards, V., et al., 1998. Relationship of childhood abuse and household dysfunction to many of the leading causes of death in adults: the Adverse Childhood Experiences (ACE) Study. Am. J. Prev. Med. 14, 245–258.

Gagnaire, J.C., Thoulon, J.M., Chappuis, J.P., Varnier, C.H., Mered, B., 1975. Injuries to the upper extremities in the newborn diagnosed at birth. J. Gynecol. Obstet. Biol. Reprod. (Paris) 4, 245–254.

Guddat, S.S., Gapert, R., Tsokos, M., Oesterhelweg, L., 2013. Proof of live birth using postmortem multislice computed tomography (pmMSCT) in cases of suspected neonaticide: advantages of diagnostic imaging compared to conventional autopsy. Forensic Sci. Med. Pathol. 9, 3–12.

Hartmann, G., Mueller, B., 1975. Gerichtliche Medizin. Teil 2. Toxikologie, Sexualpathologie, Forensische Gynäkologie, Vaterschaft. Zweite, neubearbeitete und erweiterte Auflage. Kindestötung. Springer, Berlin, pp. 1172–1211.

Heise, R.H., Srivatsa, P.J., Karsell, P.R., 1996. Spontaneous intrauterine linear skull fracture: a rare complication of spontaneous vaginal delivery. Obstet. Gynecol. 87, 851–854.

Hobbs, C., 1997. Fractures. In: Meadow, R. (Ed.), ABC of Child Abuse. BMJ Publishing Group, London.

Hong, T.S., Reyes, J.A., Moineddin, R., Chiasson, D.A., Berdon, W.E., Babyn, P.S., 2011. Value of postmortem thoracic CT over radiography in imaging of pediatric rib fractures. Pediatr. Radiol. 41, 736–748.

Hulson, O.S., van Rijn, R.R., Offiah, A.C., 2014. European survey of imaging in non-accidental injury demonstrates a need for a consensus protocol. Pediatr. Radiol. 44, 1557–1563.

Joseph, P.R., Rosenfeld, W., 1990. Clavicular fractures in neonates. Am. J. Dis. Child. 144, 165–167.

Kemp, A.M., Dunstan, F., Harrison, S., Morris, S., Mann, M., Rolfe, K., et al., 2008. Patterns of skeletal fractures in child abuse: systematic review. BMJ 337, a1518.

Kendall, N., Woloshin, H., 1952. Cephal hematoma associated with fracture of the skull. J. Pediatr. 41, 125–132.

King, J., Diefendorf, D., Apthorp, J., Negrete, V.F., Carlson, M., 1988. Analysis of 429 fractures in 189 battered children. J. Pediatr. Orthop. 8, 585–589.

Klein, W.M., Bosboom, D.G., Koopmanschap, D.H., Nievelstein, R.A., Nikkels, P.G., van Rijn, R.R., 2015. Normal pediatric postmortem CT appearances. Pediatr. Radiol. 45, 517–526.

Kleinman, P.K., 2015. Diagnostic Imaging of Child Abuse. Cambridge University Press.

Kleinman, P.K., Marks, S.C., Spevak, M.R., Richmond, J.M., 1992. Fractures of the rib head in abused infants. Radiology 185, 119–123.

Kleinman, P.K., Marks Jr., S.C., Nimkin, K., Rayder, S.M., Kessler, S.C., 1996. Rib fractures in 31 abused infants: postmortem radiologic-histopathologic study. Radiology 200, 807–810.

Kleinman, P.K., Rosenberg, A., Tsai, A., 2015. Skeletal Trauma. Cambridge University Press.

Kogutt, M.S., Swischuk, L.E., Fagan, C.J., 1974. Patterns of injury and significance of uncommon fractures in the battered child syndrome. Am. J. Roentgenol. Radium Ther. Nucl. Med. 121, 143–149.

Landin, L.A., 1983. Fracture patterns in children. Analysis of 8,682 fractures with special reference to incidence, etiology and secular changes in a Swedish urban population 1950–1979. Acta Orthop. Scand. Suppl. 202, 1–109.

Landin, L.A., 1997. Epidemiology of children's fractures. J. Pediatr. Orthop. B. 6, 79–83.

Leth, P.M., 2009. Computerized tomography used as a routine procedure at postmortem investigations. Am. J. Forensic Med. Pathol. 30, 219–222.

Leventhal, J.M., Thomas, S.A., Rosenfield, N.S., Markowitz, R.I., 1993. Fractures in young children. Distinguishing child abuse from unintentional injuries. Am. J. Dis. Child. 147, 87–92.

Loder, R.T., Bookout, C., 1991. Fracture patterns in battered children. J. Orthop. Trauma 5, 428–433.

Maresh, M.M., Deming, J., 1939. The growth of the long bones in 80 infants. Roentgenograms versus anthropometry. Child Dev. 10, 91–106.

Mendelson, K.L., 2004. The Society for Pediatric Radiology—National Association of Medical Examiners. Pediatr. Radiol. 34, 675–677.

Mendelson, K.L., 2005. Critical review of 'temporary brittle bone disease'. Pediatr. Radiol. 35, 1036–1040.

Meyer, J.S., Gunderman, R., Coley, B.D., Bulas, D., Garber, M., Karmazyn, B., et al., 2011. American College of Radiology. ACR appropriateness criteria on suspected physical abuse: child. J. Am. Coll. Radiol. 8, 87–94.

Nadas, S., Gudinchet, F., Capasso, P., Reinberg, O., 1993. Predisposing factors in obstetrical fractures. Skeletal Radiol. 22, 195–198.

Norman, W., Jawad, N., Jones, R., Taylor, A.M., Arthurs, O.J., 2016. Perinatal and paediatric post-mortem magnetic resonance imaging (PMMR): sequences and technique. Br. J. Radiol. 89, 20151028.

Offiah, C.E., Dean, J., 2016. Post-mortem CT and MRI: appropriate post-mortem imaging appearances and changes related to cardiopulmonary resuscitation. Br. J. Radiol. 89, 20150851.

O'Neill Jr., J.A., Meacham, W.F., Griffin, J.P., Sawyers, J.L., 1973. Patterns of injury in the battered child syndrome. J. Trauma 13, 332–339.

Persson, A., Jackowski, C., Engström, E., Zachrisson, H., 2008. Advances of dual source, dual-energy imaging in postmortem CT. Eur. J. Radiol. 68, 446–455.

Prosser, I., Maguire, S., Harrison, S.K., Mann, M., Sibert, J.R., Kemp, A.M., 2005. How old is this fracture? Radiologic dating of fractures in children: a systematic review. Am. J. Roentgenol. 184, 1282–1286.

Rao, D., 2013. E-book Forensic pathology. Infant Deaths. http://forensicpathologyonline.com/e-book/sexual-assaults/infant-deaths. last visited 13 Dec 2016.

Reed, M.H., Letts, R.M., Pollock, A.N., 1994. Birth Fractures. Management of Pediatric Fractures. Churchill Livingstone, pp. 1049–1061.

Rizzolo, P.J., Coleman, P.R., 1989. Neonatal rib fracture: birth trauma or child abuse? J. Fam. Pract. 29, 561–564.

Roberts, I.S., Benamore, R.E., Benbow, E.W., Lee, S.H., Harris, J.N., Jackson, A., et al., 2012. Post-mortem imaging as an alternative to autopsy in the diagnosis of adult deaths: a validation study. Lancet 379, 136–142.

Robinson, C., Eisma, R., Morgan, B., Jeffery, A., Graham, E.A., Black, S., et al., 2008. Anthropological measurement of lower limb and foot bones using multi-detector computed tomography. J. Forensic Sci. 53, 1289–1295.

Rutty, G.N., Gorincour, G., Thali, M., 2013. Post-mortem cross-sectional imaging: are we running before we can walk? Forensic Sci. Med. Pathol. 9, 466.

Scheuer, J.L., Musgrave, J.H., Evans, S.P., 1980. The estimation of late fetal and perinatal age from limb bone length by linear and logarithmic regression. Ann. Hum. Biol. 7, 257–265.

Scheuer, L., Black, S., 2000. Developmental Juvenile Osteology. Elsevier Academic Press, Bath.

Schievano, S., Sebire, N.J., Robertson, N.J., Taylor, A.M., Thayyil, S., 2010. Reconstruction of fetal and infant anatomy using rapid prototyping of post-mortem MR images. Insights Imaging 1, 281–286.

Scholing, M., Saltzherr, T.P., Fung Kon Jin, P.H., Ponsen, K.J., Reitsma, J.B., Lameris, J.S., et al., 2009. The value of postmortem computed tomography as an alternative for autopsy in trauma victims: a systematic review. Eur. Radiol. 19, 2333–2341.

Schulze, C., Hoppe, H., Schweitzer, W., Schwendener, N., Grabherr, S., Jackowski, C., 2013. Rib fractures at postmortem computed tomography (PMCT) validated against the autopsy. Forensic Sci. Int. 233, 90–98.

Sethi, D., Bellis, M., Hughes, K., Gilbert, R., Mitis, F., Galea, G., 2013. European Report on Preventing Child Maltreatment. World Health Organization, Regional Office for Europe, Copenhagen, Denmark.

Sieswerda-Hoogendoorn, T., Soerdjbalie-Maikoe, V., Maes, A., van Rijn, R.R., 2013. The value of post-mortem CT in neonaticide in case of severe decomposition: description of 12 cases. Forensic Sci. Int. 233, 298–303.

Simonson, C., Barlow, P., Dehennin, N., Sphel, M., Toppet, V., Murillo, D., et al., 2007. Neonatal complications of vacuum-assisted delivery. Obstet. Gynecol. 109, 626–633.

Thayyil, S., Sebire, N.J., Chitty, L.S., Wade, A., Chong, W., Olsen, O., et al., 2013. Post-mortem MRI versus conventional autopsy in fetuses and children: a prospective validation study. Lancet 382, 223–233.

The Royal College of Radiologists and Royal College of Paediatrics and Child Health, 2008. Standards for Radiological Investigations of Suspected Non-accidental Injury. https://www.rcr.ac. uk/publication/standards-radiological-investigations-suspected-non-accidental-injury. last visited 13 Dec 2016.

U.S. Department of Health and Human Services Administration for Children and Families, Administration on Children Youth, & Families Children's Bureau, 2013. Child Maltreatment 2012. http://www.acf.hhs.gov/sites/default/files/cb/cm2012.pdf. last visited 13 Dec 2016.

van Kan, R.A.T., Kubat, B., Haest, I.I.H., van Lohuizen, W., Kroll, J., Lahaye, M.J., et al., 2014. Comparison between radiologist and pathologist in determining trajectories in gunshot victims. J. Forensic Radiol. Imaging 2, 96.

van Rijn, R.R., Bilo, R.A.C., Robben, S.G.F., 2009. Birth-related mid-posterior rib fractures in neonates: a report of three cases (and a possible fourth case) and a review of the literature. Pediatr. Radiol. 39, 30–34.

Weber, G.W., Schafer, K., Prossinger, H., Gunz, P., Mitterocker, P., Seidler, H., 2001. Virtual anthropology: the digital evolution in anthropological sciences. J. Physiol. Anthropol. Appl. Human. Sci. 20, 69–80.

World Health Organization, 2016. Child Maltreatment. http://www.who.int/topics/child_abuse/en/. last visited 13 Dec 2016.

Worlock, P., Stower, M., 1986. Fracture patterns in Nottingham children. J. Pediatr. Orthop. 6, 656–660.

CHAPTER 12

The Storage and Long-Term Preservation of 3D Data

Kieron Niven and Julian D. Richards
University of York, York, United Kingdom

12.1 GROWTH OF 3D DATA

There has been a rapid increase in the acquisition and dissemination of 3D datasets within a number of heritage-related disciplines over the last 10–15 years. Within Archaeology in particular, 3D recording techniques such as laser scanning, photogrammetry and structured light scanning have been applied to the entire range of archaeological evidence, from small-scale cultural objects, artefacts and remains (SketchFab, 2014; Smithsonian X 3D, 2013), through to excavation trenches (McPherron et al., 2009) and large-scale buildings and monuments (Selden et al., 2014). With regard to human and animal remains, a number of projects have applied laser scanning (e.g., Betts et al., 2011), structured light scanning (e.g., Niven et al., 2009) and photogrammetry techniques (Smithsonian X 3D, 2013) to the digitization and 3D modeling of both individual and articulated bones and to complete in-context burials.

Human Remains: Another Dimension. DOI: http://dx.doi.org/10.1016/B978-0-12-804602-9.00013-8

12.2 ADVANTAGES OF 3D DATASETS

At least part of the increase in availability and application of these techniques can be attributed to decreases in the costs associated with 3D scanners and the computers and software required to acquire and process such datasets (Betts et al., 2011, p. 755). More significantly, however, Betts et al. (2011, p. 757) and Kuzminsky and Gardiner (2012, pp. 2746–2749) identify a number of crucial benefits that 3D modeling presents over traditional paper-based or 2D photographs and drawings. The most obvious of these is that 3D models are able to convey complex shapes and geometry—and can be actively manipulated through different scales and angles—at resolutions not easily obtainable in more traditional 2D forms of media.

Parallel advances in web technologies and in the availability of broadband Internet connections have also allowed much more 3D content to be made accessible online, allowing users across the globe remote and usually free, access to extensive, detailed digital collections. Sites such as Digitised Diseases (2013), From Cemetery to Clinic (2013) and the Virtual Zooarchaeology of the Arctic Project (VZAP) (2015) present virtual collections of bones as 3D models within structured online interfaces, allowing users to explore the collections via elements such as age, sex, taxa, or disease classification. The linking of 3D models to complex databases as part of online collection interfaces further enhances the idea of a reference collection by allowing faster and more complex queries to be carried out. The development of online viewers for 3D data, most notably 3DHOP (Potenziani et al., 2015; Galeazzi et al., 2016), allows for ease of manipulation of 3D models within web browsers without the need for the download of dedicated software, or for high bandwidth.

Digital 3D models also have specific advantages over physical collections of human remains (Betts et al., 2011, p. 756; Niven et al., 2009, pp. 2018–2019). In addition to free remote access, there are comparatively minor financial or physical barriers or restrictions to retaining online collections and 3D models can be "handled" with little fear of damage and "wear and tear." Where physical handling is required or seen as being beneficial, digital models can now be 3D-printed with relative ease. Such physical models can be used in teaching activities and public engagement (Selden et al., 2014, p. 21) and 3D files can be made available with associated publications (e.g., Milner et al., 2016) allowing models to be created wherever the file can be downloaded without ever needing access to the original material. Additionally, 3D printing allows objects to be recreated at differing scales, for example, smaller remains such as teeth can be reproduced at a number of times their original size to aid analysis (Niven et al., 2009, p. 2019).

12.3 IMPORTANCE OF RETAINING DATA

The advantages outlined above are, it would seem, enough in themselves to highlight the value of digital data and therefore the importance of retaining and ensuring access to such information. In addition to general advantages relating to access and use, arguments for retaining digital surrogates are particularly relevant in situations where physical remains are subject to possible future access limitations, for example, where materials are fragile or at risk from environmental damage or erosion, are under excavation and require *in situ* recording (McPherron et al., 2009), or where reburial or repatriation legislation only allows limited short-term access to remains.

Betts et al. (2011, p. 755) highlight the long-term importance of retaining these data in terms of the creation of reference collections, with such collections described as being "a crucial tool" for analysis. While physical reference collections of all types can suffer from limitations in terms of scope and variety, access to multiple digital reference collections can mean access to broader, more varied and more comprehensive examples (Betts et al., 2011; Brewer and Jansma, 2016, 1.1.3).

12.4 DIGITAL PRESERVATION, NOT DATA STORAGE

While storing digital data in the long term may, on the face of it, seem like a fairly simple case of putting the data somewhere "safe," ensuring that such data can continue to be accessed and understood indefinitely requires considerable planning and ongoing management (ADS/Digital Antiquity, 2011a). While the advantages of long-term access to digital data is becoming increasingly well known, so too is an awareness that the digital preservation and management of datasets should be considered at the start of and throughout, a project's lifecycle and that digital datasets are best stored within specialized digital repositories (Abbott, 2008; Chartered Institute for Archaeologists, 2014, pp. 6–8).

Furthermore, studies such as that undertaken on behalf of the Research Information Network (Technopolis, 2011) demonstrate that while generalized institutional repositories may be capable of safeguarding common data types, more specialized formats require curation by those with domain expertise and that by providing a critical mass of resources, domain-specific data centers also show greater data reuse by their user communities.

The Archaeology Data Service (ADS) is one such discipline-specific digital repository. Established in 1996 in response to the increase in the creation of born digital archaeological data (Richards et al., 2013) and in recognition of the associated dangers of data loss (Waters and Garrett, 1996), the remit of the ADS is to support research, learning and teaching. This is done through the provision of freely available, high-quality and dependable digital resources and by preserving, promoting and disseminating a broad range of data digital data in the long term. Over the past 20 years, the ADS has become widely recognized for excellence in digital preservation alongside its role in developing and disseminating guidance on standards for archiving, not just in the archaeological community, but on a much wider scale. In 2012, the ADS received the Digital Preservation Coalition Decennial Award for the most outstanding contribution to digital preservation over the preceding decade and the ADS has held the Data Seal of Approval since 2011.

An integral component of the ADS remit has been the lifecycle principle of preservation, curation and dissemination of data in order to enable data reuse (see the Digital Curation Centre, 2008, Curation Lifecycle Model webpage for an overview). Although much of this cycle focusses on data management within the repository, a key extension of this cycle is the process of early engagement with data creators—preferably during the project planning stages—in order to assess and plan how datasets may viably be accessioned, managed, preserved and disseminated. In order to accomplish this, the ADS provides depositors with a series of online Guidelines for Depositors (ADS, 2015) which provide detailed advice on the ADS collection policy. Key to these guidelines is the specification of accepted file formats for deposit alongside metadata schemas for the comprehensive documentation of data across a number of crucial areas. These ADS-specific depositor guidelines are additionally complimented by the online Guides to Good Practice series which aim to provide wider, more generic advice and workflows for the planning, creation and preservation of common archaeological data types.

12.5 PRESERVING 3D DATASETS

Kuzminsky and Gardiner (2012, p. 2750) briefly identify that the long-term storage of 3D datasets may be problematic but this is largely on the basis that storage media may fail over time. While certainly true for the storage of any type of digital data, wider more fundamental considerations for long-term data preservation have been identified by the digital preservation community (ADS/Digital Antiquity, 2011a).

12.6 WHAT TO PRESERVE?

The first question when archiving any dataset is "What to preserve?" Many 3D datasets have complex data creation workflows (3D-ICONS, 2014; ADS, 2016a) incorporating various stages of data acquisition, processing and output. While project "outputs," i.e., finalized 3D models, may be an obvious choice for preservation, original unprocessed data in the form of raw scans and raster images usually form the basis for all subsequent work and capture the real-world objects at the original resolution. The preservation of such raw data—as with any form of data analysis—allows any subsequent results or derivatives to be verified, recreated, or reanalyzed, possibly at a later date using improved software or computing power. With this in mind, consideration of the entire data workflow, particularly of the points at which data are created and processed, is fundamental to forming a representative and functional archive. Data should ideally be preserved in its raw state and then captured at suitable points where the application of data processing techniques, such as meshing, decimating, cleaning, etc., fundamentally change the "input" to a point where it cannot be easily recovered or documented ("Preservation Intervention Points," see ADS/Digital Antiquity, 2011b).

In addition to creating such snapshots of data, a consideration when choosing which data to archive is that archiving bodies may also specify that certain types of data (interim or draft files, files containing confidential or sensitive data) be omitted from the archive. Where sensitive or personal data such as site locations or images or names of individuals are seen to have value in the long term, such data may be anonymized for immediate release or embargoed for a fixed period of time (see ADS, 2016b).

12.7 WHICH FORMATS?

When examining a data workflow, it is also important to consider the formats in which data are to be preserved. The principle that data should be actively managed in the long term is fundamental to digital preservation; data cannot simply be saved and left. In order to accomplish this, digital datasets should ideally be deposited in an appropriate digital archive or repository where they can be properly accessed, curated and maintained for the future. When depositing with such an archive it is usually a requirement that datasets conform to specified standards and guidelines on how they should be structured and formatted (see ADS, 2015 for examples). Preferred formats are largely based on long-term sustainability, that is, the ability to access the data that they contain independent of specific software or hardware configurations (Brown, 2008, pp. 4–5). Even in cases where data are not ultimately deposited with a formal repository, ensuring that files are "preservable"—i.e., that they are in formats that can be easily and reliably accessed by intended users and, ultimately, a digital repository—will to some degree mitigate the likelihood of data loss. During the process of data creation, it is important to remember that "programs and data formats are closely connected" (Nestor, 2009) and that certain data formats may not function the same—if at all—outside of their native software. Several general file format characteristics can help decide which formats may be suitable for data preservation (Brown, 2008; NDIIPP, 2013), including a preference for formats that are:

- Based on open formats and standards, i.e., formats that are standardized, openly documented and, where possible, nonproprietary.
- Binary and plain text files, i.e., formats based on textual encoding (such as ASCII plain text or XML) and are therefore more transparent, human-readable and easily identified in terms of content and associated software, with fewer external dependencies.
- Not compressed, i.e., the content is not encrypted in any way which might magnify the effect of data loss or corruption via bit corruption (Heydegger, 2008).

With regard to 3D datasets, McHenry and Bajcsy (2008) highlight the variety of information that can be stored within a number of popular 3D data formats and the extent to which these formats are compatible (and to which conversion between formats can cause data loss). For 3D datasets arising from laser scanning and photogrammetry or structured light scanning techniques, there is a preference to preserve raw data point clouds in ASCII text formats or in a standardized format such as E57. In addition, where 3D data are generated from images, the original image files should be retained as either TIFF or DNG files. The ADS *Guides to Good Practice* for laser scanning (Payne, 2011), close range photogrammetry (Barnes, 2011), structured light scanning (Errickson, 2015) and 3D Models (Trognitz et al., 2016) provide more detailed guidance on the selection of specific preservation formats for 3D datasets in relation to the specific techniques used.

12.8 METADATA AND DOCUMENTATION

Lastly, in addition to the datasets themselves, preserved data must be "understandable." A key element to successful digital archiving is the thorough documentation of data, including elements such as how they were collected, what standards were used to describe them and how they have been managed since collection. At a minimum, metadata and documentation should provide the "who, what, when, where and how" information relating to a file or project, although metadata often comes as standardized sets (schema) of information that can be used to document, in a structured way, different aspects of data archiving at various levels. Two general categories of metadata relevant to 3D datasets are described in the Guides to Good Practice on laser scanning, photogrammetry and structured light scanning: Top-level, project-level metadata and technical (acquisition and processing) and "model" metadata.

Project-level metadata (Fig. 12.1), as described generally elsewhere in the ADS Guides (ADS/Digital Antiquity, 2011c), focusses on describing the project as a whole, including relevant subject keywords, location and date, as well as information about data creators, copyright and documentation of specific issues such as sensitive data. Project-level metadata also provides broad, top-level information for resource discovery and data accessibility. While certain technique-specific considerations may exist in this broad metadata type, ADS and other repositories have generally adopted variants of a

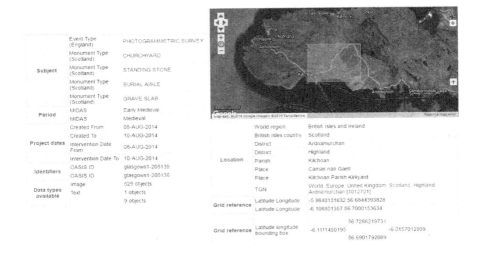

The table within the figure:

Subject	Event Type (England)	PHOTOGRAMMETRIC SURVEY
	Monument Type (Scotland)	CHURCHYARD
	Monument Type (Scotland)	STANDING STONE
	Monument Type (Scotland)	BURIAL AISLE
	Monument Type (Scotland)	GRAVE SLAB
Period	MIDAS	Early Medieval
	MIDAS	Medieval
Project dates	Created From	08-AUG-2014
	Created To	10-AUG-2014
	Intervention Date From	08-AUG-2014
	Intervention Date To	10-AUG-2014
Identifiers	OASIS ID	glasgows1-205139
	OASIS ID	glasgows1-205136
Data types available	Image	629 objects
	Text	1 objects
		9 objects

Location	World region	British Isles and Ireland
	British Isles country	Scotland
	District	Ardnamurchan
	District	Highland
	Parish	Kilchoan
	Place	Camas nan Gaell
	Place	Kilchoan Parish Kirkyard
	TGN	World, Europe, United Kingdom, Scotland, Highland, Ardnamurchan [1012701]
Grid reference	Latitude Longitude	-5.9840131632 56.6844393828
	Latitude Longitude	-6.108801357 56.7000153634
Grid reference	Latitude longitude bounding box	56.7286219731
		-6.1111450195 -6.0157012939
		56.6901792089

Figure 12.1 Example project-level metadata from an ADS archive.

standardized, generic metadata schema (such as Dublin Core) for recording this project-level metadata.

In contrast, technical metadata is highly specific to the data acquisition techniques used within a project and aims to record technical aspects such as equipment types and settings alongside information on the processes carried out on data throughout the project workflow. Detailed technical metadata specifications for 3D datasets are set out in the Guides to Good Practice on laser scanning (Payne, 2011), photogrammetry (Barnes, 2011) and structured light scanning (Errickson, 2015). For all three techniques, the aim of the metadata specifications is to record the types of equipment used for data capture (laser scanner, camera, etc.), the specific settings (resolution, etc.) used and environmental variables experienced during the capture. In addition, specific relationships between datasets should also be recorded and additional schema such as CRMdig (FORTH, 2016) may be employed to record these complex relationships (provenance) between subsets of data and the types of processing used.

12.9 CONCLUSIONS

While data storage may seem like a fairly straightforward business, proper digital preservation of any dataset requires a lifecycle approach that engages with data creators prior to the data creation stage all the way through to the creation of project deliverables. Throughout this process it is important to bear in mind that datasets should stand independent of the people and software that created them. In order to accomplish this, files should be stored in formats that are both open and standardized and should be accompanied by documentation and metadata that explain how data were created, how files relate to one another and why specific elements have been chosen for archiving. Beyond the creation of the digital archive, data should ideally be deposited with an organization that can ensure the long-term management and preservation of files and metadata and, most importantly, their continued availability.

REFERENCES

3D-ICONS, 2014. Guidelines. http://3dicons-project.eu/eng/Guidelines-Case-Studies/Guidelines2.

Abbott, D., 2008. What is Digital Curation? DCC Briefing Papers: Introduction to Curation. Digital Curation Centre, Edinburgh, <http://www.dcc.ac.uk/resources/briefing-papers/introduction-curation>.

ADS, 2015. Guidelines for Depositors. Archaeology Data Service, York, <http://archaeologydataservice.ac.uk/advice/guidelinesForDepositors>.

ADS, Preserving 3D Datasets: Workflows, Formats and Considerations. In: Johnston, L. R. (Ed.) *Curating Research Data Volume Two: A Handbook of Current Practice*, 2016a, ACRL; Chicago, 119-123.

ADS, 2016b. Guidance on the Deposition of Sensitive Digital Data. Archaeology Data Service, York, <http://archaeologydataservice.ac.uk/advice/sensitiveDataPolicy>.

ADS/Digital Antiquity, 2011a. What is digital archiving? Guides to Good Practice. Archaeology Data Service, York, <http://guides.archaeologydataservice.ac.uk/g2gp/ArchivalStrat_1-0>.

ADS/Digital Antiquity, 2011b. Data selection: Preservation intervention points. Guides to Good Practice. Archaeology Data Service, York, <http://guides.archaeologydataservice.ac.uk/g2gp/ArchivalStrat_1-3>.

ADS/Digital Antiquity, 2011c. Project metadata. Guides to Good Practice. Archaeology Data Service, York, <http://guides.archaeologydataservice.ac.uk/g2gp/CreateData_1-2>.

Barnes, A., 2011. Close-range photogrammetry: A guide to good practice. Guides to Good Practice. Archaeology Data Service, University of York, UK, <http://guides.archaeologydataservice.ac.uk/g2gp/Photogram_Toc>.

Betts, M.W., Maschner, H.D.G., Schou, C.D., Schlader, R., Holmes, J., Clement, N., et al., 2011. Virtual zooarchaeology: Building a web-based reference collection of northern vertebrates for archaeofaunal research and education. J. Archaeol. Sci. 38 (4), 755–762.

Brewer, P., Jansma, E., 2016. Dendrochronological data in archaeology: A guide to good practice. Guides to Good Practice. Archaeology Data Service, University of York, UK, <http://guides.archaeologydataservice.ac.uk/g2gp/Dendro_Toc>.

Brown, A., 2008. Selecting File Formats for Long-Term Preservation. The National Archives. <http://www.nationalarchives.gov.uk/documents/selecting-file-formats.pdf>.

Chartered Institute for Archaeologists, 2014. Standard and Guidance for the Creation, Compilation, Transfer and Deposition of Archaeological Archives. Chartered Institute for Archaeologists, Birmingham, <http://www.archaeologists.net/sites/default/files/CIFAS&GArchives_2.pdf>.

Digital Curation Centre, 2008. Curation Lifecycle Model. http://www.dcc.ac.uk/resources/curation-lifecycle-model.

Digitised Diseases, 2013. http://www.digitiseddiseases.org/.

Errickson, D., 2015. An optimum guide for the reduction of noise using a surface scanner for digitising human osteological remains. Guides to Good Practice. Archaeology Data Service. University of York, UK, <http://guides.archaeologydataservice.ac.uk/g2gp/CS_StructuredLight>.

FORTH, 2016. CRMdig: A model for provenance metadata. http://www.ics.forth.gr/isl/index_main.php?l=e&c=656.

Galeazzi, F., Callieri, M., Dellepiane, M., Charno, M., Richards, J.D., Scopigno, R., 2016. Web-based visualization for 3D data in archaeology: The ADS 3D viewer. J. Archaeol. Sci. Rep. 9, 1–11.

Heydegger, V., 2008. Analysing the Impact of File Formats on Data Integrity. Archiving 2008, Vol. 5. http://www.imaging.org/IST/store/epub.cfm?abstrid=38884.

Kuzminsky, S.C., Gardiner, M.S., 2012. Three-dimensional laser scanning: Potential uses for museum conservation and scientific research. J. Archaeol. Sci. 39 (8), 2744–2751.

McHenry, K., Bajcsy, P., 2008. An Overview of 3D Data Content, File Formats and Viewers. National Center for Supercomputing Applications, <http://isda.ncsa.illinois.edu/drupal/sites/default/files/NCSA-ISDA-2008-002.pdf>.

McPherron, S.P., Gernat, T., Hublin, J.-J., 2009. Structured light scanning for high-resolution documentation of in situ archaeological finds. J. Archaeol. Sci. 36 (1), 19–24.

Milner, N., Bamforth, M., Beale, G., Carty, J.C., Chatzipanagis, K., Croft, S., et al., 2016. A unique engraved shale pendant from the site of Star Carr: The oldest Mesolithic art in Britain. Internet Archaeol 40, http://dx.doi.org/10.11141/ia.40.8.

NDIIPP, 2013. Sustainability factors. <http://www.digitalpreservation.gov/formats/sustain/sustain.shtml>.

Nestor, 2009. Nothing Lasts Forever. Nestor/IfM. http://files.d-nb.de/nestor/ratgeber/ratg01_2_en.pdf.

Trognitz, M., Niven, K., Gilissen, V., 3D Models in Archaeology: A Guide to Good Practice, Guides to Good Practice, 2016, Archaeology Data Service, University of York;UK, <http://guides.archaeologydataservice.ac.uk/g2gp/3d_Toc>.

Niven, L., Steele, T.E., Finke, H., Hublin, J.-J., 2009. Virtual skeletons: Using a structured light scanner to create a 3D faunal comparative collection. J. Archaeol. Sci. 36 (9), 2018–2023.

Payne, A., 2011. Laser scanning for archaeology: A guide to good practice. Guides to Good Practice. Archaeology Data Service, University of York, UK, <http://guides.archaeologydataservice.ac.uk/g2gp/LaserScan_Toc>.

Potenziani, M., Callieri, M., Dellepiane, M., Corsini, M., Ponchio, F., Scopigno, R., 2015. 3DHOP: 3D heritage online presenter. Comput. Graph 52, 129–141.

Richards, J.D., Niven, K., Jeffrey, S., 2013. Preserving our digital heritage: Information systems for data management and preservation. In: Ch'ng, E., Gaffney, V. (Eds.), Visual Heritage in the Digital Age. Springer-Verlag, London, pp. 311–326.

Selden Jr., R.Z., Means, B.K., Lohse, J.C., Koenig, C., Black, S.L., 2014. Beyond documentation: 3D data in archaeology. Texas Archaeol. 58 (4).

SketchFab, 2014. British Museum user page. https://sketchfab.com/britishmuseum.

Smithsonian X 3D, 2013. Tour: The Jamestown Chancel Burials. http://3d.si.edu/tour/jamestown-chancel-burials.

Technopolis, 2011. Data Centres: Their Use, Value and Impact. Research Information Network. JISC, <http://www.rin.ac.uk/system/files/attachments/Data_Centres_Report.pdf>.

Virtual Zooarchaeology of the Arctic Project (VZAP), 2015. http://vzap.iri.isu.edu/.

Waters, D., Garrett, J., 1996. Preserving Digital Information. Report of the Task Force on Archiving of Digital Information, Report 63. The Commission on Preservation and Access. <https://www.clir.org/pubs/reports/pub63watersgarrett.pdf>.

CHAPTER 13

Management of 3D Image Data

Summer Decker and Jonathan Ford
University of South Florida Morsani College of Medicine, Tampa, FL, United States

In previous chapters, this text has discussed some of the applications of three-dimensional (3D) imaging capture methods including medical imaging (X-ray/CT/MRI), 3D surface or laser scanning, 3D photography, and microscopy. In this chapter, you will learn more about the actual 3D data in what the possibilities are with image manipulation, how to manage and store it, as well as some potential issues of specific interest to forensic researchers and practitioners to be aware of when working with 3D data. While the focus will be on 3D data in a funerary context, the information is applicable to many other fields. In order to fully understand the potential of 3D data, one must have an understanding of what exactly "3D data" is and how you can interact with it.

13.1 WHAT IS 3D IMAGE DATA?

3D data in context of this chapter is computer based and derived from the numerous imaging modalities previously discussed in this book. Standard 3D data file formats include, but are not limited to,

Human Remains: Another Dimension. DOI: http://dx.doi.org/10.1016/B978-0-12-804602-9.00014-X

DICOM, JPEG, TIFF, STL, VRML, and OBJ. File formats will be dependent on the type of image capture method and what the desired postcapture analysis or interaction method will be. The level of resolution of the scan or image will directly affect the size of the data file. Once data has been captured and saved, it can then be viewed and manipulated in three dimensions and exported to external software packages for editing, modeling, measurement, or long-term storage. Additionally, the vast amount of packages that are on the market to create and manipulate those files will have their own proprietary file format alongside the field standards (McHenry and Bajcsy, 2008).

13.1.1 File Types and Metadata

"3D volumetric data" is the type of data that is the output of current 3D image acquisition devices used in medical imaging modalities like magnetic resonance imaging (MRI) and computed tomography (CT). DICOM (Digital Imaging and Communications in Medicine) format is the current accepted standard file format for most medical imaging modalities including X-ray, CT, MRI, ultrasound, angiography, and microscopy. It was established as the field standard in 1993 in an effort to make scanner data more consistent across the different brands of scanners so patient information would not be separated from the image file itself making it transportable to other image viewing packages. Inside every DICOM file is metadata that provides a tremendous amount of useful information on the scan, the scanner itself and patient or object being scanned (Udupa and Herman, 1999). Data fields such as XYZ-coordinate location, Gantry Tilt, and pixel data can assist in 3D reconstruction. Some of this information is captured automatically while other portions are entered by the radiographer at the time of the scan. The 3D volumetric images from medical scanners are created from tiny cubes called voxels which are reconstructed to create 3D models of the 2D and 3D images taken from the scanner (Bronzino et al., 2005).

TIFF or Tagged Image File Format is a widely used computer file format used for image data by photographers, graphic artists or illustrators, and many software packages that use and manipulate image files. JPEG, PNG, and more recent JPEG 2000 are common file formats for digital images with varying levels of image and loss compression. Like in DICOM, both TIFF and JPEGs have embedded metadata that captures information such as GPS coordinates of the image's location, the date and time taken, the camera's resolution, and other technical information about camera and its settings.

STL (stereolithographic) files, VRML (virtual reality modeling language) files, OBJ (object files), IGES (initial graphics exchange specification), and STEP (standard for the exchange of product data) are the most common output file types used in computer-aided design (CAD) software, 3D visualization packages, and 3D printing software. It is the expectation for most software packages to at least have the ability to export a 3D object in one or more of the standard file types. STLs are 3D triangulated meshes made up of three ordered points and an external surface. STLs maintain an object's relative scale and XYZ-coordinate location provided from the scanner at the time of the scan.

3D laser scanners will often use OBJ or VRML for 3D point cloud data. However, it is important to note that many laser, photogrammetrics, or surface-scanning cameras will use their own proprietary file formats that may have to be converted to a more standard file format before it can be used in an analysis package. OBJ and VRML files contain geometric vertices, internal and external information as well as texture (UVW) information. In addition, VRML files contain information regarding specular or "shininess," bump information, transparency, and other surface-related data.

Overall the most fundamental requirement of utilizing 3D data files is to have a strong computer system to interact with and analyze the data on. Until recently, technological restrictions such as computer processor speed and scanner resolution have limited 3D applications of the data. A strong video card, sufficient RAM, and processor speed are musts when dealing with large files of 3D data. With advances in computer and imaging technologies and reduction in technology costs, higher resolution images and models are now able to be run on commercially available computers. This has sparked enormous growth in 3D volumetric data, quantitative analyses, and 3D design (Swennen et al., 2007; Vaidyanath and Temkin, 2005).

13.2 LARGE DATASET STORAGE

Each of the 3D data capture modalities that have been discussed in this book create very large data files. A full body CT scan completed at a thin slice thickness, for example, can easily have between 1000 and 1500 images at a file size in the gigabytes. Meshes generated from laser or surface-scanning methodologies can contain millions of triangles and texture information which also take up substantial digital storage space. 3D models can be in the high megabytes or even gigabytes in size depending on the level of detail and size of the model. Therefore, it is important to plan in advance for data storage. This should be done by anticipating your long-term storage needs as well as who will need access to the data.

13.2.1 Storage Options

Storage options for 3D data can range from simple external hard drives to more complicated and expensive PACS systems. The amount of data being captured and its purpose will dictate storage requirements. External hard drives are an affordable and entry-level option for practitioners and researchers with limited data and funding. Larger external drives in the multiple gigabyte size can be purchased at most computer stores or online. If the 3D scans are only periodic and data sharing is not needed, then this can be a long-term option for most people. Users of this option should also consider a backup hard drive to protect their data as hard drives are known to fail and get lost. Another economic option might be cloud-sharing services such as Dropbox, OneDrive, GoogleDrive, and Box. This option also allows for easy data sharing and collaboration between individuals regardless of location. Downside of these services is that online storage space can be limited and is Internet access dependent.

If an institution or individual is starting a long-term, larger scale forensic imaging project or practice, then more advanced level, secure storage should be considered. Most radiology and clinical imaging facilities maintain a PACS (Picture Archiving and Communication System) that stores all of scans done for diagnostic purposes for a certain period of time required by that country's laws. A PACS system usually consists of a storage system or server and a network of computers that communicate with that system to send, query, and receive patient scans and records. They can be very expensive and require institutional support to get established. In a general workflow, scans series are completed on the scanner and once complete, those images are automatically sent to the data storage server via a secured network. PACS systems will also contain patient electronic medical records so that series of scans on the same patient can be kept together for reference. Most of these systems are stored in highly secured storage facilities such as data centers with backup power and built-in storage redundancy to account for any errors or failures that might occur on the main system. Depending on the size of the system, they often take up a large footprint and require special electrical plugs, network access, and storage racks to function. PACS systems are most often run by a PACS administrator who is responsible for keeping the system stable and functioning as needed. This individual or team are often in the IT department of an institution but need specialized training in data storage. It is possible to hire outside PACS administration for your system but those usually require virtual or remote access to your system or cloud storage. For individuals setting up a new forensic imaging enterprise, it is recommended that they reach out to their institution or hospital to see if there is an existing PACS infrastructure that they can use or merge their workflow in.

Many facilities are transferring data storage responsibilities to virtual PACS or large-scale data cloud storage as the cost of off-site storage and management becomes more affordable. Researchers or practitioners conducting forensic 3D data research without an existing PACS might find this option more feasible and practical. With virtual PACS, data is sent from the scanners to the server much like in a local PACS but the data center is not located at your facility. As with smaller scale cloud storage, data access and transfer speeds are Internet and provider dependent.

Whatever the selected method of storage is, it is important to make sure that the storage plan includes sufficient space for future scans and data as well as anticipates potential data storage issues.

13.3 ISSUES TO CONSIDER: DATA MANAGEMENT

There are any number of issues that can arise when working with 3D data files. Beyond storage constraints, access, and security, how to maintain evidence and records and data ownership are all topics of special concern to forensic practitioners.

13.3.1 Access and Security

Defining who needs or should to have access to 3D data files is important to consider at the beginning stages of any 3D forensic imaging project. Security is a huge concern that must be addressed often before the first scans are completed.

Internationally there are laws that regulate access to protected private medical data including image scans. Medical images, microscopy, and even 3D surface scans or photographs are included under the category of protected or private information. In the United States, HIPPA or the Health Information Protection and Portability Act (A. Act, 1996) requires academic and hospital institutions to review all projects that include human subject data records. Institutional Review Boards will review in detail the data security plans submitted by investigators to insure that an individual's, living or deceased, privacy remains strictly protected. It also requires that all investigators or researchers working with protected data be certified in data security and ethics. The European Union's Data Protection Directive (E. Directive, 1995) and the United Kingdom's Data Protection Act (D.P. Act, 1998) have similar safeguards for the regulation and protection of data access. It is important for individuals to check their country's laws on data protection before getting started as these will dictate the type of storage and security measures that will be needed.

Data security and access can be managed by password protecting all devices that contain the image data as well as keeping all computers used to interact with the data in locked, secured locations. For individual's using external hard drives, keeping them in a locked desk or closet can be an option. PACS systems, physical and virtual, have federally required security measures and the administrators or institutions control access. Making sure that everyone associated with the project has been properly trained in data security is the first step to insuring that your data will remain properly protected and secure. Revoking access to anyone who violates these policies will be key to keeping your project in regulation.

13.3.2 Maintaining Evidence and Records

Due to the nature of forensic imaging, case files and associated images need to be maintained long term for legal purposes (Decker et al., 2009). One of the benefits of 3D data is that it can be maintained long after a body has been returned to the family. Analyses on virtual human remains can be done years later as new technologies emerge. Therefore, it is important that 3D data files be treated the same as with any forensic evidence. In addition to being careful to use accepted practices for scanning in a specific modality, extensive records on the scan itself and any data manipulation such as postprocessing should be maintained. As there is no universal agreement in how long forensic evidence should be maintained, you should check your country or region's guidelines or laws on record retention.

13.4 CONCLUSIONS

As new technologies arise, the applications of 3D imaging and data will only continue to grow. Considerations for the management and storage of 3D data and their analytical derivatives must be given before conducting research studies and casework. This chapter has provided a broad overview of the different types of 3D data as well as what infrastructure is necessary to maintain and work within a forensic context.

As 3D forensic fields develop and new laws emerge, it is the investigator's responsibility to follow the evolving laws specific to their country governing sensitive data, data security, and the maintenance of 3D forensic evidence. As juries become more educated on the potential of 3D data, they will expect the level of analysis and presentation, such as the case examples shown in this text, that only 3D data can provide.

REFERENCES

A. Act, Health insurance portability and accountability act of 1996. Public Law 104 (1996), 191.

Bronzino, J., Enderle, J., Blanchard, S., 2005. Introduction to biomedical engineering. Innovation 62, 2.

Decker, S., Ford, J., Hilbelink, D., 2009. Maintaining custody: a virtual method of creating accurate reproductions of skeletal remains for facial approximation. Proceedings of the 61st Annual Meeting of the American Academy of Forensic Sciences American Academy of Forensic Sciences, Colorado Springs, CO, p. 334.

Data Protection Act, HMSO, London, 1998.

E. Directive, 1995. 95/46/EC of the European Parliament and of the Council of 24 October 1995 on the protection of individuals with regard to the processing of personal data and on the free movement of such data. Official Journal of the EC 23.

McHenry, K., Bajcsy, P., 2008. An Overview of 3D Data Content, File Formats and Viewers, 1205. National Center for Supercomputing Applications.

Swennen, G.R., Barth, E.L., Eulzer, C., Schutyser, F., 2007. The use of a new 3D splint and double CT scan procedure to obtain an accurate anatomic virtual augmented model of the skull. Int. J. Oral Maxillofac. Surg. 36, 146–152.

Udupa, J.K., Herman, G.T., 1999. 3D Imaging in Medicine. CRC Press.

Vaidyanath, S., Temkin, B., 2005. Registration and segmentation for the high resolution visible human male images. Stud. Health Technol. Inform. 119, 556.

CHAPTER 14

Ethical Considerations: An Added Dimension

Nicholas Márquez-Grant and David Errickson
Cranfield University, Cranfield, United Kingdom

14.1 OUR ETHICAL RESPONSIBILITY TO HUMAN REMAINS

In bioarchaeology there have been a number of ethical issues surrounding the excavation and analysis of human remains (Fforde, 2004; Sayer, 2010; Fossheim, 2012; Lohman and Goodnow, 2006), and more recently they have focused on aspects of documentation, dissemination, curation, and repatriation (Buikstra, and Gordon, 1981; Larsen and Walker, 2005; Giesen, 2013; Taylor, 2014; Lambert, 2016). These issues and some added challenges have also been extended to forensic anthropology (Blau, 2016a,b). These ongoing discussions in physical anthropology include both academic and museum settings, incorporating the way bodies are captured and displayed. Unfortunately, often the decisions the deceased themselves made during their life (with regard to their own funerary rites) are not always considered, and in these situations we ask: Should we be considering, above all, our own personal motivations just because the past cannot speak to us anymore? For example, Charles Byrne is currently displayed in the Hunterian Museum, Royal College of Surgeons, London, against his own wishes (Doyal and Muinzer, 2011).

However, the past does speak to us. The skeleton is a "repository" of data for understanding social, biological, and cultural information

Human Remains: Another Dimension. DOI: http://dx.doi.org/10.1016/B978-0-12-804602-9.00015-1

(Gowland and Thompson, 2013). It is paramount that human remains are accessible to study so that researchers can place their findings into a wider context, furthering our current understanding of past and present populations. In forensic anthropology, methods developed from human remains can assist in the identification of the deceased, closure for families, and justice where applicable. However, human remains are a limited resource. More to the point, to study human remains is a privilege (BABAO, 2010) as these were once living individuals and therefore, should still be treated with respect.

The body has long been a curiosity, whether displayed in Gunther Von Hagen's "BODYWORLDS" or the local archaeological society's findings. Museums often display human remains for educational purposes. Consequently, it has long been understood that these displays increase everyone's (including the general public) understanding of past and current contexts. However, in this process, there is still a need to ethically study and display human remains.

Throughout this book, the potential of three-dimensional (3D) imaging and printing technologies has been demonstrated. Advantages include improving access to skeletal remains, minimizing the destructive analysis of human remains (including autopsies) which may also be an ethical issue in itself, using the data as an education resource, and enhancing the user's knowledge and learning experiences (Brown, 2000; Frantini et al., 2008; Kuzminsky and Gardiner, 2012; Woźniak et al., 2012). There are a number of guidelines that can be referred to in relation to displaying, handling, and evaluating actual human remains (DCMS, 2005; BABAO, 2010; English Heritage, 2013); however there are no such guidelines that touch upon the digital data collected. Therefore, this chapter aims to consider the challenges of representing human remains through the use of advanced imaging and printing practices.

14.2 THE ROLE OF IMAGING

As observed in this volume, physical remains can be represented in a number of ways including photographic imaging, radiographs, 3D scanned data (surface and internal), and as a printed model (see chapters by Errickson; Wilson et al.; Godhino and O'Higgins; Ulguim in this volume). Recently, the analysis of human remains via internal and surface documentation has demonstrated valuable benefits that include digitizing, exposing, comparing, reconstructing, materializing, and sharing objects (Weber, 2014). However, as researchers we have a responsibility to justify our decision making process, whether it is a method of presenting an image or manipulating the dataset (Comstock, 2013). For justification there must always be a good aim. These reasons may include recording the human remains before they are (further) altered by external influences, permanent capture of the remains prior to repatriation and/or reburial, obtaining statistical data, presentation in education, or to reconstruct a fragmented skeleton. This is furthered by the very fact that the data is present long after the remains have been (re)buried (see, e.g., discussion on Richard III— Bonney, 2015).

Whatever the case, the British Association of Biological Anthropology and Osteoarchaeology's (BABAO) codes of ethics state that analyzing human remains:

> is a privilege and not a right ... and ... should always be treated with dignity and respect.
>
> *BABAO, 2010, p. 1*

It could be argued that many 3D imaging techniques maintain respect to the actual human remains as they are noninvasive, limit handling, and therefore reduce any further destruction to the individual's remains. As a result, digital data capture is becoming progressively common and the availability of 3D digital data is increasing (Ulguim, 2016). Consequently, we may view these techniques as reformatting the remains of an individual into another form. Fundamentally, this form of data is the digital record of a person who had once lived, so a key consideration is to also treat this representation with as much dignity and respect as the body itself. It appears to be increasingly common that human remains are routinely captured without good justification. It is paramount that at the outset there is an intended goal for undertaking such imaging of the remains.

We believe some key considerations into the undertaking of digital capture should include:

- Is it necessary to capture the human remains in this format? (Are the remains fragile? Are they of great significance to the wider

understanding of cultural and historical contexts? Will the remains be reburied?)
- Who is the custodian of the data?
- Who is curating this information?
- Who can we share the data with?
- Once accessed, what can be done with this information? (Can it be used for teaching, publication or display?) How long for?
- Would imaging be a compromise if human remains were to be reburied?
- Can we 3D-print the datasets? Can these be used for teaching, research, and display?

Still, on top of these considerations, the data must also be stored ethically and securely; and if it is intended for research it must be accessible to other researchers as long as there is some regulation (with regard to social media and who can handle the data). There are repositories (such as the archeology data service) where this information can be stored and protected. It must be noted that all contextual information should also be included as absence of this also defies the contemporary meaning of the collection. With regard to storing the metadata, the archeology data service has a series of guides that should always be followed (see chapter by Niven and Richards in this volume).

14.3 REPLICAS, RECONSTRUCTIONS, AND REPRODUCTIONS

The ethics behind the use of human remains (especially within anthropological and archeological contexts) have become:

complex, fluid, ambiguous, politicized, and confusing.
White and Folkens, 2005, p. 24

This is furthered by the apparent stages different disciplines are at. Commonly, scientists are starting to discuss ethical concerns and practices, but there is a call for more communication between institutions (e.g., museums), anthropologists, forensic scientists, anatomists, historians, archeologists, and other academics alike, as well as with the public and any known relatives of the deceased. As discussed in Section 14.2, there are great benefits to 3D scanning and a large part of this is the advancement of knowledge through the worldwide availability of the data, especially the increasing collaboration. However, when the British government (Pearson et al., 2011; McKie, 2010)[1] stated that all:

> human remains archeologically excavated should be reburied after a two year period of scientific analysis.

Recognition of the undertaken procedures within the United States should be observed. Digital scanning is becoming particularly important for documenting objects and human remains within the ethical and political context of North America, in which many objects and skeletal collections have been repatriated to Native American tribes under the Native American Graves Repatriation Act (NAGPRA) (Hollinger et al., 2013).

The resulting digital data can still provide researchers with detailed morphological information, concerning, for example, nonmetric skeletal variants or pathological lesions.[2] Likewise, metric data can still be recorded as accurately from scans as the original bones. In addition, the data can also be printed. Some institutions currently 3D-print digital versions of skeletons to use as an alternative teaching collection (AbouHashem et al., 2015). What is more, this data can be used in the forensic context within a courtroom for visualizing evidence or demonstrating pathological lesions and/or trauma analysis (March et al., 2004; Errickson et al., 2014).

Although this technique will never replace the observations that can be made on an actual skeleton; it can importantly minimize the risk of damage to the human remains (Caffell et al., 2001), and become an alternative if the actual human remains are no longer available (Ebert et al., 2011). The NAGPRA law was enacted to ensure that every culture with a religious/spiritual reverence, such as Native Americans, will have their culturally affiliated items and human ancestors returned to them. Likewise, repatriation of ancestral remains of indigenous groups is common in Australia and New Zealand (Arts.gov.au, 2016; Wellcome, 2016). NAGPRA states all human remains and "cultural items" must be returned to the indigenous groups for repatriation if ownership can be claimed. However, this statement opens up the question: Is digital data a replication, reproduction, or a reconstruction of the original object?

---

[1] https://www.theguardian.com/science/2011/feb/04/archaeologists-forced-to-rebury-finds; https://www.theguardian.com/science/2010/oct/10/burial-grave-mike-pitts-stonehenge.

Likewise, if human remains have been reformatted through another mode of representation, then should we be also giving back this wealth of information too? The answer is possibly more complex than the question, and ultimately the answer is probably not, yet, it does question ethical boundaries and opens up conversations that have currently not happened and clearly further discussion and understanding is needed. This dilemma is furthered with the use of 3D printing (Killgrove, 2015). A 3D-printed model acquired as a result of scanning an individual is almost certainly a replica, due to its physical qualities. However, it is a layered buildup within the 3D printing process and thus can also be classed as a reconstruction. Due to this rapid movement in "virtual anthropology and archeology" (e.g., see Weber, and Bookstein, 2001) there is also a call for a better understanding of terminology.

The advantage of 3D printing is all the possibilities that can be achieved with it. For example, a 3D-print can be scaled to be a smaller version of the object, or even enlarged to look at physical characteristics in much more detail (Liscio, 2013). Cases of trauma in forensic anthropology can be, with all the permissions in place, 3D-printed to show to a jury or for teaching (Errickson et al., 2014). Furthermore, it would be easier to transport 3D models than actual human remains. However, replicating human remains in this way has yet to be fully tried and tested. Cornwall (2016) stated that worldwide, many laws agree that body parts cannot be sold for commercial gain, but the sale of images arising from donated cadavers has yet to be investigated (Hugo, 2016). Consequently, very little is understood as to what is acceptable with regard to 3D printing of body parts.

Indeed, most of the general public are keen to see skeletons and mummified remains in museums (Mays, 2014). This has been established by surveys undertaken by museum visitors who have demonstrated an overwhelming majority in support of their public display (Pearson et al., 2011), and up until now, the use of human remains for museum exhibitions has been highly favorable to attract and captivate the public. However, displaying human remains has also brought up other ethical quandaries (see, e.g., discussion on the Egyptian Mummy—Egypt Manchester, 2008).

14.4 DISSEMINATION AND DISPLAY

Once the data has been collected, with the advancement of technology and the availability of social media, disseminating information is now easier than ever. This technological progression has pushed for the Internet to be used as a facilitator for researchers to display their findings. But in turn, it also allows our society to place pictures of mummified remains, skeletons, and individual bones online too. As authors of this chapter, our standpoint is that sharing data in this way can lead to increasing discussions. For example, increasing discussions between scientists has led to the creation of a JISC discussion forum (DigitalOsteo[2]) in the United Kingdom. With this in mind, we believe sharing must be done in an ethical manner. For example, the avoidance of Hamlet type poses and untasteful exhibition of human remains (especially display without reason). This may extend to academic PowerPoint presentations in which human remains seem to be used to make things more attractive. Moreover, in an institute where the remains may be identifiable, permissions from the family should be sought first as a sign of respect. For that reason, the question we must ask, similar to photographs, is it necessary for the images to go online? And what is the intended goal?

Ancient human remains are not owned by anyone, but the information that they hold are important to many people including academics and practitioners for educational use. This has been demonstrated with an increasing number of available web resources that form actual 3D data directly taken from physical remains (e.g., Digitised Diseases,[3] Dactyl[4]). These tools are important as they have a purpose. These resources capture pathological conditions and anatomical variants that complement the new wave of education. For example, within medical schools there has been an increase in the use of the virtopsy approach which means they now rely less on actual cadavers (Thali et al., 2007, 2009). In addition, not all institutions have direct access to physical remains. Therefore, students, and the public can use these resources as a revision and research tool.

Then, if data is becoming increasingly available to view online, why are museums feeling the pressure to remove bodies from display?

[2]Digitalosteo@jiscmail.ac.uk
[3]http://www.digitiseddiseases.org/alpha/
[4]http://www.anthronomics.com/

Whether it is to do with culture or the removal for burial, Søren Holm states it is nothing to do with respect, but the argument of necessity:

> It is not in any obvious sense disrespectful to display a skeleton of someone long dead, if the display has a valid purpose. After all, in Catholic countries the display of relics, often said to be bones of the saints, is still commonplace.
>
> Holm, 2011, p. 1

With this in mind, most museums do try to address the many concerns from repatriation to display. For example, the British Museum has held human remains since 1753 and in 2014 published a collection of articles regarding the treatment of the dead within their institution (Fletcher et al., 2014). These chapters discuss the broader aspects of curating, displaying, analyzing, storing, and imaging human remains.

Alternatively, 3D printing human remains may provide a solution for museums that do not wish to display actual human remains. This practice is comparable to medical applications in which a 3D-print can be used as an accurate and effective substitute if cadavers are not accessible due to their limited availability and/or ethical constraints (McMenamin et al., 2014). Yet, if these replicas are as good as the original human remains, why exhibit the remains in the first place? Furthermore, where is the 3D printing boundary and how long until we can download them and print them out? The *Digitized Diseases* team feels very strongly about this and state on their Web site[2]:

> any misuse of material (e.g. creation of artwork / installations or printing of 3D models) from this resource will be taken very seriously ... and is obliged to inform the HTA [Human Tissue Authority] of any misuse of images involving their modern human remains.

Thus, *Digitized Diseases* leave it to the individuals to act "responsibly," though by doing this we assume that the public know how to act responsibly when it comes to human remains. Yet, a recent stroll around Spitalfields Market demonstrates that some individuals cannot be left to act responsibly as the visit found a significant amount of human remains on display and for sale in a number of businesses. This is a global issue (Hugo, 2016). Furthermore, online resources are globally accessible which raises the question of the Human Tissue Authority's legislation over internationals (Human Tissue Act, 2004).

On the other hand, Anthronomics states on their Web site[3] (Anthronomics, 2016) there is a need for social responsibility by those that are providing the resource:

> We believe that all companies have a responsibility to their community. We take that responsibility very seriously, and so donate time and resources for a number of educational workshops to allow more people to access to the human skeleton, or their shared heritage.

This statement demonstrates the need for communication between researchers and the public. How can individuals act responsibly, if they are unaware of any misdoings? The authors believe that if an increased dialog between practitioners, academics, and the public is accomplished, and time is taken to inform, discuss, and debate, future guidelines can be established that will benefit all individuals worldwide.

14.5 CONCLUSIONS

As scientists we have an ethical responsibility with regard to caring for the dead, but the ethical debates surrounding human remains are far from transparent. The authors of this chapter believe that the most important aspects that require significant consideration are necessity and consent. There must always be a good reason behind displaying, curating, and the destructive analysis of human remains, whether it is for educational or research purposes. In addition, there must be consent from any living relatives prior to undertaking analysis on human remains, specifically in repatriation cases. From this, we can increase communication between scientific disciplines and the public in the form of discussions and debates, therefore establishing good practice guidelines for the future.

In summary, we want to highlight the following:

- We all have an ethical responsibility when dealing with the remains of the dead.
- There is an advantage to imaging human remains; however, there must always be a justified value to undertaking 3D documentation. This value must be for education and/or research and also serves to protect the human remains by limiting further handling and transportation. The public should be informed about this approach.

- Taking and using images (especially in the public domain such as on social media) with no good valid reason is not justifiable. Ethical concerns about these must also be considered and discussed with colleagues, living relatives, or groups affiliated to the remains.
- Protocols need to be put in place with regard to images of human remains. Such protocols include use, data storage (including length of storage), data sharing, and security of information.
- There must be an improved effort to ensure standardization of terminology.
- Communication between professionals and the public should increase to ensure everyone is familiar with current ethical discussions and concerns. This could be done in the form of workshops or roundtable discussions at different institutions.
- There must always be some form of consent from living relatives with regard to documentation, data storage, and display, etc., of human remains.

REFERENCES

AbouHashem, Y., Dayal, M., Savanah, S., Štrkalj, G., 2015. The application of 3D printing in anatomy education. Med. Educ. Online 20, 10.

Anthronomics, 2016. http://www.anthronomics.com/ (accessed 04.07.16).

Arts.gov.au, 2016. Indigenous Repatriation | Department of Communications and the Arts [online]. https://www.arts.gov.au/what-we-do/cultural-heritage/indigenous-repatriation (accessed 26.09.16).

BABAO, 2010. http://www.babao.org.uk/assets/Uploads/code-of-ethics.pdf (accessed 08.08.16).

Blau, S., 2016a. More than just bare bones: Ethical considerations for forensic anthropologists. In: Blau, S., Ubelaker, D.H. (Eds.), Handbook of Forensic Archaeology and Anthropology, 2nd ed. Routledge, Abingdon, pp. 593–606.

Blau, S., 2016b. La ética y el antropólogo forense: Una variedad de consideraciones. In: Sanabria-Medina, C. (Ed.), Patología y Antropología Forense de la Muerte: La Investigación científico-judicial de la muerte y la tortura, desde las fossa clandestinas, hasta la audiencia pública. Forensic Publisher, Bogotá, pp. 25–36.

Bonney, H.E., 2015. Richard III: Skeletal evidence of perimortem trauma. Lancet 385 (9964), 210.

Brown, J.R., 2000. Enabling educational collaboration—a new shared reality. Comput. Graph. 24 (2), 289–292.

Buikstra, J.E., Gordon, C.C., 1981. The study and restudy of human skeletal series: The importance of long term curation. Ann. N. Y. Acad. Sci. 376, 449–465.

Caffell, A.C., Roberts, C.A., Janaway, R.C., Wilson, A.S., 2001. Pressures on osteological collections—the importance of damage limitation. Br. Archaeol. Rep. 187–197.

Comstock, G., 2013. Research Ethics: A Philosophical Guide to the Responsible Conduct of Research. Cambridge University Press, Cambridge, UK.

Cornwall, J., 2016. The ethics of 3D printing copies of bodies donated for medical education and research: What is there to worry about? Australas Med. J. 9 (1), 8−11.

DCMS, 2005. Guidance for the care of human remains in museums. https://www.britishmuseum. org/pdf/DCMS%20Guide.pdf (accessed 04.07.16).

Digitised Diseases, 2016. http://www.digitiseddiseases.org/mrn.php?mrn=xx (accessed 04.07.16).

Doyal, L., Muinzer, T., 2011. Should the skeleton of "the Irish giant" be buried at sea? Br. Med. J. 343, 1290−1292.

Ebert, L.C., Thali, M.J., Ross, S., 2011. Getting in touch—3D printing in forensic imaging. Forensic Sci. Int. 211, e1−e6.

Egypt Manchester, 2008. Covering the mummies. https://egyptmanchester.wordpress.com/2008/ 05/06/covering-the-mummies/ (accessed 03.07. 16).

English Heritage, 2013. Science and the dead: A guideline for the destructive sampling of archae-ological human remains for scientific analysis. http://www.archaeologyuk.org/apabe/pdf/ Science_and_the_Dead.pdf (accessed 04.07.16).

Errickson, D., Thompson, T.J.U., Rankin, B., 2014. The application of 3D visualisation of osteo-logical trauma for the courtroom: A critical review. J. Forensic Radiol. Imaging 2 (3), 132−137.

Fforde, C., 2004. Collecting the Dead: Archaeology and the Reburial Issues. Duckworth, London.

Fletcher, A., Antonine, D., Hill, J.D., 2014. Regarding the Dead: Human Remains in the British Museum. 4 edge Ltd, Hockley.

Fossheim, H., 2012. More Than Just Bones: Ethics and Research on Human Remains. The Norwegian National Research Ethics Committee, Oslo.

Frantini, M., Crescenzio, F., Persiani, F., Gruppioni, G., 2008. 3D restitution, restoration, and prototyping of a medieval damaged skull. Rapid Prototyping J. 14, 318−324.

Giesen, M. (Ed.), 2013. Curating Human Remains: Caring for the Dead in the United Kingdom. Boydell Press, Martlesham.

Gowland, R.L., Thompson, T.J.U., 2013. Human Identity and Identification. Cambridge University Press, Cambridge.

Hollinger, R.E., John, E., Jacobs, H., Moran-Collins, L., Thome, C., Zastrow, J., et al., 2013. Tlingit-Smithsonian collaborations with 3D digitization of cultural objects. Museum Anthropol. Rev. 7, 1−2.

Holm, S., 2011. Removing bodies from display is nonsense. New Scientist 2803. https://www. newscientist.com/article/mg20928030-100-removing-bodies-from-display-is-nonsense/.

Hugo, K., 2016. Human skulls are being sold online, but is it legal? http://news.nationalgeo-graphic.com/2016/08/human-skulls-sale-legal-ebay-forensics-science/ (accessed 23.08.16).

Human Tissue Act, 2004. https://www.hta.gov.uk/policies/human-tissue-act-2004 (accessed 31.05.16).

Killgrove, K., 2015. How 3D printed bones are revolutionizing forensic and bioarchaeology. http://www.forbes.com/sites/kristinakillgrove/2015/05/28/how-3d-printed-bones-are-revolutioniz-ing-forensics-and-bioarchaeology/#3a76b4d86811 (accessed 04.07.16).

Kuzminsky, S.C., Gardiner, M.S., 2012. Three-dimensional laser scanning: Potential uses for museum conservation and scientific research. J. Archaeol. Sci. 39, 2744−2751.

Lambert, P.M., 2016. Ethics and issues in the use of human skeletal remains. In: Grauer, A.L. (Ed.), Companion to Paleopathology. Wiley-Blackwell, Chichester, pp. 17−33.

Larsen, C.S., Walker, P.L., 2005. The ethics of bioarchaeology. In: Turner, T.R. (Ed.), Biological Anthropology, and Ethics: From Repatriation to Genetic Identity. SUNY Press, Albany, NY, pp. 111−119.

Liscio, 2013. http://www.forensicmag.com/article/2013/06/forensic-uses-3d-printing (accessed 08.08.16).

Lohman, J., Goodnow, K. (Eds.), 2006. Human Remains, and Museum Practice: Museums and Diversity. first ed. UNESCO, Paris, Museums and Diversity, no. 2.

March, J., Schofield, D., Evison, M., Woodford, N., 2004. Three-dimensional computer visualization of forensic pathology data. Am. J. Forensic Med. Pathol. 60–70.

Mays, S., 2014. Part one—holding and displaying human remains. In: Fletcher, A., Antonine, D., Hill, J.D. (Eds.), Regarding the Dead: Human Remains in the British Museum. 4edge Ltd, Hockley, pp. 1–2. 2014.

McMenamin, P.G., Quayle, M.R., McHenry, C.R., Adams, J.W., 2014. The production of anatomical teaching resources using dimensional (3D) printing technology. Anat. Sci. Educ. 7, 479–486.

McKie, R., 2010. Burial law is threatening archaeological research, say experts. <https://www.theguardian.com/science/2010/oct/10/burial-grave-mike-pitts-stonehenge> (accessed 20.12.16).

Pearson, M.P., Schadla-Hall, T., Moshenska, G., 2011. Resolving the human remains crisis in British archaeology. Papers from the Institute of Archaeology 21, 5–9. Available from: http://dx.doi.org/10.5334/pia.369, http://discovery.ucl.ac.uk/1419102/1/343-767-1-PB.pdf.

Sayer, D., 2010. Ethics and Burial Archaeology. Gerald Duckworth & Co, London.

Taylor, J.H., 2014. The collection of Egyptian Mummies in the British Museum: Overview and potential study. In: Fletcher, A., Antoine, D., Hill, J.D. (Eds.), Regarding the Dead: Human Remains in the British Museum. The British Museum, London, pp. 103–114.

Thali, M.J., Jackowski, C., Oesterhelweg, L., Ross, S.G., Dirnhofer, R., 2007. VIRTSOPY—the Swiss virtual autopsy approach. Leg. Med. (Tokyo) 9 (2), 100–104.

Thali, M.J., Dirnhofer, R., Vock, P., 2009. The Virtopsy Approach: 3D Optical and Radiological Scanning and Reconstruction in Forensic Medicine. CRC Press, Boca Raton, FL.

Ulguim, P., 2016. https://bonesburialsandblackcoffee.wordpress.com/2016/04/01/models-and-metadata-how-are-3d-models-of-human-remains-and-funerary-archaeology-shared-on-a-digital-platform/ (accessed 20.07.16).

Weber, G.W., 2014. Virtual anthropology. Yearbook of Physical Anthropology 59, 22–42.

Weber, G.W., Bookstein, F.L., 2001. Virtual Anthropology: A Guide to a New Interdisciplinary Field. Springer-Verlag, New York.

Wellcome, 2016. Repatriation of Māori/Moriori ancestral human remains held by the Science Museum on behalf of the Wellcome Trust | Wellcome. https://wellcome.ac.uk/funding/managing-grant/repatriation-maorimoriori-ancestral-human-remains-held-science-museum-behalf-wellcome (accessed 26.09.16).

White, T.D., Folkens, P.A., 2005. The Human Bone Manual. Academic Press, New York.

Woźniak, K., Rzepecka-Woźniak, E., Moskaøa, A., Pohl, J., Latacz, K., Dybala, B., 2012. Weapon identification using antemortem computed tomography with virtual 3D and rapid prototype modeling—a report in a case of blunt force head injury. Forensic Sci. Int. 222, 29–32.

Printed in Great Britain
by Amazon

61430593R00129